THE LIFE AND TIMES
OF A VICTORIAN OFFICER

Lt. Col. D. B. A. Donne, 1899.

THE LIFE AND TIMES OF A VICTORIAN OFFICER

being the journals and letters of

Colonel Benjamin Donisthorpe Alsop Donne, CB.

Edited and with additional notes by

Alan Harfield

Photography of the Donne collection by
Geoff Parselle

THE WINCANTON PRESS
OLD NATIONAL SCHOOL, NORTH STREET
WINCANTON, SOMERSET BA9 9AT.

Also by Alan Harfield

The Royal Brunei Malay Regiment
Fort Canning Cemetery, Singapore
Headdresses, badges and embellishments of the Royal Corps of Signals
A history of the village of Chilmark
Christian Cemeteries and Memorials in Malacca
British and Indian Armies in the East Indies [1685-1935]
Blandford and the Military
Bencoolen – the Christian Cemetery and the Fort Marlborough Monuments
Early Christian cemeteries of Singapore

INTERNATIONAL STANDARD BOOK NUMBER 0 948699 01 9

 Typeset in a Linotype 'Garamond' face by Irene Howard at SOS Typesetting, Bell Street, Shaftesbury, Dorset. Layout and design by the publisher, Rodney Legg, at Wincanton Press. Colour plate separations by Wessex Reproduction of Bristol. Assembled by Andrew Johnstone and Jonathan Bristow at Wincanton Litho, Wincanton, Somerset, where it was printed by Steve Taylor

Contents

Preface

I FIRST became aware of Colonel Donisthorpe Donne whilst serving in Cyprus in 1974 when I visited an exhibition of his paintings. Miss Anne Cavendish, who had organised the exhibition, obtained permission for me to photograph a number of the water colours dealing with the military subjects in Cyprus and I was subsequently able to write a short article dealing with the Cyprus Pioneer Corps and Cyprus Military Police.

After my return to England in 1978 I made contact with Lieutenant Colonel William [Tom] Donisthorpe Shaw, the Grandson of Donisthorpe Donne, and it was then that the idea of publishing the Donne Journals and letters, illustrated with many of his water colours and sketches, was first discussed. The idea greatly appealed to me as, whilst in Cyprus, I had visited many of the places mentioned in the Cyprus portion of the Journals. I commenced work on the project that year and found the subject completely absorbing. Donisthorpe Donne's journals, letters and many of the family documents were loaned to me by Tom Shaw and over the past five years, whilst working on the manuscript journals and letters, I feel that I have come to know this typical Victorian officer.

The best description of Donisthorpe Donne's temperament and career comes from a letter written to his sister Rose on the day following his unexpected demise. The writer comments "...his was a most lovable nature, so winning and unassuming, self never thought of, just a straightforward gallant soldier, making light of all toil and danger gone through in his country's service...".

I am most grateful to Miss Anne Cavendish, Mr H. M. Williamson, Mrs L. Shoosmith, Miss M. Zenonos and Mrs G. Lasselle, all of whom have made Donne water colours available to me for inclusion in this publication. The majority of the illustrations of Donne's work are from the collection of his work owned by Tom Shaw who has given me unrestricted access to his collection.

My sincere and grateful thanks are extended to Miss D. M. Moore, Mrs J. Norman and Miss M. Shaw, all of whom kindly allowed me to photograph the Donne Paintings in their homes.

The Donne sketches and paintings that were located in the U.K. were photographed by Mr G. Parselle and I am most grateful for the care and expertise that he used to ensure that the best possible reproduction was obtained from the original paintings. I am also extremely grateful to Mrs Michelle Cooper who very kindly undertook to photograph those items that were located in Cyprus and without her help it would not have been possible to have included the seven sketches and paintings in this book.

I would also like to thank Mr P. B. Boyden, BA, of the National Army Museum and Major J. M. A. Tamplin, TD, of the Army Museum Ogilby Trust for their help and advice.

Finally I would like to acknowledge the help and encouragement that I have received from my wife, June. It is due to her endless help with research, photography, checking of typing etc, that the book finally reached completion.

April 1985

Chronological list of sketches and paintings by Donisthorpe Donne included in the book

Heidelberg Ruins, April 1875
Barbarossa Tower, North Germany, 1875
Tower of Barbarossa , April 1875
Rothenberg, 1875
Ruins of Rothenburg Castle, 1875
Pitz Termoggia and Fex Thal, Engadine, August 1876
Kingston Harbour, Jamaica, 1878
Riding along the track to the camp at Newcastle, Jamaica, 1878
Signal School, Aldershot, 1879
Ear of Dionosius, October 1879
Stromboli, December 1879
A night on Mount Etna, December 1879
The Greek Theatre, Taormina, December 1879
Temple of Juno, Lucinia Girgenta, December 1879
The Temple of Jupiter, December 1879
Tent in the Officers' Lines at Polymedia Camp, Cyprus, 1880
Donne in his tent at Polymedia Camp, 1880
View of the coast, with Limassol on the left, as seen from Donne's tent at Polymedia Camp, November 1880
View of Mount Troodos from Polymedia Camp, 1880
Akrotiri after rain, November 1880
The Tower of Colossi, November 1880
Kyrenia, 1881
Monastery at Bella Pais, 1881
The Cyprus Pioneer Corps, Limassol, February 1881
Cypriot workmen, 1881
Santorin Island, Cyclades, April 1881
Volcanic Island, Santorin Island, 1881
Tayorsin, 1881
Island of Melos, April 1881
Seen from the Orient Express – four studies of uniforms, 1881
The Breithorn, 1881
Mountain View, 1881
Sunset, August 1881
Sunset off Crete, August 1881
Limassol Bay, 1881
Turkish Zaptieh, 1881
Zaptieh on patrol, 1881
Approaching the cave, 1881
The fight in the cave, 1881
Entrance to the Nicosia mosque, 1882
Macheras Monastery, 1882
Donne's quarter at Limassol, Cyprus, 1882

After the battle of Tel el Kebir, September 1882
Looking across the Nile Valley from the Great Pyramid, 1883
The Nile Valley, after the rains, 1883
Going up stream – three masted Nile craft, 1883
Entrance to the small Temple of Thotmes, 1883
Portion of the Rammeseum, Thebes, January 1883
View of the Temple of Luxor, January 1883
Statue at Luxor, 1883
The Ptolemaic Temple of Edfou, from the Nile, January 1883
Two winged globes over the entrance of the temple of Kom Ombos, 1883
Nile craft, 1883
View of the Pyramids, 1882.

The Sphinx, 1883
The Sphinx from the rear, 1883
On the Acropolis, Athens, May 1883
Outward bound from Naples, 1883
The Egyptian Camel Corps, 1883
Camp of the Egyptian troops at Assouan, under Colonel Duncan, March 1884
Castle, near Sarras, Batu el Hazar, Lower Nile, 1884
Donne's tent at Korosko, 120° in the shade, 18 June 1884
Two unfinished sketches by Donne – Dongola, April 1885
Unfinished sketch by Donne – Nile craft, 1885
Unfinished sketch by Donne entitled 'Two more of the guns', 1885
The interior of an Officer's mat hut, Kajbar, April 22, 1885
The Nile expedition, 1885
*The Nile expedition – conveying stores to the front along the Abu Fakmak, Dongola
    Reach,* 1885
A soldier of the 10th Sudanese Battalion, 1885-88
10th Sudanese Battalion going down river, near Arment, 21 November 1888
    en route to Kosseir
*Relief of Suakin – 10th Sudanese Battalion marching across the desert from the Nile
    to Kosseir on the Red Sea,* 1888
*10th Sudanese Battalion at halt in the desert near Bir el Morela at a rain pool after a
    2 day hard march,* November 1888
Suakin during the investment by the Dervishes, 1888
A sortie from Suakin before the battle of Gemaizah, 1888
Looking across the Red Sea 1888
Three soldiers of the 10th Sudanese Battalion, 1888-91
The Mosque, Cairo, 1891
Cairo, the Citadel, early morning, 1891
Cairo, the Citadel, midday, 1891
Alexandria, 1891
Aboukir Bay, 1892
Aboukir Fort, 1892
Cairo, a street scene, 1892
The Pyramids, 1892
Unfinished sketch by Donne, the Pyramids, 1892
Local ships, 1892
The Valley of the Kings, 1893

Karnac, Luxor, 1893
An Egyptian village scene, 1893
Jerusalem, a street scene, 1893
Jerusalem, the Dome of the Rock, 1893
Lebanon, Beirut, 1893
Damascus, Courtyard of the Great Mosque, 1893
Mar Saba, 1893
Baalbeck, 1893
Baalbeck, the Temple of Jupiter, 1893
A Crusader Castle, 1893
Limassol from the Acropolis of Amathus, 1893
Limassol from the sea, 1893
Cape Gata and Mount Troodos, 1893
Rhodes, as seen from the anchorage, 1893
Rhodes, 1893
The Gateway, Rhodes, 1893
Greek island craft at Smyrna, 1893
Island craft at Smyrna, 1893
The Island of Imbros, 1893
The sea of Marmora, 1893
Coastline of the Sea of Marmora, 1893
The Golden Horn of Scutari, 1893
Bagnoli, near Naples
Gibraltar, The Rock, 1896
Malta, HMS Ramillies in the Grand Harbour, 1896
P & O liner 'Himalaya' leaving Valetta, 1896
Egypt, Cairo, 1896
Red Sea, Jedda, 1896
The colours of the 107th Regiment of Foot, 1896
The Taj Mahal, 1897
Fort Jamrud, North West Frontier, 1897-98
The Red Fort at Agra, 1898
Mussoorie, 1898
The Taj Mahal with cranes in flight, 1898
The Taj Mahal in early morning mist, by H. B. Donne, 1898
Off Cape Town, the tablecloth mist, 1898
Looking across the town of Heidelberg, South Africa, 1898
Sailing ships – the Sail Squadron, Royal Navy, 1903
HMS Implacable, 1904
The old Arethusa being towed away in Portsmouth Harbour, [undated]
Flagship off Malta in the 'Fifties', [undated]
Man of War leaving harbour, [undated]
Cleaning ships, [undated]
Ships on a Beach, [undated]
The colours of the 35th Regiment of Foot, [undated]
Second study of the colours of the 35th Regiment, [undated]

Where known the above titles are those given to the various paintings and sketches by Donisthorpe Donne and have been obtained either from an inscription on the work itself, or from his own manuscript list of paintings and sketches.

Additional illustrations

Map of Donisthorpe Donne's travels in the Middle East.
Self portrait by Donne as a young man
Embarkation order for Barbados on H.M.S. Simoom, 9 October 1876
Embarkation order, 14 October 1876
Photograph sent to his younger sister Mary Rose Donisthorpe Donne, April 1879
Certificate from Army Signalling School Aldershot, 14 August 1879
The Troopship 'Tamar'
The British occupation of Cyprus – General view of the landing place, Larnaca
    [Illustrated London News]
Landing Place and Piers at Larnaca from the House used by H.R.H. The Duke of
    Edinburgh, 1878 [Illustrated London News]
Disembarkation of horses at Larnaca [Illustrated London News]
Polymedia Camp, with the walled cemetery in the foreground, circa 1881
The British Camp at Larnaca with the Salt Lake and the aqueduct in the foreground,
    1878 [Illustrated London News]
Sketch of Donisthorpe Donne by Lieutenant Allan Gilmore – Limassol, 1881
St Sophia Cathedral converted into a mosque, 1878 [Illustrated London News]
Illustrations of Cyprus, including the Mosque of St Sophia, Nicosia [The Graphic,
    10 August 1878]
An artist's impression of Kyrenia, 1878 [Illustrated London News]
Entry of Captain Swain into Levcaro, Cyprus, 1878 [London Illustrated News]
Kitchener's house at Limassol [By courtesy of Mr H. M. Williamson]
Photograph of a picnic at Troodos, June 1882
Portrait of Donne by Donne's elder sister Anna. It is probable that the title was added
    later as the rank shown is not contemporary with the painting, which is dated 1882
Photograph of Donne, 1883
Photograph of War Office letter, 14th March 1883
Photograph of Donne as a Major Egyptian Army, sent to his elder sister Anna, 1883
Photograph of Donne as a Major in the Egyptian Army, 1883
Photograph inscribed on the reverse 'Stationed at Absarat on the Nile' February 1885
Two photographs of Donne in his Egyptian Army uniform These were taken at the
    'Alexander Bassano Studio, 25 Old Bond Street, London W', November 1885
A further study from the Alexander Bassano studio, 'Xmas 1885'
Special Certificate for the Examination for Promotion, 15 February 1886
Contract for service with the Egyptian Army, 1888-89
The 10th Sudanese Battalion on parade at Luxor
The Band of the 10th Sudanese Battalion
Photograph of Donne, 1891
Types of the Egyptian Army by R Simkin
Two photographs of Donne, circa 1895
Colours of the 35th Regiment of Foot
2nd Battalion, 35th Regiment at Fort Jamrud, North West Frontier, 1897
Lieutenant Colonel B. D. A. Donne at Malta

Lieutenant Colonel and Mrs Donne
Portrait of Donisthorpe Donne by M. Donne, 1899
Memorial stone of Colonel B. D. A. Donne at Heston Church cemetery
Photograph of Ghikko monastery, 1983
Photograph of the old church at Dali, 1983

List of abbreviations used by Donne in his Journals

Battn, Batt'on(s)	*Battalion[s]*
Captn	*Captain*
CO	*Commanding Officer*
Col	*Colonel*
Comt, Comdnt, Comdant	*Commandant*
Commt	*Commissariat*
Cr Sergt	*Colour Sergeant*
Detment	*Detachment*
Genl	*General*
Hd Qtrs	*Headquarters*
LCMP	*Local Commandant of Military Police*
Lt	*Lieutenant*
Lt Col	*Lieutenant Colonel*
PMO	*Permanent Medical Officer*
Qtrs	*Quarters*
Regt	*Regiment*
Sergt	*Sergeant*
Subtns, Subtrns	*Subalterns*
2IC, 2nd In Comd	*Second in Command*

Map of Donisthorpe Donne's travels in the Middle East.

1   Early days and Commissioning

BENJAMIN DONISTHORPE ALSOP DONNE was born in London on 4th October 1856, the son of Benjamin John Merifield Donne and Jane Donne of Crewkerne, Somerset. Benjamin Donne, the senior, was brought up by a wealthy Great Aunt, Mrs George Donne, and as heir to her estate was able to live a life of leisure and indulge in his love of painting, angling, yachting and travel. He was an accomplished artist, although self-taught. This talent was inherited by his son Donisthorpe who later became a very talented watercolour artist, although he did not develop this skill until after he was twenty years old.[1]

Donisthorpe Donne was educated at Wellington College and left the College sometime after 1870. A letter, written by him, to his two sisters Anna and Rose, dated "Sunday, September 26th" (1872) reveals that he was at that time attending Eastmans Royal Naval Academy, at Southsea, Hampshire, and was preparing for entry into the Navy. His letter gives an interesting insight into the daily life at such an Academy "... in the morning the doctor took all our chaps (eighteen in number) to see the Armoury. The guide said that there were more than eighteen thousand breech loading muskets & the whole of the middle of the room was filled up by them. There was a good deal of ancient armour and weapons, pistols, canons excetra, and he showed us the working of revolvers and breech loading muskets. Afterwards we went to Seagroves outfitting shop for the Navy and army and saw the different kinds of badges and uniforms that is (sic) worn. The Doctor then took us to a pastrycook shop (and) treated us each to a sixpence worth of sweets! ..."

By 1873 he was continuing his education at Sherborne School Dorset, and it was at the age of sixteen years that he started writing his Journal. The first entry is dated January 1873 and at that time he records that he was 'at home' at Merifield, Torquay, Devon.

From the early entries in the Journal it is obvious that Donisthorpe Donne was a keen observer and chronicler. The early notes in his Journal deal with his school days at Sherborne, social events, and a detailed account of a visit to Switzerland. On 22nd April 1874 he left Sherborne School and on 5th May set off from Crewkerne, where he had been staying with relatives, to Germany. On the 9th May he recorded that whilst at Niedersachswerfen, Hannover –

"... I stopped with this homely family for nearly a year, soon getting accustomed to German ways & generally spent most of the morning & p.m. studying French & German ..." During his stay in Niedersachswerfen he noted that on 14th September 1874 he travelled to Hannover, with C.F. Tufnell, to see the manoeuvres of the 10th Prussian Army Corps, noting that –

"... (we) passed several Regts coming home from march past & saw Emperor William[2] and his staff ...".

On the following day, 15th September, his entry reads

"... off at 5.30 a.m. to the review ground marching there alongside a Regt. There was a big sham fight of about 40,000 men engaged. Had a good view of the Emperor William ..." This was, without doubt, an impressive sight to a young man who was destined to become an officer in the British Army. Donisthorpe Donne eventually left the family at Niedersachswerfen on 21st April 1875 and returned to England via Heidelberg, Cologne, Amsterdam and Rotterdam to London.

His entry for 13th May 1875 showed him to be resident in London and had commenced to "... cram up for the Army Exam ..." On 15th July the entry shows:

Heildelberg Ruins, April 1875.

Barbarossa Tower, North Germany, April 1875 [above, left]. Tower of Barbarossa, April 1875 [above].

Rothenburg, 1875.

"... today the examination commenced at Burlington House, and lasted until the 19th and I found I had succeeded so far as passing the qualifying exam ...". The results were published in the national papers on 12th August which confirmed his acceptance into the Army. On 10th September 1875 Donne was Gazetted as a Sub Lieutenant in the Army on the Unattached List and on the following day he travelled to Sandhurst and joined the College. On the 12th September he recorded "... The course of studies, parading, riding etc now began, General Sir D Cameron commanding the College ..."[3] Soon after his arrival he travelled over to Wellington College to renew acquaintances with the staff who were still there from the days of his term at the College. On the 16th September he noted "... 1st riding lesson ..." The entry for 18th December, 1875 reads: "... *Sandhurst – London.*

Sir R. Airey[4] came down & inspected the Sub Lieuts on parade after which the Xmas vacation began ..." During the Christmas vacation Donne remained in London until 1st January 1876 and then visited Cheltenham, Exmouth, Torquay and Crewkerne. He returned to Sandhurst on 14th February 1876 –
"... *London – Sandhurst.*

Went back to Sandhurst as one of the Senior term. Riding and other courses went on as usual ...". He continued his training and only at odd intervals does he mention the type of training and recreational pursuits but these do give an insight as to the activities of the young officer under training at Sandhurst at that time. Brief entries include:

March 1876

11. "Walked to Aldershot with King and Cruse.
     (Poor Cruse was afterwards killed in India).[5]
18. Walked to Windsor with King and Cruse & back over Bagshot.

May 1876

1. Survey at Barehill. 1st parade with rifles.
2. Drove over to Aldershot Long Valley with others & saw march past before the Queen.[6]
3. Fortification scheme at Sandhurst vill[e]. (sic)
18. First riding lesson with stirrups – what a treat the fellows thought it! ..."

**Ruins of
Rothenburg Castle,
1875.**

and by way of recreation –

26.   "Sandhurst – London. Up to town with Eccles[7] to see a Cricket Match at Lords.
      London – to see the Queens parade at Horse Guards & then to Wilkinsons to inspect
      swords ..."

Donne had returned to Sandhurst by 31st May and on that date he records –

31.   "Pontoon bridging with casks on the lake.

June 1876
4.   Walked to Wellington College with Frith.
      (Frith was killed in Zulu War 1879 as Adjt 17th Lancers).[8]
20.   Advance Guard scheme at Haivley Hill.

July 1876
1.   Outpost scheme with troops from Aldershot.
      Went up to town and saw the Great Volunteer Review in Hyde Park.[9]
13.   Riding inspection at School.
25.   Passing out Exam commenced and lasted till 28th.
29.   *Sandhurst – Sherborne.*
      Public day. General Parade. My last day a(t) Sandhurst. I was sorry to leave, my time having
      been almost the most pleasant I can remember, and the fellows left to await appointment
      to Regts in different parts of the world, and many probably never to meet again. Most of my
      batch took appointments direct to the Indian Staff Corps. Went down to stop at
      Hetherington's for the break up of Sherborne School ...

August 1876
2.   *Crewkerne – London.* Started on a continental trip to join my people prior to joining a
      Regt abroad."

At this stage of his journal Donne obviously reviewed all that he had written and
commented –

"... Now that I have got thus far in my journal, I think it would be as well to improve my style a
little, and not only make entries of dates and doings, but also to make a picture to myself of my
thoughts and feelings of what I may see and do in the World, where ever Her Majesty's Service
may call me for if I were to continue to enter the perhaps monotonous routine of daily life in the
Service I should soon tire of it, and it would then cease to be natural ..."

   Donne left England on his tour of Germany and Switzerland on the 4th August and
returned on 17th September. During this leave he stayed at Dusseldorf on the night of
5th August and commented that the town appeared to house a large Garrison "... from
the numbers of German soldiers about ...". Whilst in Switzerland Donne spent some
time climbing peaks and in his journal he noted that on 29th August he attempted to
reach the top of Pitz Margna alone but had to turn back not far from the top due to the
recent fall of snow. On 2nd September Donne set off with a guide and reached the top
of Pitz Termoggia. On 3rd September he had news that he had been appointed as a Sub
Lieutenant in the 35th Royal Sussex Regiment which was then stationed at Barbados in
the West Indies. Donne commented that "... my people did not exactly relish the idea of
my going to such an outlandish place, and one so generously reputed as being
unhealthy, but the idea of adventure delighted me muchly ..." Donne spent the time
whilst he was waiting for sailing orders visiting friends and relatives at Crewkerne and
Exmouth. He finally received his orders to embark on the 15th October 1876. He was to
embark on HMS Simoon at Portsmouth on 23 October.[10] On 20th October Donne
revisited Sandhurst and dined in Mess once more. On 21st he travelled by rail to

Portsmouth and stopped overnight at the George Inn. On Sunday 22nd October he reported on board HMS Simoon which was, at that time, moored alongside the Dockyard jetty.

Notes to Chapter One

1. Letter from Donne to his daughter Grace, written from South Africa on 28th June 1902.
2. Kaiser Wilhelm I, King of Prussia and German Emperor (1797-1888).
3. The Annual Army List, 1874 by Colonel H. G. Hart, shows Lieutenant General Sir Duncan A. Cameron, KCB as Governor of the Royal Military College.
4. General Sir Richard Airey, GCB, Adjutant General to the Forces. Army List, July 1875.
5. Henry King was commissioned into the 6th Regiment of Foot with a seniority date of 10 April 1876. Clifford Cruse commissioned into the 11th Regiment of Foot with a seniority date of 12 February 1876. On leaving Sandhurst joined his regiment in India and died shortly afterwards at Poona on 11 December 1877. (Army List, February 1878).
6. The Illustrated London News, No. 1919, Vol. LXVIII of May 6, 1875. "... The Queen, accompanied by Princess Beatrice went to Aldershot on Tuesday and reviewed the troops in camp ... (she) was received on arrival at Farnborough Station by Lieutenant General Sir T. Steele, KCB, and staff who attended the Queen, escorted by a detachment of the 5th (Royal Irish) Lancers, ... at half past three accompanied by Field Marshal the Duke of Cambridge reviewed the troops of the Aldershot division in the Long Valley."
7. Richard H. Eccles commissioned into 97th Regiment of Foot with a seniority date of 10 September 1875. Army List, November 1877.
8. Frederick J. Cokayne Frith. Commissioned into 17th Lancers with a seniority date of 12 February 1876. (Army List, November 1877). Frith was serving as Adjutant of the 17th Lancers when he was killed. An account of his death appeared in 'The recollections of Miles Gissop with the 17th Lancers in Zululand" – edited by D. Clammer and published in the Journal of the Society for Army Historical Research, Vol. LVIII, No. 234, Summer 1980. In his account Glissop records Frith's death as follows – 5th June 1879 – "... half the men dismounted and commenced firing, the Zulus firing smartly in return but the bullets passed over our heads. Lieut & Adjt Frith was on the left with the Col and the latter was just saying "You are all right men. You are all right they are all passing over your heads," when a bullet pierced the heart of our poor Adjt. He only exclaimed 'Oh! I'm shot' and dropped dead off his horse ..."
9. The Illustrated London News, No. 1928. Vol. LXIX, July 8, 1876. "... The Great Volunteer Review in Hyde Park, on Saturday in honour of the Prince and Princess of Wales, proved a complete success. The assembled forces of volunteers, yeomanry cavalry and militia, comprised not less than seventy-four regiments with a nominal strength of about, 30,000 men besides regular troops ..."
10. The movement order gave the following embarkation details.

> "Horse Guards
> War Office
> 14th October 1876
>
> Sir,
>   Passage to Barbados having been provided for you on board HMS 'Simoon'.
>   I am directed by the Field Marshal Commanding in Chief to request that you will proceed to Portsmouth in time to embark in the above vessel by 2 pm on the 23 Instant reporting yourself before embarking to the General Officer Commanding the Troops at the Station.
>   You must not take with you more baggage than 45 cubic feet ..."

Pitz Termoggia and Fex Thal, Engadine.   August 1876.

Self portrait of Donne as a young man.

Provisional and final movement orders,   **October 1876.**

2 Service in the West Indies – Barbados

DONNE'S FIRST sea voyage to join his Regiment began on the 23rd which he recorded in his journal.

October 1876

23. "Reported myself to the CO where I met several others who were about to embark. I went on board ship where I met a draft of the 35th for Barbados under Capt Lloyd & Lt Thomson & found myself in a cabin with Mills 102^d, George 102^d & Thomson (35th).[1]
    In the afternoon we cast off and went out to Spithead for orders.

24. H.M.S. Simoon. I had the morning watch from 4 to 8 going down channel & in the afternoon we rounded close to the Lizard & the Landsend bound for Pembroke Dock, the weather remaining perfect.

25. We anchored off the dockyard and took off more drafts for Gibraltar, so now we were packed pretty full. In the eve we started again down Milford Haven protected by forts on all sides, & saw the 'Great Eastern' laid up at Milford. About sundown we saw the last of the British coast & headed for Kingston, where we found ourselves next morning after a calm crossing.

26. Kingston, Dublin. I went up with George to explore the Irish capital, & we did not bring away the best opinions with us of Dublin ...

27. Had the watch from 8 to 2 pm and more Drafts having been embarked for Gibraltar, we finally set sail at 3 pm & shortly afterwards passed the spot where the 'Vanguard' went down. On the 29th we experienced a stiff breeze & swell in the 'Bay' and several fellows were ill, but I just managed to keep my equilibrium. The next day we were in sight of Cape Finistere and kept along the coast.

    On the am of the 31st we were off Berlingas Isles & coasted along close to the Portuguese coast passing the Castle of Cintra, Cape Roca, & Lisbon.

November 1876

1. Then we passed the ever memorable Trafalgar Bay & shortly afterwards rounded Cape Tarifa the most southerly of Europe, and at the end of a lovely day sighted the rock of Gibraltar.

2. Simoon, Gibraltar. The Channel Squadron was at anchor in the Bay, and we went alongside the New Mole and landed all the drafts for the different Regts in Garrison (23rd, 69th, 102^d, 4th R.B.).[2] I walked in town with Johnstone A.H.C.[3] & out to (the) Neutral Ground & North Front where the Rock above is pierced with numerous batteries & in eve (sic) to Europa point where the 102^d were quartered.

3. Gibraltar. I started to go to the top of the Rock, 1600ft, & from the Signal Station had a superb view of the Mediterranean & Country around & Africa to the south. The Regt^s in Garrison were now marching down to the Neutral Ground below, for a grand review and the ships at the same time were landing 2 Naval Brigades, & the Spanish Gov^{nr} of Algeciras landed below at the Ragged Staff. So I made my way down to the Neutral Ground to see the march past, before the Gov^{nr}, Lord Napier of Magdala, which was a goodly show.

4. Ship coaled today & in consequence almost untenable.

5. Sunday. La Touche, 2^d W.I. Regt[4] & self crossed the Bay to Algeceras in Spain to see a bull fight, which to say the least it was tame & disgusting but as an Englishman was the bull fighter it was said to be more than usually interesting & we had the celebrity of lunching with this fellow at an Inn there, & came back after with several fellows of the Simoon having had a most festive day of it.

6. Today we were to sail for Barbados but had to first land an officer who was taken suddenly ill, at 2 pm we cast off & coasted along the African shore of Morocco, until night put the land out of sight & we were fairly on our way across the Atlantic.

7. I have now a good cabin to myself, and we ran 190 miles with Barbados 3056 more.

9. On the 9th a gale of wind sprang up which continued 3 days, & I had a regular dose of mal

de mar. The sea ran very high, & we were blown out of our course and lost (a) jib boom.

12.   ...I came on deck again the sea going down fast. The next day a Marine died, & we put him over the side, the sea still running high, & the ship rolling tremendously & dipping her boats, we now headed for Cape de Verde Isles to coal.

16.   The sea had now quite gone down, & we were in the land of Flying fish which were in shoals all around. We sighted the Cape de Verde Islands, and anchored in the fine harbour of St Vincente. The island(s) were very high & mountainous, & of a rugged volcanic appearance.

17.   Cape de Verdes. Went on shore, and explored the squalid looking Portuguese town, & up to the British Consul's, & Telegraph Stations, which were the only decent places on the Island. There was not a single lady in the place! We weighed again at 8 pm, & steered for Barbados about 9 days voyage.

19.   H.M.S. Simoon at sea. We were now in the tropics & it was 84° in the shade. The trade winds were now in our favour so we set sail, & ran 277 miles – Barbados 1600. The weather was perfect throughout this passage & nothing occurred to mar our tranquility & we made on the average about 240 miles a day. When about 300 miles to (the) east of Barbados the colour of the sea suddenly changed which no one could explain satisfactorily, but I imagine it had something to do with the great rivers of South America. We sighted no single craft.

25.   Wind changed with heavy showers which betokened the proximity of land.

26.   H.M.S. Simoon – Barbados. This morning on going on deck I found the island of Barbados full in sight & this was my first view of the tropics & West Indies. It seemed highly cultivated & very green with the ripe sugar cane fields & groups of cocoa nut trees along the shore, but the island was flat, & I can well imagine how disappointed Kingsley was when a few years ago he visited it after his glowing account in Westward Ho. Before dropping anchor in Carlyle Bay at 10 am we had some heavy tropical showers. The Col & Adjt^5 came off soon after, & at 4 in the aft(ernoon) I landed with the draft of 90 men on the Engineers Wharf, & marched up to the Bks headed by the Band of the Regt, & were inspected by the C.O. Col Tisdall. I dined with the Regt that night, the custom with all fellows on first joining, & put up in Courtenay's room.^{6} I was introduced to our friends the mosquitos for the 1st time that night having no nets to sleep under, & they evidently seemed to enjoy a newcomer, for I did not get much sleep.

27.   Drove into Bridgetown (Capital of Barbados) with Chapman^7 & (went) on board the Simoon.

28.   The Regt played the 'Simoon' fellows at cricket, & I dined at the RA & RE Mess at the stone barracks that eve.

29.   Today I think it was that Ma Genl (sic) Farren^8 inspected our draft on the Savannagh^9 together with two Comp^y of the 2nd W.I. Regt who were going to the West Coast.

December 1876

1.   The Gov^{nr} Pope Hennesy, whom the Barbadians seemed cordially to detest & who is credited with having been the cause of the late riots in the island left for England.

2.   Called on the Genl & others.

3.   Subaltern of the day for the 1st time, and walked down to the usual rendezvous at the 'Rocks'. I took over quarters now at the Stone Bk^s the other end of the Savannah, and went on with recruits drill, & attending courts martial etc.

8.   The Lt Gov^{nr} Dundas^{10} gave a Levee to which we went in full tog.

10.   Walked with Imbusch into the country. The Regt still kept up two Dett^{mts} in the interior at Gun Hill & Moncrieff.

12.   Dance at the Gov^{ors} at Government House & made many acquaintances.

16.   Went to the Island Horticultural Show in Bridgetown where there was a large assortment of Tropical produce on show.

19.   Mails arr.(ived) & Gov^{nr} Strahan landed. Guard of honor (sic) etc.

22.   Into Bridgetown & to 'Ice House', which out here is an indispensible institution but a very

expensive one.

25.   Xmas Day. Went round the Barracks (with the) mens dinners with the Governor & ladies, & went on board the German training ship 'Nymphe' in aft.
26.   The officers of (the) German ship 'Nymphe' dined with the Regt.
27.   Small hop at the General's.
31.   St Ann's, Barbados. The old year out, which ended a fairly eventful one for me.

January 1877

1.   New Year's day in the Tropics. Although much hotter than our ordinary summer at home, this was the cold season in the West Indies. During most of the day there was generally a pleasant land or sea breeze blowing, dying away towards evening, and although the men used to play cricket all day long on the Savannah even without hats on, they never seemed any the worse for it, and since the Garrison has been properly drained, the scourge of yellow fever has been unknown in Barbados. The road to Bridgetown, called Bay Road, was very hot to walk on, and I often used to go in and out on foot although most fellows indulged in 'Buggies'. The odors too, coming from the shanties on each side of the way was not particularly enhancing to the route. The great promenade of the Barbadians or 'Bims', was a place called the Rocks bejoining the Garrison of St Ann's at a suburb called Woking. I think Chester in his 'Transatlantic Sketches' is rather hard on Barbados for we always found the planters very hospitable although entertaining a too high idea of their noble island. We had muster parade today, & I dined on board the German ship 'Nymphe', & went afterwards to the Serg[ts] dance which I had occasion to regret the next morning, however experience is a good thing in its way."

For the next three months Donne spent his time at St Ann's Barbados carrying out his duties as a subaltern and enjoying the social life of the island. Entries in his journal show him attending dinners, dances and with the arrival of the West Indian fleet on the 20th January the Garrison played the fleet at cricket and generally acted as hosts to the Naval visitors. The fleet departed for Trinidad on 30th January. On the 23rd February Donne

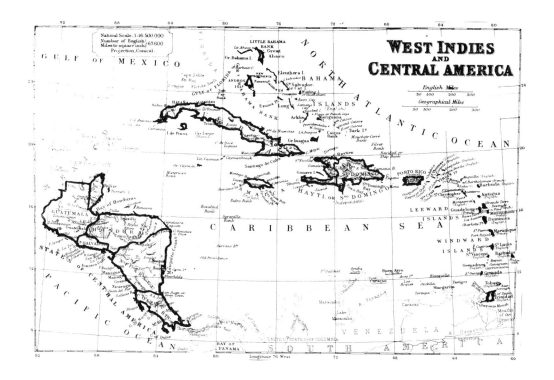

recorded in his journal "...I was highly delighted today to find myself on orders to go to Jamaica to join the half batt^n of the Regt there when the 'Simoon' returned..."

The 'Simoon' arrived back in Barbados from Africa on the 20th March with the 1st West India Regt on board. The journal shows Donne as boarding the vessel on the following day.

March 1877

21.   "Packed my baggage off to the 'Simoon' & went to the Gov^{nr} & others & in the eve the 1st W.I. Regt dined (in the 35th Regt Mess) which was my last at H^d Q^{rs} & I went on board the 'Simoon' with them.

22.   H.M.S. Simoon We set sail in the morning for Jamaica & it was not long before the fishes became aware of my presence on board, but I soon pulled round & appeared that night all right at dinner. Barbados soon began to get dim to leeward but for hours after the smell of the sugarmaking from those crowded estates was wafted over to us, and was anything but pleasant. When at a distance one gets a very poor idea of their size and shape of that little sugar manufactory. The islands of St Vincent and St Lucia were now towering up in front of us – links that reminded one so much of that wonderous chain of islands forming the West Indies and Windward Groups as when the old Bucaneers & the Pioneers to the New World sailed through them & made their wonderful discoveries & where later on the Fleets of England won such splendid victories over the French and Spanish.

The high rugged outline and crater of St Lucia with wreaths of cloud below & a glassy sea beneath gave a wierd grandeur to the outline of that beautiful island over whose possession so much British blood had been shed. As the sun went down we found ourselves in the Caribbean Sea. Most of the 1st West fellows slept on deck being literarily eaten out of their cabins by the numbers of 'Norfolk Howards' introduced by the black soldiers, but (I) had the luck to get a cabin with a Dr Chalcomb who embarked at Barbados. For the next four days we sailed along the same glass calm sea & played ciots (sic) most of the day. It rained most of the 26th & this obscured the high land of Jamaica in front.

27.   When I came on deck at 6 am we were going alongside the dockyard at Port Royal and I beheld one of the finest sights I have ever seen. The magnificent harbour of Kingston, perhaps one of the finest in the world, with the Liquanca plains & the Blue Mountains in all their majestic beauty beyond. At that early hour there seemed such a tranquil hazy loveliness about the scene which in the many books I have read I have never found adequately described. My destination in the Mountains, Newcastle, where the white troops are quartered was then pointed out, and looked like a stray flock of sheep on the steep hillside above the clouds which were circling round the lower valleys of the Port Royal Mt^s and the mountains and mangrove swamps were reflected in the waters of the harbour that looked like an immense landlocked lagoon and it was some time before I could pick out the way I had come in. This then was the Island of the Antilles so deadly and treacherous to Europeans! and over which my friends had congratulated me on *not* being sent to! I went up to Kingston the Capital, in the cutter & and put up (in) a lodging house in Duke St patronized by the Military and kept by one Miss Smith. It is curious that the Landladies in Jamaica seem always to prefer the maiden prefix! There is nothing whatever noteworthy about Kingston, & the streets are the worst I have ever seen, being watercourses or drains. I drove to Up Park Camp & found most the 1st West[11] officers sitting outside their Mess or sitting down in their new Q^{trs} ... the Regt had previously landed & marched out under Major Niven."[12]

Notes to Chapter Two

1. Captain Thomas Lloyd, 35th Regt of Foot. Sub Lieutenant Arthur George, 102nd Regt of Foot. Lieutenant George Arthur Mills, 102nd Regt of Foot. Lieutenant George Leonard Thompson, 35th Regt of Foot. Hart's Army List, 1876, pages 279 and 348.
2. The regiments were the 23rd (Royal Welsh Fusiliers) Regt of Foot, 69th (South Lincolnshire) Regt of Foot and 102nd (Royal Madras) Fusiliers. Donne appears to have made an error in his numbering of the fourth regiment. The 2nd Battalion, the Rifle Brigade (The Prince Consort's Own) was stationed at Gibraltar at the time of Donne's visit and the Battalion had been on station since 1874. The 4th Battalion had, at this time, been stationed in India since 1873.
3. Lieutenant of Orderlies George Johnston, Army Hospital Corps. Hart's Army List, 1879, page 381.
4. Captain George Digges La Touche, 2nd West India Regiment. Hart's Army List, 1877, page 361.
5. Commanding Officer – Lieutenant Colonel Archibald Tisdall
    Adjutant – Lieutenant Herbert Langdon Sapte, appointed adjutant from 12 August 1876. Hart's Army List, 1877, page 279.
6. Lieutenant Edward James Courtenay. Hart's Army List, 1877 page 279.
7. Lieutenant Arthur Thomas Chapman. Hart's Army List, 1877, page 279.
8. Major General Richard Thomas Farren, CB, Commanding the Forces, West Indies. Hart's Army List, 1877, page 126.
9. Savannah – a grassy plain with scattered trees.
10. Lieutenant Governor – George Dundas Esq. Hart's Army List, 1877, page 126.
11. 1st West India Regiment. Hart's Army List, 1877, page 360.
12. Major Knox Rowan Niven, 1st West India Regiment. Hart's Army List, 1877, page 360.

Merefield House, the Donne home at Crewkerne, Somerset. The drawing shows the east wing, 1948.

3   Jamaica 1877 and 1878

DONNE REMAINED in Jamaica for almost two years and his journal reveals that although the posting was uneventful as far as soldiering it had moments of crisis when yellow fever became prevelant within the regiment. The journal for Jamaica commences with Donne collecting his heavy baggage:

March 1877

29.   "The next morning I went to Ordnance Wharf to get at my baggage & then with Lowry 1st West[1], lionized the town, or city, as it is called and were photographed, I indulging in a big helmet for which I had to give the exhorbitant sum of £2. I then started for Newcastle driving to the Gardens near Gordon Town at the foot of the hills, the road ends here, & one has to ride the remaining 5 miles (up a) steep hill, & a very grand & picturesque ride it is, the hills of rocks being covered with the most luxuriant tropical vegetation, and the peeps between the overhanging ledges of rocks are grand beyond measure. To a newcomer it requires a good nerve to ride along some of the ledges, & I arrived up in 1½ hrs. My baggage being brought up on the heads of women. I found most of the Officers of the Dett[t] at the Mess. Lt Col Hackett[2] in Command.

30.   I shook down into Campbell's[3] Qtrs & my heavy baggage arr(ive)d on the 30th. The view from the elevated station of 4,000 ft up is vast & magnificent one which will always remain fixed in my mind. The immense vista of land & sea I should imagine could rarely if ever be equalled. The horizon when visible being nearly 80 miles off, & the plains with villages & towns scattered about lying below like a map spread out. The miles of Palisados farming, the harbour with Port Royal at the end looking dizzy in the heat & Fort Augusta opposite, then Kingston, Up Park Camp & Spanish Town.

During all the time I remained at Newcastle I never tired of this splended erie (sic) which was often rendered doubly sublime by clouds & thunder storms rolling down. In the aft(ernoon) I took my first walk around the celebrated fern walks which are one of the sights of the West Indies where ferns & parasites of every size and sort grow in wild disorder and the apparent entire absence of birds or sounds adds to the enchantment of the scene.

April 1877

1.   Walked with Keighley 2[d] W.I.[4] to Craigton where we arr(ive)d dripping with sweat and stopped to lunch at the Lacocks. Craigton is one of the prettiest places in the hills & used to belong to the Gov[or].

5.   Rode to Greenwich... & called on Col Cox.[5]
     Called on Mrs Hackett.

8.   Newcastle, Jamaica. Walked round to St Catherine's peak. Grand view of Yallah's River and Blue Mountain Range beyond.

11.   Today several of the 1st West India fellows came up to lunch, & we had a ladies lawn tennis day.

13.   Col Cox CB inspected the Half Batt[n] on parade.

16.   Campbell & his dett[mnt] returned from Nassau.

17.   Capt Osmer left.[6] On account of a money robbery in my Qtrs by my servant the police Sergt came up next day & took my black servant off to jail at Gordon Town.

19.   Rode to Gordon Town & then up a valley to Le Reys the magistrate with the prisoner then on to Half Way Tree in the plains & further to Up Park Camp. Lunched here & then took train into Kingston & (back) again & rode up the hill in time for mess.

20.   Newcastle, Jamaica. Changed into better Qtrs at the top of the hill..."

Donne continued to spend his spare time visiting various scenic spots, within the immediate area of the camp, and attending social lunches and dinners. He attended court at Gordon Town when his servant was remanded for the Quarter Session. The

Queen's birthday was celebrated on 24th May with a parade. The journal entry for that day reads:

May 1877

24. "Queen's birthday and general parade under Ballingall..."[7]

On 27th May Donne comments on the local weather:

27. "The rains continued more or less every afternoon with now and then a vivid thunderstorm and some striking effects which continued until the middle of June..."

and then in the latter part of June the season for pigeon shooting brought the following comments in the journal:

June 1877

20. "Out to Hardware Gap pigeon shooting. These ring tail pigeons are one of the delicacies of Jamaica, and this is the season for them to fly over the Gaps in the mountains down to Buff Bay.

23. Into Kingston with the Col. Lunched at 40 Duke Street with Halldine, & rode out again. Gen Farren[8] arr[d] to inspect..."

The journal continues to record various social activities and Donne's servant was finally dealt with on the 28th June, when he was found guilty of theft and sentenced to a years jail. The journal then moves into July:

July 1877

4. "Gen Farren inspected the half Batt[on] which lasted 'till 4 pm.

5. Inspection continues. Trafford[9] & self rode off to Ropley to see the Brooks & stopped the night.

6. After a very slow day & oceans of rain I started to walk back to Newcastle in the deluge & got back soaked..."

The next entry in the journal of any military interest is at the end of July when Donne records:

July 1877

22. "... I began a course of Signalling now which lasted a month ..."

Although Donne commented in his journal that the Barbados camp was free from yellow fever this was not the case in Jamaica and in August one of the officers of the 35th Regiment of Foot died.

August 1877

10. "Lieut Gordon Rushworth died, & was buried, of yellow fever ..."

Two other entries of note for the month of August are:

23. "The new Gov[or] Sir A Musgrave arr[d] in the island amid much negro rejoicings.

28. Regular signalling by day & night was now installed between us (at Newcastle Camp) and Up Park Camp, except when interrupted by the cloud or mist ..."

Donne had, by this time, taken an interest in the many varieties of ferns and he, and some of his fellow officers spent their free time out in the bush collecting the varieties and he comments that his collection "...amounted to about 200 species...". On 12th September Donne went to Up Park Camp to take his Lieutenants examination and dined with the 1st West India Regiment that night. The entry reads:

September 1877

13. "Set too at answering 100 questions, & in the aft(ernoon) drilled a Company of the 1st West India... Board consisted of Lt Col Niven, Capt Platt RA & Capt Pollard 1WI.[10]

14.   Returned to Newcastle.
17.   In the aft. There was a very clear view of Arnotts Bay from The Gap. Near the Gap is a
      cemetery where a large number of the 84th Regt[11] were buried during a yellow fever
      epidemic 8 years ago ..."

Normal military training and duties continued and these together with the social
events were recorded by Donne. The entry for 19th October not only covered the
military aspect but also gives details of a possible yellow fever epidemic. The entry
reads:

October 1877

19.   "Ma Gen Fellowes (sic)[12] inspected the Half Batt[on] & I shifted into the Qtrs vacated by
      Buscarlet[13] who went home sick. Grove[14] was also very bad with fever now & this was
      indeed the beginning of the yellow fever epidemic which was said to attack the hills about
      every 10 years, and no ease had been known for nearly that time above a certain altitude,
      and since the Lt Gov[ors] death it had been gradually stealing up house by house, although
      it had not yet attained Newcastle. Capt Mackay[15] the Brigade Major & one of the little
      Lacocks at Craigton died on the 21st & then we were placed in quarantine or kept in the
      Cantonments. It lasted off and on for many months during which time we had a very slow
      time of it.
30.   Mrs Lacock died at Craigton today.

November 1877

5.   Handed over the Barracks & started at mid-night with E Compy under Gem[16] for Port
      Royal for Musketry. Marched down to Kingston during the night arriving at (the) Wharf at
      5.30 am & were taken down by gun-boat to Port Royal, and after taking over Bks & Qtrs
      which were in a very antiquated and wretched condition; lunched and dined on board the
      Guard ship 'Urgent' which was the one saving point about the place. We dined on board
      every night & went on the range at day break & sun set, even then it was awfully hot work,
      the range being one of the worst imaginable. Grove[17] started for England in the 'Moselle'
      having just scraped through his fever.
11.   Port Royal, Jamaica. I hired a boat & sailed over to a place opposite called Port Henderson
      which in the old days of Jamaica prosperity was the watering place of the Spanish Town
      people, & a sugar wharf, but now was reduced to almost nothing. I had a bath in a very cool
      spring in the rocks here which is the only recommendation to the place & went up to the
      12 Apostles Battery, now deserted. Then I sailed along to the once celebrated & notorious
      Fort Augusta where the tombs on the shore attest the havoc yellow fever played amongst
      the Troops here. The fort, which once mounted 100 guns is now gone to rack and ruin &
      suggestive of melancholia in the extreme. I sketched some of the tombs on the shore &
      after a blazing hot day, rowed back.[18]
17.   Up Park Camp. Came up to Camp by market boat, & put up with Loveridge, 1st WI[19] &
      walked round the camp in afternoon.
18.   Port Royal. Back again to Port Royal in eve taking boat from Kingston.
19.   Yellow fever broke out at last at Newcastle. Sergt RA died. So it was impossible to say how
      long we should be detained here.
22.   Up to Kingston by the Market boat, I lunched at the familiar 40 Duke Street.
27.   Rode round the Palisades through grave yards, swamp & cocoanut (sic) trees to the Plum
      Point Lighthouse & back.

December 1877

4.   In the Gazette today I was promoted to be Lieutenant in the Regt with seniority from 10th
      Sept 1875.
6.   Port Royal. The English Mail came in, and brought Vandeleur, Barnes, Thomson and
      Powell,[20] from H[d] Q[rs]. I went on board the 'Nile' to meet them & up to Kingston, &
      brought Bt Ma (sic) Barnes[21] back by (the) market boat to take command of the Co[y] at

Kingston Harbour, Jamaica, 1878.

Port Royal. We were to march up to Newcastle on Saturday 8th.

8. Port Royal – Newcastle. After lunch at the Lloyds[22] we left at 3.30 in (the) steam launch and left Kingston for the march up at 5pm. I marched the Dett[t] to Gordon Town & then rode up the hills on my pony with Barnes, & after a wet & cold ride arr(ive)d at the Mess at 12.30 am wet through. It continued to rain without ceasing for nearly a week.

11. Took over Act Q[r] M[r]-ship from Campbell during his absence at Port Royal.

13. Yellow jack broke out again & two more men died, so we were more isolated than ever, & many of the men put under canvas at Farm Ridge etc. In fact now that the fever seemed to have settled upon the Cantonment it was considered expedient to put the men of every hut that was affected under canvas immediately and this was found to check it considerably, for none of the men took it after going under canvas. The married men were moved higher up the hill, & subsequently placed under canvas, and on the 14th the R[l] Art[y] (Royal Artillery) who had lost several men were suddenly marched down the hill to camp in the plains.

15. Two more men died today of Yellow fever ...

19. 1 Gunner died ...

21. 1 man died (of) Yellow fever. Thomson[23] & self rode down to Yallah's River ..."

Donne records that on Christmas day a ladies dinner night was held in the Mess and during the remaining days of 1877 his journal shows him riding around the area visiting friends. On the last day of 1877 he records:

31. "This the last, was the coldest day in the year, & a heavy norther was blowing ..."

Donne dined with his Commanding Officer on New Year's day, 1878, and in his journal for the 2nd January he notes:

January 1878

2. "Glass down to 55°. Continued to be Act. Q'Master with extra pay etc until Campbell came back from Port Royal.

8.   Departure of Major & Mrs Ballingall[24] for England on retirement. A touching adieu on their leaving the Reg[t]. Many invalides were sent off next day.

15.   The Artillery were marched off to Camp of Isolation. On the 16th Mrs Hackett had her school fete on the Tennis ground, & the married people were put under canvas on the 18th.

24.   Today we lost our CO Col & Mrs Hackett[25] leaving for Barbados. Major Vandeleur took command of the Dett[mt.]

      B[t] Major Barnes commanding (the Company)."

In his journal entry for the 4th February Donne comments that he "... heard of Clifford Cruse's death in India ...".[26] The first event of military note in his journal for February was on 11th February when "... the General and staff came & inspected the yellow fever encampment...", and after that date Donne's entries were confined to his social visiting until the 27th when once again he was sent off to the Port Royal rifle ranges. The journal records his detachment as follows:

February 1878

27.   "Port Royal. Started on my second expedition to Port Royal in command of D Co[y] marched off at midnight. Took over Qtrs & took to dining on board the 'Urgent' again. We did our shooting as before at 5 am & 4 pm, it being impossible to do anything in the middle of the day. Tennis & bowles at the Dockyard were the only amusements ..."

During March 1878 a number of ships visited the port, including the British West India fleet, which led to parties, visits to the naval vessels, cricket matches etc. On 17th March, a Sunday, Donne records:

March 1878

17.   "Marched the Dett[t] to church which edifice is solely remarkable for the number of its monuments to yellow fever victims...

18.   Finished the musketry course & on the 19th yellow fever appeared in the Dock(yar)[d].

21.   Port Royal – Newcastle. Started with the Comp[y] on board the 'Heron' for Kingston and after giving up (the) arms at the Ordnance marched to camp, & left again for Newcastle by the short cut through the jungle and arr(ive)[d] up about 9.30 taking over lines under canvas ...

April 1878

1.   Lt Gen Farren[27] inspected us. Full parade at 4.30 pm.

2.   Inspection continued & the Gen[1] dined."

Apart from the entry for 20th April which recorded that his Company moved location, involving the striking and re-erection of tents, little other than social events appear in the journal until 24th May.

May 1878

24.   "Celebrated Her Majesty's B-day (sic) by getting an awful soaking on parade in a heavy thunderstorm ..."

The months of June, July and early August passed without any entries of note. Donne continued to keep up his military training and attend all the social events which followed a seasonal pattern in Jamaica. The entry of 10th August showed that the yellow fever epidemic had not yet finished.

August 1878

10.   "On the 10th (went) to Gordon Town to shoe pony. One of the final acts of the yellow fever tragedy was poor Robinson's[28] death at Port Royal, where he had gone a few days ago. He went with the idea of never getting out alive, & we saw his funeral through the big telescope. He was buried where many hundreds of soldiers & sailors were buried before

him for the same fatal disease – cut off in the prime of life without much warning. Has God created this fair island paradise to be a scourge to the desecrating hand of the white man? ..."

His diary soon returned to its normal recordings of the round of social events.

21.   "Rode down to Lady Smith's Tennis, and on to camp to dine with Burke, 1st West,[29] an old Sherburnian...

22.   Up Park Camp – I rode in the most infernal downpour of rain imaginable, & had to stop at Camp for the night & tool up the next am.

25.   On the 25th to Ropley ...

28.   Gordon Town in heavy rain, & drove to Lady Smith's Lawn Tennis afternoon, & a dance at the Aughton's in eve. (My pony Kisber had to be shot today, glanders having set in. So he was a dead loss to me). Breakfast at Jamaica Club, and also with Thomas, who afterwards wanted to enlist in the Regt, & then called at Belair, & up to the Hills.

September 1878

10.   Rode to Kingston and Camp calling on R. E. Tons of rain all day. The Mann's gave a dance at Mt Mansfield on 12th a most successful one.
Rode home by 4 am.
Winter of the 1st West[30] came up sick & took my vacant room.

19.   I took over the Quarter Master duties from Campbell with extra pay at 6/-.

**Self portrait of Donne riding to the
camp at Newcastle, Jamaica.**

October 1878

9. Issued the new long bayonet to the men and I made up the mail budget.
20. Transfer & Settlement documents arr(ive)[d] by mail from Lukin to sign & Chapman arr(ive)[d] from England & took over D Company.[31]
25. A speciman day for Jamaica, as I had to attend at Gordon Town District Court on charges of slander from a nigger servant. I was defended by Mr McDougall, and judgement was given in my favour with costs. Drenching rain riding up the hill ..."

In November Donne was again unfortunate when he had his quarter robbed, for the third time, and he wrote in his journal:

November 1878

12. "This was a sorry day for me as my house was entered by burglers whilst at Mess, through the window, and most of my property sacked, including many valuables... although I immediately stirred up the police about it and everything to catch the rascals, they only succeeded in finding out that it was my discharged servant Low who had done it. One or two of the articles were found in his shanty, but he had decamped ..."

After a few entries dealing with social events Donne records his second piece of bad-luck that occurred during November:

25. "In riding round St Katherines peak today my horse slipped into the gully, but I got him up uninjured luckily, and myself with a slightly sprained leg ..."

The entries in the journal for the remainder of the year are confined to social events and visits to various camps on the island. On the 1st January 1879 Donne comments:

January 1879

1. "The regime of the 35th Regt in Jamaica is now fast drawing to a conclusion and now I have been here longer than any of the other officers. All the original lot have gone. How intensly I love the Island for its gorgeous scenery. ... I may as well mention here that the rain fall gauged at Newcastle for 1878 was 179 inches. Such a fall had not been known for years. On the 1st I was at Camp with Thomson and the 1st West gave a capital hop in pm ...
11. General Court Martial at Camp on Pte Samons, 35th, 5 years penal servitude. Drove into Kingston & went to performance at the Theatre in pm and met the Smiths. Rode up to Ropley on Sunday lunched as of yore with old Kerr and put up at Ropley.
    Rode next day to Gordon Town with Mrs Brooks & Miss Allwood...
16. On the 16th I went to Gordon T(ow)n to shoe the pony, and then up the Hills round by Raymond Hall, where I found the inmates at home...
    Escort duty to Gordon Town and coming round the corner of the hospital on return the pony tripped in a drain and I went over his head, but no damage ..."

By the end of January 1879 the regiment was preparing to leave and the events are chronicled by Donne:

25. "News arr[d] that the 'Orontes' troopship was to arr[e] in a day or two which took us greatly by surprise, so my occupation was principally at the store sending off baggage as fast as possible down the hill ...
26. My last Sunday at Ropley, we had to work with a will now to prepare for marching out and handing over to the 4th Kings Own Royals[32] who were to relieve us.
28. On the 28th the bulk of the baggage went on, and I rode to the Picquet House to superintend it, and up to Ropley and Ellerslie to stop. Mess was broken up.
29. The 'Orontes' appeared in sight off the Palisadoes, with the H[d] Q[trs] 35th and (a) wing (of the) 4th on board, and went alongside at Port Royal in evening.
30. Luckily during these movements the weather remained supremely fine The married people were got rid of today, and I went to a farewell picnic given to us at Ellerslie by the Mann's. Escorted two of the girls to Gordon Town afterwards and waited for the advance

party of the 4th to arrive, and found Pote[33] in command of them, but we did not get up to Newcastle 'till midnight.

31.   The Dett[t] 4th Regt took over Farm Ridge Bks.

February 1879

1.   & 2. I commenced handing over the Barracks and Cantonment to Pote & Taylor[34] of the 4th, after which I went to Ropley to supper, and at 10 pm we could hear the drums of the 35th strike up and the men cheer as the sound came across the valley in the still moonlight night, which meant that the Dett[t] had commenced their night march to Kingston. In riding up to Newcastle Hill I met the men coming down, and I put up that night with Taylor of the 4th.

3.   On Monday we finished the handing over and finally quitted the old hill, being the last 35th-er in the place. I did not get on board the Troopship until 1 o/c the next morn, driving 1st to camp & calling on the Allwoods & O'Malleys and dining that evening at Camp for the last time with the 1st W.I. Regt & I got down to Port Royal by ferry boat.

4.   H.M.S. Orontes – Got a cabin with Young.[35]
      Came up to Kingston by ferry once more and after lunch at Camp called to say G.B. to the Kembles & Lucie Smiths, and after a look in at Hirst's Lawn Tennis returned to the Orontes by launch with O'Donnel and Brown, 1st West ...".[36]

Notes to Chapter Three

1.   Sub Lieutenant Thomas Pepper Ernest Lowry, 1st West India Regiment.
      Hart's Army List, 1877, page 360.
2.   Brevet Lieutenant Colonel Simpson Hackett, 35th Regiment of Foot.
      Hart's Army List, 1877, page 279.
3.   Lieutenant Francis Selwyn Campbell, 35th Regiment of Foot.
      Hart's Army List, 1877, page 279.
4.   Lieutenant Herbert Hope Keighley, 2nd West India Regiment.
      Hart's Army List, 1877, page 361.
5.   Colonel J. W. Cox, CB, late 13th Foot, Colonel on the Staff, Jamaica.
      Hart's Army List, 1877, page 125.
6.   Captain James John Osmer, 35th Regiment of Foot.
      Hart's Army List, 1877, page 279.
7.   Major William Henry Ballingall, 35th Regiment of Foot.
      Hart's Army List, 1877, page 279.
8.   Major General Richard Thomas Farren CB, Major General Commanding the Forces, Jamaica. Hart's Army List, 1877, page 126.
9.   Lieutenant Lionel J. Trafford, 35th Regiment of Foot.
      Hart's Army List, 1877, page 279.
10. Lieutenant Colonel Knox Rowan Niven, 1st West India Regiment.
      Hart's Army List, 1877, page 366.
      Captain Wadham Pigott Platt, served in Jamaica from February 1876 until November 1880.
      Royal Artillery Officer List 1716-1899, page 80A.
      Captain Henry William Pollard, 1st West India Regiment.
      Hart's Army List, 1877, page 360.
11. 84th (York and Lancashire) Regiment of Foot.
12. Major General Edward Fellowes,
      Hart's Army List, 1878, pages 14 and 28.
13. Lieutenant Jules Robert Bowen Buscarlet, 35th Regiment of Foot.
      Hart's Army List, 1877, page 279.
14. Lieutenant Henry Charles Grove, 35th Regiment of Foot.

Hart's Army List, 1877, page 279.

15. Captain Hugh Allen Mackay, RA, Brigade Major, Jamaica.
    Hart's Army List, 1877, page 125.
16. Lieutenant Arthur S. H. Gem, 35th Regiment of Foot.
    Hart's Army List, 1877, page 279.
17. See note 14.
18. There appears to be no trace of the sketch of the tombs, nor can Donne's Grandson, Lieutenant Colonel W. D. Shaw, remember having seen any such work.
19. Captain Charles Gooden Loveridge, 1st West India Regiment.
    Hart's Army List, 1877, page 360.
20. Brevet Major John Ormsby Vandeleur
    Brevet Major Edward Robert Bigsby Barnes
    Lieutenant George Leonard Thomson
    Sub Lieutenant Robert Edward Powell
    – all 35th Regiment of Foot.
    Hart's Army List, 1877, page 279.
21. Donne uses a variety of unusual abbreviations in his diary and Bt Ma Barnes refers to Brevet Major E. R. B. Barnes.
22. Captain Thomas Lloyd, 35th Regiment of Foot.
    Hart's Army List, 1877, page 279.
23. Lieutenant George Leonard Thomson, 35th Regiment of Foot.
    Hart's Army List, 1877, page 279.
24. Brevet Major William Henry Ballingall was appointed Ensign 5 April 1844, and saw service with the regiment during the Indian Mutiny.
    Hart's Army List, 1877, page 279.
25. See note 2.
26. Clifford Cruse died at Poona on 11th December 1877.
    Notification of his death appeared in the Monthly Army List for February 1878.
27. See note 8.
28. Robert Robinson, born 27 September 1845. Appointed Surgeon 4 February 1877, died at Port Royal Jamaica on 11 August 1878.
29. Donne appears to have misspelled this name. The officer was Sub Lieutenant Henry B. Bourke who was at that time serving with the 1st West India Regiment.
    Monthly Army List, May 1878, page 360.
30. Sub Lieutenant Francis Bathie Winter, 1st West India Regiment.
    Hart's Army List, 1877, page 360.
31. Lieutenant Arthur Thomas Chapman, 35th (Royal Sussex) Regiment of Foot.
    Hart's Army List, 1878, page 279.
32. 4th (The King's Own Royal) Regiment.
    A Register of the Regiments and Corps of the British Army, by A. Swinson, Archive Press, London 1972.
33. Captain Charles St Clair Pote, 4th (Kings Own Royal) Regiment.
    Monthly Army List, October 1880, page 226.
34. Lieutenant George Goodwin Taylor, 4th (Kings Own Royal) Regiment.
    Monthly Army List, October, 1880, page 226.
35. Sub Lieutenant James Charles Young, 35th (Royal Sussex) Regiment of Foot.
    Monthly Army List, May 1878.
36. Sub Lieutenant George Boodrie O'Donnell and Sub Lieutenant Thomas Henry Browne, 1st West India Regiment.
    Hart's Army List, 1877, page 360.

4   Malta and the Continental Tour

DONNE DEPARTED from Jamaica on 5th February 1879, but he was a very different Donne from the young inexperienced subaltern who had arrived in the West Indies some two and quarter years before. He had, during that time advanced from being the junior officer of the regiment to being the eighth Lieutenant in the regiment which had at that time thirteen full Lieutenants. He had also become proficient in his duties and had gained much in the social graces which were so important in overseas stations during the Victorian era. He had learned to love the islands and even his dislike of the local inhabitants, which had probably been soured by his experiences with an unfortunate succession of unreliable servants helped to mould him into the efficient officer that he was later to become. It is unfortunate that from this first military posting only two small paintings have survived.

Donne records his departure from Jamaica as follows:

February 1879

5. "Next morning we finally cleared the Port Royal Point with the whole Regt of 900 men on board and soon found ourselves on the ocean swell outside the Palissados (sic) waving goodbye to the old island. The white lines of Newcastle with all the familiar hills and valleys soon passed out of sight round the Hills above the Yallah's River as we shaped our course for Malta. But all the lovely prospects of the island coast (which only darkness finally hid from our view) were very soon dissipated by that hell of all soldiers afloat, Mal de Mer, my old 'familiar' which stuck to me like a leech for two days, for we had a strong head wind, and the joys of watch keeping did not enhance it.

6. 7. & 8. On the 6th we had the dim land of St Domingo on the Port bow and on the 7th we saw the last of the Caribbean Sea. We passed through the Mona Passage about 4.0 a.m. 8th and being on the morning watch I could see the land of San Domingo and Porto Rico on both bows. My last glimpse of the West Indies. When morning dawned we were clear on the 'broad' Atlantic once more with a clear 3446 miles to run to the 'Pillars of the Mediterranean', as Gib was the lst land we expected to see.

10. On the 10th we passed the line of the Tropics and the 12th brought a perceptible change in the temperature.

16. We had 1650 miles to run to Gibraltar and passed through a good deal (of) Sargasso weed each day.

20. & 22. Sighted a large German ship, and 22^d the wind came more aft, so sail was set and we made 267 miles.[1]

23. Sunday we had a taste of some heavy squalls and strong wind, the ship rolling heavily. Gib 251 off.

24. The African Coast was sighted in the a.m. and passing Cape Tarifa, we dropped anchor off Gibraltar at 2.30 where we heard of the disaster at Isandhlwana,[2] in South Africa.
    Went on shore, and after going to the library, I drove to Europa Point to see Shewell R.A.[3] who was down with Rock fever in his Qtrs. Dined at the Hotel with Thomson[4] and after a near shave at being locked in the fortress (we managed to catch the Capt^s boat at the New Mole) got on board at 9. The weather was very cold here, after coaling ship, started at 11 p.m. for Malta.

25. Down the Mediterranean with a very cold N wind after us from the Snow M(oun)t(ain)s of the Sierra Nevada on the Port beam. Made 304 miles, the longest run of the voyage.

26. Coasted along the African Shore where the hills were covered with snow and very cold on deck.
    Passed lots of vessels beating up for Gib.

27. 27th the African coast was still in sight and passed between the small islands of Galita and Galena, and Cape Bon and Pantillarie at 2 a.m. 28th.

28.   We sighted the highland of Gozo and arrived in the Grand Harbour of Valetta at 4 p.m. with band playing etc. The General and officials came off, and congratulated us on the termination of our long voyage, and the ship was soon swarming with touts and tradesmen. The Regt was again fated to be split up.

March 1879

1.   We were all eager to land the next a.m. and I marched with the H^d Qtr^s and 3 Coys to be quartered at Fort Ricasoli at the entrance of the harbour, where we shook down into substantial stone barracks, floors and roof being all alike. The rest of the Regt marched out to Pembroke Camp. The Grand Harbour of Malta is magnificent and the view from the upper Barracks is (one) of Naval and Military grandeur. A mass of forts and batteries bristling with cannon etc wherein there is nothing of nature to catch the eye. But that soon palls after going there a few dozen times! We were in time for most of the winter festivities of the place, and as is usual balls and prances were the order of the day and night ashore and afloat. We of course found the weather very cold and fires 'de regeur' (sic).

4.   The officers of the 'Orontes' dined with us on the 4th and I took over command of 'B' (Trinidad) Coy from Dowdall.[5]

7.   On the 7th I dined at the R.A. Mess with Guthrie, RA,[6] and got home rather mixed up at about 5 a.m.

12.   The Regt was also served out with white helmets in place of the Shako and appeared on parade for the 1st time on the 12th.

13.   Called on the 61st Regt.[7]

16.   Sunday. Walked with Russell[8] to a fort to the eastward.

18.   Went on board the 'Jumna', Shot at Camp and to the 98th dance in the evening.

20.   Big concert at the palace in eve.

23.   Walked to San Rolo Fort with Guthrie and sailed back in a Joe's punt.

25.   General Sir A Borton and Gen. Fielding[9] inspected the Regt and dined.

27.   Regt out route marching to Zabbar Village and I had the pleasure of doing the Road report.

30.   Sunday. Called on board the new Torpedo ship 'Hecla' with Guthrie.[10] Then went to Fort St Angelo and called on Col Cary RA.[11]

April 1879

7.   During this week the Rifle Meeting at Pembroke Camp was on, and I met Mortimore of Sherborne School and lunch on board the 'Cruiser' on 6th.

8.   The Channel Squadron came in (Minoteur, Agincourt, Defence, Shannon). Cricket match and lunch with the 61st Regt.

11.   Called on board the new ironclad 'Shannon' and after on the 10th Regt[12] at Verdala. The Alexandra arr(ive)d with Admiral Hornby on board. There were now four Admirals flags flying in the harbour with 12 ironclads.

18.   The $H^d Qt^{rs}$ of the Regt moved to Pembroke Camp and took over quarters there. Court Martial at Verdala Fort on 19th which lasted all day.

23.   Went on Guard at (the) Palace for the 1st time with Cary.[13] (The Guard was a 24-hour duty).[14]

24.   Duke and Duchess of Connaught arr(ive)d and I drove in from Pembroke to the Grand Reception in p.m. The bands were massed on the Square, with illuminations etc.

25.   Grand Parade on Floriana before the Duke, the Regt marched (from Pembroke Camp) to Fort Manoel and crossed to Valetta side in boats, and home the same way.

28.   Sailed round the Grand Harbour with Thomson and Trafford[15] yacht hunting.

May 1879

1.   From the 1st May I had obtained 6 months leave of absence to go home, and handed over command of my $Comp^y$ B to Freeman.[16] I left with Vandeleur and Thomson[17] by the Italian mail str 'Leone' for Syracuse. The sea was heavy and the wretched str rolled & pitched causing as usual a horrid irruption of my interior ...”

Donne travelled overland from Naples, taking time to visit the ruins at Pompeii and the Colliseum at St Peters at Rome, then via Turin and Paris finally arriving in London on 11th May. His entry in the journal for that date gives an interesting comment on the cost of travelling:

11.   "London. I found England a cold country and my own people round a fire at 28 Hogarth Rd, on this occasion of my return home which was before I was expected, as I had hurried over the last part of journey. My expenses were £17. 5. 6d.

24.   ... my unfortunate port manteau arrived with most of the contents spoilt from immersion on its way home, including a collection of Jamaica ferns, and other nic nacs uniform etc..."

Only one water colour and one sketch appear to have survived from his tour of duty in the West Indies. It is therefore reasonable to assume that any he had painted, or sketched, such as the tombs adjacent to Fort Augusta, would have been transported in the port manteau and damaged beyond repair. The journal continues:

26.   "I was presented to H.R.H. Prince of Wales at the levee at the Court of St. James by General Renny, CSI, Col of the Regt.[18] There were an immense No of other presentations and the sight one not often witnessed. The same p.m. the Regtl Dinner came off at the Grosvenor Restaurant 2O past and present turning up ..."

On 2nd June 1879 the DAQMG of the Quarter-Master Generals Department wrote to Donne at his London address informing him that in response to his (Donne's) letter of 20th May, there are "... unexpected vacancies in the Army Signalling Class now assembling at Aldershot having taken place, there will be no difficulty in your being attached to it for instruction, provided you report yourself to the General Officer Commanding at Aldershot forthwith ..."[19]

Signal School, Aldershot, 1879.

Left: Donne in 1879, a photograph from Malta sent to his younger sister, Mary Rose Donisthorpe Donne, in April. Above: Certificate upon qualifying as an Instructor in Army Signalling, August 1879.

Donne joined the course and his entry in his journal reads:

June 1879

4.   "... went down on the 4th (to Aldershot) and was attached to our link Batt[n] the 107th Bengal Infantry,[20] in the 1st Brigade, South Camp and attended the Signalling class everyday under Major Le Mesurier, R.E. and remained there until the 8th August, taking an instructors certificate in Army Signalling. I went to Town Friday each week and remained till Sunday night. I generally paired of(f) in the class with Money of the 43rd."[21]

Whilst in London for weekends Donne continued to live a full social life, frequently dining at various clubs with a wide range of friends. The signalling course finished on 8th August and Donne successfully became qualified to act as an Instructor.[22] On completion of the course Donne spent from 15th August until 4th October visiting friends and relatives in the West Country. He commenced his journey back to Malta on 18th October travelling from Victoria Station, London to Dover; Dover to Ostend by boat and then taking time to visit the site of Waterloo on the afternoon of 19th October. His journey then took him to "... Coln and on to Coblenz on the Rhine ..."; on then to Heidelberg. From Heidelberg he travelled to Munich, Innsbruck, Verona, Florence, Rome and finally to Naples where he embarked on 28th October for Malta on the SS 'Etna' arriving on 30th, where he found "... my Regiment quartered in Lower St Elmo Barracks Valetta and I took over Qt[rs] accordingly... ". During the leave period Donne painted a number of small water colours, of which two have survived, these being 'The Signal School, Aldershot, 1879' and one entitled 'Ear of Dionesius, October 1879', which he had visited on 29th October. Donne resumed his military entries in the journal on his return:

October 1879

30.   "Commenced duty again & being attached to B[t] Major Gratton's (H) Coy.[23]

Ear of Dionosius, October 1879.

November 1879

3. Marched with Major Gratton's Coy to Pembroke Camp for the Annual musketry course, during which time we had some very heavy storms. I became a marksman by scoring 135 points.
20. On the 20th we marched back to St Elmo.
24. On the 24th I was appointed Instructor in Signalling to the Regt. Up to the close of the year we were mostly occupied with Garrison duties such as Public Guard Mounting in St George's Square, parades at Floriana and the Marso, at which latter we were brigaded with the 98th and 61st Regts.

December 1879

29. The 'Jumna' arrived with Money,[24] and several other fellows on board for India, but being quarantined, could not board her.
31. The bells of St. Paul's chimed out the old year and I could but reflect what a pleasant and changeful year 1879 had been to my humble self and B.D.G. Donne!"

Donne obviously wrote up his journal periodically probably from a daily diary kept in a rough form. His entry first for 1880 gives a brief resume of his activities:

January 1880

1. "I indulged in sketching more than usual, and put several courses through signalling and commenced regular practice days with flags on Monday, and every now and then brigade signalling with the other Regts, our chief station in the summer being the palace tower signal station, where there is a grand view of all Malta. The winter season was as gay as ever, with the fleet under Sir B Seymour generally in Harbour, and the usual number of Troops going to and from India.
13. I was a week on the sick list from the 13th to 17th.

February 1880

9. We were shocked at the sudden death at Sliema of Lt Col Blyth of the 35th;[25] this put the

Stromboli, December 1879.

officers in mourning for a month, and the funeral parade at which all the Regt. attended marched all the way from Sliema to Ta Braxia cemetery where he was interred at sundown. Several hundreds of naval and military officers attending.

March 1880

7. Being Officer of the Main Guard I dined with his Excellency the Govn^r, Sir A Borton at the palace.

23. 2^d Lt Newton King[26] of the Regt died at Baviere, the Regt being once again placed in mourning. He was buried with Mil^y Honours at Ta Braxia on the 24th.

27. The Gov^{or} had the whole of the Inf^y Bde out on review at the Marsa Ground.

April 1880

1. This was the first day of the Malta annual rifle meeting at Pembroke Camp and I won the Valetta Cup value 7£ (sic) against all comers Army & Navy at 500 (yards) getting 46 points out of a possible 50. There were 110 competitors. Also the 2nd Officers prize (silver cigarette case) against about 50 competitors. Shot also next day in the Gov^{nrs} and Champion prizes.

5. The inter Regt[1] Match came off, the RE winning with 98th, 35th, 1st, 10th and 61st.,[27] in succession. This concluded the Shooting Season.

8. The prizes were presented in the Gymnasium by Lady Fielding.

9. Today we held the Reg^{tl} Sports at Floriana, which was a great success and well attended, lunched with Hunter[28] at (the) 98th Mess.

12. Examination in Morn at St Elmo under Col Byron,[29] and passed for rank of Capt.

13. 13th and 14th were the Garrison Sports at the Marsa, in which the Reg^t came well to the front in the Tug of War.

16. Nearly all the 98th dined, Hunter with me.

30. Saw Gem[30] off for England on board Steamer.

May 1880

12. The 'Euphrates' arr^d from India and I came across King of the 6th,[31] and Foss S.C.[32]

A night on Mount Etna, December 1879.

The Greek Theatre, December 1879.

29.   The Queen's B'day was celebrated today the Troops lined the ramparts of Grand Harbour, and firing a feu de joie. The Regt marched home through Valetta.

June 1880

4.   Commenced a course of big gun drill at St Jame's Cavalier which went on till 1st July. Old Tailor (sic) (Taylor) of the 101st[33] dropped in on board the Himalaya on his way to join the Bengal Staff Corps and came to breakfast & lunch on 5th after which I saw him off on board ship.

13.   News of Barnes[34] death at the Cape which put the officers again in crepe. Grattan filling his majority.

July 1880

5.   Today Campbell[35] & self started on a 3 weeks trip to Sicily by the Italian mail boat, and landed next a.m. at Syracuse ..."

Donne completed a number of water colours during this leave. He had, however, painted a water colour of Stromboli in December 1879. Four paintings exist dating from the leave in Sicily these being:

— night on Mount Etna.
— The Greek Theatre, Taormina.
— Temple of Juno, Lucinia, Girgenta.
— Temple of Jupiter.

The journal gives a graphic account of the journey through Sicily.

6.   "We made straight for Catania where we found the heat nearly suffocating.
At noon next day we started on our projected trip to the top of Etna, taking with us a major domo to act as interpreter. After driving to Nicolosi began the real part of the ascent on mules, after passing through the charming and changeful scenery of the slopes of the m(oun)t(ain) we arr(ive)d at the Casa del Boseo and then continued our ride up to the Casa Inglese. After clearing the forests we gradually rose to the desert regions where all traces of vegetation soon disappeared and nothing but a dreary waste of lava and ashes met the view. At 10 p.m. long after dark we arr(ive)d at the Casa Inglese, half benumbed by the cold which was a severe test to the constitution after the great heat of the plains. After passing a very uncomfortable night during which my companion went sick, we found Etna clouded but shortly after the clouds cleared off.

8.   I started alone for the summit with the guide. After a hard climb up the last 1000 feet we gained the ridge of the crater, and I at length stood on the *summit of Etna.* nearly 11,000 feet above the sea. The scene from this lofty pinnacle which stands alone in its majesty, is one of indescribable spendour, and although I did not actually witness the sunrise, the scene was striking enough to be printed on my memory for many a day. On the one side with the apparently bottomless crater vomiting forth volumes of sulphur clouds, obscuring the view of the opposite side, and thus giving the mind even a vaguer idea of its great depth and vastness; in all other directions an unrivalled map of land, sea islands and clouds vanishing on the horizon, and thus the combination which it commands of the sublime and the beautiful can scarcely be rivalled. The great shadow of the Mt was projected half across Sicily as the sun rose, and looking in this direction I had the luck to see a *mirage,* with myself and the guide reflected in it. We then turned down again and after a rapid glissade down this very steep cone soon regained the Casa Inglese. Here I found Campbell no better so we decided on a hasty departure, and after some hours riding regained the Casa del Boseo, where matters improved, and on reaching Nicolosi a country meal soon set matters right again. Here we again took trap, and were soon rattling through the Via Etna of Catania once more. There is little vestige of life in Catania during the heat of the day, all offices and shops being closed. We determined to make for Taormina that night, and accordingly took the train along that lovely coast in the evening and esconsed

Temple of Juno, December 1879.

Temple of Jupiter, December 1879.

ourselves about dark in the Bella Veduta of that charming little town.

9. Here we remained 3 nights, the heat being such that there was not one other visitor in the Hotel. I sketched the old Greek Theatre one morning, and in the evening we climbed up to the village of Mola, perched on a rocky crag some distance above, and commanding a fine view.

10. Taormina – Messina. Continuing our way along the coast, we arr^d at Messina and put up at the Victoria. We crossed the Straits of Messina the same afternoon, and saw Reggio. In the evening a fine military band played in the square.

12. After booking our passages we started in the steamer 'Drepano' for Palermo. The night was perfect, and we dined on deck.

13. Palermo. We arr(ive)d in port at 7 a.m. and went to Hotel Trinacria, and explored the Museum & Cathedral. The town was en fete, and full of visitors and country people to see the Feast of Sta Rosalia, the Greek patron saint of Palermo. The illuminations at the Flora Gardens at night were wonderful, and all Palermo seemed to turn night into day, no one thinking of going home before day break.

14. Today we drove out to see the Chapel Royal at the palace, a gem of its kind, and the Capuchin Catacombs, a most extraordinary sight. That night there were brilliant illuminations and fireworks on the Corso, which all Palermo flocked out to see by thousands, and which terminated the Gala week. During the following days we visited Monreale, the road to which was guarded against brigands by sentinels at regular intervals the great Mosaic Cathedral being the chief point of interest apart from the lovely view seawards, which is best from the Cathedral roof. We also drove to St Maria Di Jesu, a conspicuous object in the scenery round Palermo.

17. Saw us training across the Island to Girgenti, the ancient Agrigentium. We passed Jesmini on our way, a town noted for its baths on the N. Coast, and after a long hot journey got to Girgenti, and put up at the Locanda Bellaveduta, the best we could find. We started immediately for the Temple ruins, 3 or 4 miles off, the vast number of ruins of which have rendered them the most noted in Europe. The picturesque ruins of Juno Lucinia situated on the edge of a precipice were indiscribably lovely, and as we proceeded along the city walls the splendid ruins of Concord, Hercules, and greatest of all Jupiter Olympus opened themselves one after the other to our view. The colossal remains and vast ruins of the latter attest its ancient splendour, the flutes of the columns measuring 20 ins across. I managed to make some sketches the next day, although the heat was intense. Then we travelled all next day through the Island back to Catania, including 4 hrs diligence from Caldari to Cannicatti, a hot drive through a parched country, escorted by Dragoons for safety against Brigands – we were glad of our fine Qrs at the Grande Hotel after such a day.

21. After resting a day and patronizing the band in evening, we left on 21st by the 'Leone' for Syracuse. We met the Baron D'Amico on board, and landed at Syracuse with this pleasant family after dinner. The sequel to their return to Malta after a few days in England only, soon revealed itself, although we could not discover it at the time. He was simply going back to die in his own Island, and after entering his house the next morning in Valetta never left it again and I heard of his decease shortly after arrival in Cyprus. They were one of the most pleasant families in Malta, and this fearful lingering malady, which no human power could stop, made the case a distressingly sad one.

22. We were under the walls of St Angelo next morning and soon after at Breakfast in the Baviere, & (home after) a pleasant fortnight in Sicily, but a very hot one! Shortly after the 61st & 98th Regts were ordered to India in consequence of General Burrowes (sic) disaster at Candahar.[36] (sic).

August 1880

3. When on the Main Guard I had the officers of the German Man of War 'Victoria' up, and several others, but the expected illuminations of the square did not come off. I was relieved by Carey, 98th Regt, of Zulu War fame.[37]

16. Several Troopships passed through with the 23rd, 24th & Rifles[38] for India, and on the

17th the 98th dined with us prior to sailing and we had one of the biggest 'nights' on record with our 'pall' (sic) regiment. On the 19th I was on Guard of Honor over the Gov[or] at the Marina, and the same evening we said farewell to the 98th on board the 'Euphrates' for India. Ordinary Garrison life continued, having been on board the 'Invincible' in dock and sketched our old 'orange' colours in the palace armoury a piece of which I brought off. Our time in Malta was also drawing to a close.

September 1880

7. On the 7th we were placed under orders to go to Cyprus our new possession.[39] Headquarters and 5 companies were ordered, the rest to stop at Malta. Nothing particular happened before our departure. The first autumn shower fell on the 26th and whilst on Baggage fatigue all morning of 29th, it fell heavily.

29. Having packed up, I slept at the Club that night.

30. We paraded on the French Curtain, and marched through Valetta & the old Strade Reale for the last time, played out by the pipers of the 26th Cameronians.[40] The splendid discipline in which Col Hackett[41] had the Regt was evinced by the way the men marched out. It was like a Floriana parade not a move in the ranks, not a wave of the hand to show the bystanders that the Royal Sussex was off. We embarked from the Marina on board the Troopship 'Tamar',[42] and 3 p.m. rounded Ricasoli point, en route to Cyprus, not sorry to see the last of Malta."

The Troopship 'Tamar';
photograph courtesy of the Nationsl Army Museum.

Notes to Chapter Four

1. HMS 'Orontes' was a twin funnel, three masted vessel. In Colonel H.C.B. Roger's book *'Troopships and their History'* (Seeley Service, London, 1963) there is an excellent illustration of the 'Orontes'. (Plate VII).
2. The casualties for the disaster at Isandhlwana, which took place on 22nd January 1879, are given in David Clammer's book *'The Zulu War'* (David & Charles, 1973) as 52 Officers and 806 Non-commissioned officers and men killed, 471 natives were also killed.
3. Lieutenant Harry W Macan Shewell, Royal Artillery.
    Monthly Army List, April 1880, Col 169.
4. Lieutenant George Leonard Thomson, 35th (Royal Sussex).
    Army List, April 1880, Col 279.
5. Captain Aylmer Peter Gerald Dowdall, 35th (Royal Sussex).
    Army List, April 1880, Col 279.
6. Captain James Dunbar Guthrie, Royal Artillery.
    Army List, April 1879.
7. 61st (South Gloucestershire) Regiment of Foot.
    A Register of Regiment and Corps of the British Army by A Swinson,
    The Archive Press, 1972.
8. Lieutenant William James Dacres Russell. 35th (Royal Sussex).
    Army List, April 1880, Col 279.
9. General Sir Arthur Borton KCB,
        Governor and Commander-in-Chief.
    Major-General The Hon P.R.B. Fielding, CB.
    Army List, April 1879.
10. See note 6.
11. Lieutenant Colonel William Cary, Royal Artillery.
    Monthly Army List, October 1880, page 153.
12. 10th (North Lincoln) Regiment of Foot.
    Swinson, op cit.
13. Captain Byron Plantaganet Carey, 35th (Royal Sussex).
    Harts Army List, 1878, page 279.
14. Donne wrote to his sister Rose on 20th April but did not complete the letter until 24th in which he says "... being on the Palace Guard Valetta today, or since 10 a.m. yesterday ...". In the same letter he comments on Pembroke Camp "... I don't like this place so well as Fort Ricasoli, for it is far from the centre attractions, Valetta, but it is very breezy, close to the sea, and swarming with mosquitos. Col Hackett (Lt Col Simpson Hackett) has arrived out and takes over command of the Regt ...
    Colonel Hackett is rather keen on my going to the Musketry School at Hythe during the leave season but as it would cut out quite two months of the time, I do not endorse his ideas quite so readily as others ...". The view from his room is described in the same letter "... My room looks out over the musketry ranges and the Island of Gozo, between which is St Paul's Bay, the reputed spot where the above Saint was cast ashore ..."
    The letter is part of the Collection of Donne *Family* letters.
15. Lieutenant George Leonard Thomson
    Lieutenant Lionel J Trafford, both from 35th (Royal Sussex).
    Monthly Army List, April, 1880.
16. Lieutenant George Charles Peere Williams-Freeman 35th (Royal Sussex).
    Monthly Army List, April 1880.
17. Captain John Ormsby Vandeleur and Lieutenant George Leonard Thomson, both from 35th (Royal Sussex).
    Monthly Army List, April 1880.
18. General Henry Renny, CSI,

Colonel of the 35th (Royal Sussex) Regiment.
Harts Army List, 1878, page 279.

19.   Horse Guards letter 44/Classes/66 dated 2nd June 1879.

20.   107th Regiment of Foot (Bengal Infantry).
Harts Army List.

21.   Captain Arthur Campbell Money, 43rd Regiment.
Army List, 1879, page 912.

22.   School of Instruction in Army Signalling, Special Form 15 dated 14th August 1879, signed by Major F. A. Le Mesurier. (Major Frederick Augustus Le Mesurier, Royal Engineers, Hart's Army List, 1879, page 883).
The form certified that "... Lieutenant D. A. Donne, 35th Regiment has passed through a course of instruction in Army Signalling at Aldershot Camp, and that he is hereby qualified to act as Instructor in Army Signalling.
No of marks out of 600 – 340.
No of words a minute. – Sending 8.06
                                      – Reading 8.6 ..."

23.   Captain Henry Gratton, 35th (Royal Sussex).
Army List, 1879, page 909.

24.   Captain Arthur Campbell Money, 43rd Regiment.
Army List, 1879, page 912.

25.   Lieutenant Colonel Samuel F. Blyth died 9th February 1880.
Monthly Army List, March 1880, page 896.

26.   2 Lieutenant Richard Newton King, 35th Regiment, died 23rd March 1880.
Monthly Army List, April 1880, page 903.

27.   The 98th Regiment (Prince of Wales's),
1st (The Royal Scots) Regiment,
10th (North Lincoln) Regiment, 2nd Battalion,
and the 61st (South Gloucestershire) Regiment were all shown as being stationed in Malta in the Monthly Army List for January 1880.

28.   Lieutenant Ralph J. Hunter, 98th Regiment.
Monthly Army List, October 1880, page 343.

29.   Lieutenant Colonel John Byron. 10th (North Lincoln) Regiment.
Monthly Army List, April 1880, page 238.

30.   Captain Arthur S. H. Gem, 35th (Royal Sussex),
Army List, 30th June 1880, page 909.

31.   Lieutenant Henry King, 6th Regiment,
Monthly Army List, October 1880, page 229.

32.   Lieutenant Kenneth M. Foss, Madras Staff Corps.
Monthly Army List, October 1880, page 543.

33.   Lieutenant Morris A. F. Taylor, 101st (Royal Bengal Fusiliers) Regiment,
Army List, 30th June 1880, page 932.

34.   Major Edward R Bigsby Barnes, 35th (Royal Sussex).
Monthly Army List, June 1880, page 279.

35.   Captain Francis Selwyn Campbell, 35th (Royal Sussex).
Monthly Army List, June 1880, page 279.

36.   Donne refers to the Battle of Maiwand. Lieutenant General James Primrose commanding the Force at Kandahar despatched an Anglo India brigade, some 2,500 strong, under command of Brigadier General G. R. S. Burroughs to oppose the Force of Ayub Khan at Maiwand and halt the Afghan advance on the capital. On 27th July 1880 Burroughs attacked the Afghan force but the British Artillery ran out of all its ammunition and a subsequent flanking movement by Ayub's force shattered the Indian troops. The one British infantry battalion was surrounded and practically annihilated. Ayub then advanced and besieged Kandahar.

37.   Captain Jahleel B Carey, 98th (Prince of Wales's) Regiment.

Army List, June 1880, page 931.

38.   23rd (Royal Welsh Fusiliers) Regiment and the 24th (2nd Warwickshire) Regiment and
       'Rifles' were the 1st Battalion, The Prince Consort's Own Rifle Brigade.
       Swinson, op cit.

39.   An agreement between Great Britain and Turkey was reached on 4th June 1878. This was
       known as 'The Cyprus Convention' under which Britain agreed to come to the aid of
       Turkey should that country be attacked. In return His Imperial Majesty, The Sultan, agreed
       to assign the island of Cyprus to the British and for the island to be occupied and
       administered by the British.
       A History of Cyprus, Vol IV (1571 – 1948).
       by Sir George Hill, KCB, FBA.
       Cambridge University Press, 1952, pages 269 and 300.

40.   26th Cameronian Regiment served in Malta.
       Monthly Army List, October 1880, page 270.

41.   Lieutenant Colonel Simpson Hackett, 35th (Royal Sussex).
       Monthly Army List, October 1880, page 279.

42.   The Troopship 'Tamar' was also used to transport the 71st Highlanders to Cyprus during
       the initial occupation of the island.
       Troopships and their History.
       by Colonel H. C. B. Rogers, OBE.
       Seeley, Service, London, 1963, page 143.

Donne's
home at
Crewkerne,
drawn
in 1948.

View from Road

5   Cyprus and the Cyprus Pioneer Corps

DONNE was always a bad sailor and his entries in the diary after having left Malta on the troopship 'Tamar' reflected his dislike of sea voyages.

October 1880

1. "The 1st two days was the usual hellish experience of redcoats afloat, the sea running pretty high.
3. On (the) 3rd when off Crete it cooled down. We coasted along the fine high mountains of Crete.
5. Sighted Cyprus on the 5th and rounded Cape Gata, dropping anchor off Limassol in the evening.
6. The morning we landed in Cyprus was a dead calm and the process of shifting baggage ashore by means of native lighters began early. We were the first English troops to land at this place and our destination, Polymedia Camp, which was in sight in the hills a few miles out of the town. The background was mountainous crowned by Mount Troodos 6000 feet, a long ugly mountain not looking nearly its own height. The town straggled along the shore of the bay. In slinging the chargers overboard Sapte's[1] charger was killed through the sling slipping and breaking. Several pieces of baggage including the Armourer's forge also fell through the pier into the sea. Cyprus had only been occupied by England since August 1878[2] and of all the big occupation force sent there at the time the troops were now reduced to our half Battalion and some Engineers. The country looked very much parched up after the long hot summer when it never rains. We marched straight up to the Camp on landing, and many men fell out from the excessive heat. We took over Quarters in tents, Indian Sepoy ones left by the Indian troops, and remained under canvas all the winter.

The British occupation of Cyprus – general view of the landing place, seen from the anchorage. Illustrated London News, July-December 1878.

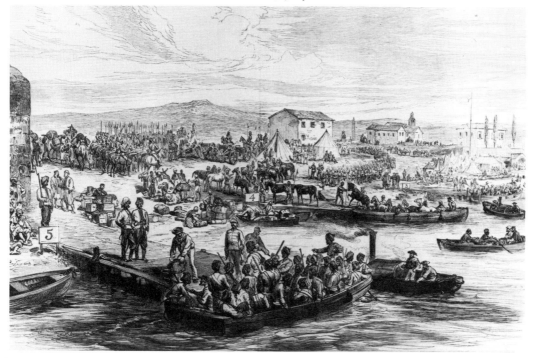

**Above: The British occupation of Cyprus,
disembarkation of horses at Larnaca.**

**Below: The landing-place and piers at Larnaca from the house
used by HRH The Duke of Edinburgh, 1878.
Both are from the Illustrated London News July-December 1878.**

7.   I marched down to Limassol with a fatigue party to land baggage and out again. The 20th Regiment[3] whom we relieved had sailed overnight in the 'Tamar'. In the afternoon Sir R. Biddulph, The High Commissioner[4] rode out and inspected the Half Battalion on parade, and was entertained in our temporary mess hut.

8.   Once having shaken down to our new camp life, the monotony of life was not much varied. Sunday church parade was conducted in the open by a remarkable looking Armenian Chaplain, the Reverend Galboushian whom we christened the 'Missionary'. Walks and rides about the country and up the Troodos road, the only one in the district, were our principal afternoon employments. There was little or no attraction in Limassol.

25.   The rains began today, the forerunner of what was in store for us during the winter, and on the 26th we had a heavy storm in the a.m. which introduced itself through my canvas.

28.   Walked into Limassol and called on R. E. fellows and Mrs. Hackett.

November 1880

1.   Tremendous thunderstorm which soaked everyone and washed down many houses in Limassol.

6.   Walked into Limassol to see Gilmore[5] at the Konak.

19.   With Chapman, Sapte and Ashurst[6] on our first expedition to the Salt Lake, lunching at a place we called Bleak House.

22.   Commenced the old signalling game again, which went on till the end of the year. I established regular communication with Limassol.

December 1880

4.   Nearly all the English of Limassol and Polymedia met at a picnic at Kolossi where there is a fine old Venetian Tower, now turned into a farmhouse, about 6 miles out ..."

During the three months of 1880 that Donne spent in Cyprus he produced five water colours and a black and white sketch.

These were of the following subjects:

(His) Tent at Polymedia Camp, dated 1880.

Donne's Tent in the Officers' Lines at Polymedia Camp, 1880.

Donne in his tent at Polymedia Camp, 1880.

Above: View of the coast, with Limassol on the left, as seen
from Donne's tent at Polymedia Camp, November 1880.
Below: View of Mount Troodos from Polymedia Camp, dated 1880.

DD in (his) tent at Polymedia Camp.
View of Limassol from Polymedia Camp, November 1880.
View of Mount Troodos from Polymedia Camp, dated 1880.
Akrotiri after rain, November 1880;
and a black and white sketch:
Tower of Colossi (Kolossi).

**Above: Akrotiri after rain,
November 1880.
Courtesy of H. M. Williamson.**

**Right: The Tower of Colossi,
November 1880.**

Donne's journal continues:

December 1880

4. "I had now purchased Thornton's pony.[7] Cyprus was certainly far preferable to Malta. A fine mountainous country with lots of interest historical and natural and any amount of riding.

11. On the 11th it blew a gale which made the tents very wretched and blew down several, besides driving one or two craft ashore in Limassol Bay. On Christmas Eve the worst storm I ever remember came over us. Coming up from the west it continued for 3 hours with great fury in huge hail stones, which literally darkened the air and deluged the country. Had there been any wind not a vestige of the camp could have remained. The ground was covered by inches of hail and when it abated the country round Limassol was a vast lake and the destruction in the town tremendous. 10 lives were lost and 96 houses washed down. The river overflowed and communication with the town was cut off. In 3 hours 6 inches of rain was gauged!

25. In spite however of our damp and uncomfortable condition and the impossibility of a plum pudding we spent a very jovial evening in the mess hut.

28. I went down to see the destruction in Limassol on (the) 28th, the whole streets being washed away. The High Commissioner came down to see it on the 30th and inspected the regiment at the same time.

31. The Sergeants had their usual dance on the last day of the year after which we let the old year out and the new year in at the mess hut.

Exit MDCCCLXXX.

January 1881

1. 1881 begins in Cyprus and likely enough will end there too and will contain sufficient body matter in between to fill many pages – the Levant is a big field and I saw a good deal of it.

3. HMS 'Monarch' arrived at Limassol on the 3rd January, bringing Sir A. Cunningham, late C. O. at the Cape.

4. Col Hackett[8] had an inspection parade in his honour on the 4th and we gave the officers a big lunch. Marriott, R. M. A.[9] came and I met an old 'Simoom' friend Chamberlain, Sub-Lieutenant on board. Having got leave to go to Larnaca with her I squared up my accounts and prepared for a trip to see something of the island.

5. I went on board early on the 5th and had a capital trip down the coast as Marriott's guest. Strangely enough I stumbled across another whilom (sic) friend Tufnell, Sub-Lieutenant of the 'Cygnet' a brother of my companion at N. Sachwerfen in 1874. By him I learned he was married and in India. We had a rattling Gun-room lunch on the strength of it. Arrived in Larnaca roads we landed in the Cutter and the middy getting us broadside on in the surf, we got no small ducking including the old veteran Sir A. Cunningham. Tufnell dined with me in the Club and I put up at Quesley's Army and Navy Hotel, if such it could be called being a relic of the occupation 2 years before but now of the past. On landing I was handed a telegram from Col Hackett offering me the Command of a Pioneer Detachment at Limassol if I like to return forthwith. Although this knocked my trip on the head I naturally jumped at it and wired back 'Yes'.

6. So I started off back the next morning at 8 a.m. arriving at Limassol about 7 p.m. having done the nearly 50 mile ride on a small mule. I naturally saw little of Larnaca but much of the country between it and Limassol. It is a monotonous journey skirting the coast most of the way and passing through only one village Zee,[10] about half way where I lunched. It is here that the Telegraph wire from Alexandria lands. The country is flat all round Larnaca the road passing the Salt Lakes, which make the place very unhealthy in summer. Monte Stavro Vouni, or 'the Sacred Cross' stands out by itself inland, and having once passed Zee the country becomes more mountainous. Limassol is first sighted about 10 miles off from a gap. Commanding a good view of the bay. One then rides down to the plains of Paleo

**Polymedia Camp, with the walled cemetery in the foreground circa 1881.
Courtesy of the National Army Museum.**

Limassol, past the site of the ancient Amathus and through a flat thickly treed and cultivated plain into Limassol. I took over my command next morning from Gilmore,[11] Local Commandant which consisted of two native officers and 100 N.C.Os and men of the Cyprus Pioneer Force,[12] who had been sent down from Nicosia to work on the improvements for the prevention of further flood destruction in the town. I had command of them until the end of March and rode into Limassol every morning from Polymedia. The weather was very wet and nasty but during this time the men worked well and cut a canal into the river to draw the water off from the town. At some times there was considerable discontent among them owing to their little pay and hard work. They were a mixed force of Greek and Turks and I had to do everything through an interpreter, which of course handicapped me very much.

16. Owing to a row in the Greek Quarter of the town 6 men deserted on the 16th but they were all brought back at different periods and sent to prison. I conducted my office work in Gilmore's office. The men also, principally the Greeks, took to malingering to get off the works but having made a good example of one man, it stopped the rest.

19. On the 19th I rode out to Episkopi village with Gilmore and in trying to ford the river, which was very high, was nearly washed down and we had to cross higher up by the bridge. Episkopi is one of the prettiest villages in the Island, surrounded by orange gardens etc. The Turkish Mucktar (sic)[13] was very hospitable and entertained us. Then we rode on to see the ancient ruins of Curium, on a promontory commanding a fine view. The place was noted in the ancient history of the Island and was probably a large town when St Paul passed that way on his journey from Salamis to Paphos. It was here that De Chesnola found his great Treasure in 1875 underneath the ruins of a temple. Large mounds of ruins and heaps of rubbish were strewn about and marble and fluted columns were plentiful; we also found some fine fragments of tesselated pavement. The Cyclamen was growing in great abundance and we took some roots back with us.

March 1881

1. The men were afterwards employed in clearing the course of the river out. Capt Chetwynd, 61st Regt, Second-in-Command of Military Police[14] came down and inspected the men at the Konak.

The British Camp at Larnaca 1878, with the Salt Lake and with the aquaduct in the foreground. From the Illustrated London News, 1878.

2.   On the 2nd I struck the camp at the Konak and marched to Hiafila[15] 3 miles out.

14. Cut a quarry road, on which they were employed till the 14th having shifted the camp back to Limassol again on the 11th.

15. On the 15th, having received orders to march the men back to Nicosia the camp was finally struck on the 16th.

16. I set out for Nicosia with the party. The first night we stopped at Jochni[16] a village in the Larnaca District and slept in a native house where I was almost eaten alive.

17. Started at 7 a.m. on 17th across the mountains to north of Stavro Vouni mountain through a fine country and arrived at Visu[17] in the Messaria plain in the evening. I preferred to sleep out in a tent and passed a very cold night on the ground. Left early next a.m. and after a very cold ride marched into Nicosia the capital of the Island.

18. We entered by the Famagusta Gate and I handed over the force to Capt Croker[18] Adjt, 93rd Regt and put up with Chetwyd and Gordon[19] the Commissioner. Nicosia is a beautifully situated town in the middle of the Messaria plain one of the richest granaries in the world, and at this time looking its best. It is unique in one respect as being perhaps the only city in the East where Mohomedan and Christian religions are tolerated side by side. The old Cathedral of Santa Sophia is now a mosque and above the walls of the town Greek Church spires rise up side by side with Moslem minarets, and in the busy picturesque bazaars Greek and Turk are freely mixed. A grand view is obtained of the Northern Range and distant Carpas, and altogether I was immensely pleased with Nicosia. I dined with H. E. the High Commissioner one night and at Mr. King-Harman's[20] another, and met most of the English officials of the Capital.

22. I started on the 22nd for Kyrenia on the North Coast. The road takes one over the Northern Range and the view from the top of the pass is very grand, the peaks of St Hilarion rising perpendicularly to the right, the lovely plains of Kyrenia spread out like a map below, with the small town and its big fort in the centre. It looked altogether like a sort of small fairyland shut out as it is from the rest of the Island and bursting on one's view in such an unexpected and delightful manner. The coast of Karamania and Asia Minor is very plainly visible to the North. I put up with the Scott-Stevensons in their charming house close to the fort and looking over the little harbour.

23. I went over the old fort and castle with Scott-Stevenson,[21] Commissioner. I had a long day of it the 23rd starting early with a zaptieh as guide for the Monastery of Bella Pais. This is one of the most lovely spots imaginable – a fine old ruin with a grand view looking north. I stopped an hour to sketch it, then rode on up the side of the mountains to a place in the pass I had come over the day before, and met Houston a Scotsman settled pro tem at Kyrenia, who had brought out lunch. So we feasted on 'foie gras' and then rode up to St Hilarion. The glorious view from the craggy heights of the splendid ruins of the old castle, built as it is on almost inaccessible points of rock 3000 feet above Kyrenia I cannot

St Sophia Cathedral converted into a mosque, 1878.
From the Illustrated London News, July-December 1878.

Illustrations of Cyprus, including the Mosque of St. Sophia, Nicosia.
From "The Graphic", 10th August 1878.

Kyrenia, 1881.

adequately describe. I should like to have camped there a week, but could barely spare more than an hour as I had to get back to the pass again, and then a long ride to Nicosia. I could only hope to visit it again some day – I parted from Houston in the pass, who returned to Kyrenia, and after a farewell glimpse at the bright little fairyland from the top, rode off to Nicosia and got in just in time for dinner.

24.   I dined with Nicolle[22] next evening and left Nicosia on the 25th for Limassol.

25.   I slept that night at Cofinu[23] and got into Limassol next day after a capital ride through the country. After taking over my old company from Powell[24] I started another signalling class: but this one I never completed having got leave of absence for four and half months before its completion.

April 1881

17.   Having made my arrangements to go home by Constantinople and see as much as possible of the Levant while out there I left by the SS 'Fortuna' on the 17th, Grattan and Trafford[25] going by the same boat, the latter for Malta ..."

During his visit to Kyrenia Donne completed two water colours, one of Kyrenia and the other of the Monastery of Bella Pais. In February 1881 Donne painted two men of the Cyprus Pioneer Corps which give an excellent record of the uniform of this very short-lived unit.[26] It was during this period that he also painted a study of three Cypriots.

An artist's impression of Kyrenia, 1878. Illustrated London News, July-December 1878.

Monastery of Bella Pais, 1881.

Cypriot workmen, 1881: left is a Greek on Limassol works, centre Ibrahim Mustafha, the Cyprus Pioneer Regiment, right Turks at Limassol.

Notes to Chapter Five

1. Lieutenant Herbert Langton Sapte, 35th (Royal Sussex)
   Monthly Army list, September 1880, 279.

2. The first British force to land on the island consisted of British and Indian Troops under the command of Lieutenant General Sir Garnet Wolseley. After assembling at Malta the force departed from there on 18th June and arrived off Larnaca, on the south coast of Cyprus, on 23rd July 1878. The disembarkation commenced on that day and continued over the next few days.

3. 20th (East Devonshire) Regiment of Foot.
   A Register of the Regiments and Corps of the British Army.
   by Arthur Swinson, London, 1972, page 110.

4. Brigadier General (Local Major General) Sir Robert Biddulph, KCMG, CB, late Royal Artillery.
   High Commissioner and Commander in Chief, Cyprus.
   Monthly Army List, May 1881, 117.
   Appointed Commissioner Nicosia from 7th August 1878 (Cyprus Gazette No 1, 5th November 1878).
   Appointed as High Commissioner of Cyprus from 23rd June 1879. He continued in that post until 9th March 1886.

5. Lieutenant Allan Gilmore, 61st (South Gloucestershire) Regiment.
   Monthly Army List, August 1880, 307.
   Appointed Local Commandant, Military Police Nicosia from 28th August 1878 (Cyprus Gazette No l, 5th November 1878).
   Appointed Local Commandant, Military Police, Limassol from 8th August 1879 (Cyprus Gazette No 33, 8th August 1879).

6. Captain Arthur Thomas Chapman,
   Lieutenant Herbert Langton Sapte and 2 Lieutenant Charles H. Ashurst, all of the 35th (Royal Sussex).
   Monthly Army List, September 1880, 279.

7. 2 Lieutenant Frederick G Todd-Thornton, 35th (Royal Sussex)
   Monthly Army List, September, 1880, 279.

8. Lieutenant Colonel Simpson Hackett, 35th (Royal Sussex) Regiment. On his arrival in Cyprus Lieut Colonel Hackett assumed the appointment of Senior Officer in Command of Her Majesty's Troops in Cyprus. He was appointed as a Member of the Executive Council from 6th October 1880. (Cyprus Gazette No 60, 25th October 1880). During Sir Ralph Biddulph's absence from the island Lieut Colonel Hackett held the post of Officer Administering the Government of Cyprus under the authority of the Cyprus Gazette Extraordinary dated 11th July 1881, and held the appointment until 9th September 1881. (Cyprus Gazette No 77, 19th October 1881).

9. Lieutenant Reginald Adams Marriott, Royal Marine Artillery.
   Monthly Army List, August 1880, page 512.

10. An edited version of the journal was published in the 1969 edition of the Journal of the Society for Greek Cypriot Studies. The article only dealt with the Cyprus episode of the Donne journals and was edited by George Georghallides, PhD. In his notes he relates Donne's village of 'Zee' to the present day 'Zyyi'.

11. See note 5.

12. In 1880 Cyprus had two separate Police forces. One was the Cyprus Military Police which, although increased in size and reformed since the British Administration, was basically the old unit of Turkish Zaptiehs.
   The second force was the Cyprus Police and Pioneer Corps which had been formed under the Ordnance of 1879 and consisted of one-third Turkish and two-thirds Greek-Cypriot recruits.

13.   Mukhtar (Mouktar.). After the Tanzimat of 1839 a popularly elected headman (Mukhtar) was appointed in all the villages of Cyprus. His duties were administrative and fiscal (See 'A History of Cyprus' Vol IV, by Sir George Hill, Cambridge University Press, 1952, page 8). The British authorised the continuance of the Mukhtar's office in the Administrative Divisions Ordnance of 1878 and successive laws gave the Mukhtar added responsibilities including the welfare and health of his villagers.
      (Georghallides, op cit, page 45.)

14.   Captain The Hon E. J. Chetwynd, 61st (South Gloucestershire) Regiment.
      Monthly Army List, August 1880, page 307.
      Chetwynd held a succession of posts under the British Administration of Cyprus, these being:
      Local Commandant, Military Police, Larnaca from 6 December 1879 (Cyprus Gazette No 41, 30th December 1879).
      Adjutant in the Police and Pioneer Force from 1st January 1880 (Cyprus Gazette No 42, 13th January 1880).
      Second-in-Command and Paymaster in the Police and Pioneer Force from 18th April 1880 (Cyprus Gazette No 52, 20th May 1880).
      In addition he held the post of Second-in-Command and Paymaster in the Cyprus Military Police from 1st December 1880. (Cyprus Gazette No 63, 8th December 1880).
      He resigned that appointment on 1st September 1881 on being appointed Assistant Commissioner, Nicosia from that date. (Cyprus Gazette No 78, 8th November 1881).

15.   Ay Phyla. Georghallides, op cit, page 45.

16.   Tochni, a mixed Greek and Turkish village.
      Georghallides, op cit, page 45.

17.   The Greek Village of Lysi
      Georghallides, op cit, page 46.

18.   Captain E. W. Dunlop Croker, 93rd (Sutherland Highlanders) Regiment.
      Monthly Army List, August 1880, page 338.
      Croker was appointed Adjutant and Quartermaster in the Cyprus Police and Pioneer Force from 18th April 1880. (Cyprus Gazette No 52, 20th May 1880). He was also appointed Adjutant and Quartermaster in the Cyprus Military Police from 1st December 1880 (Cyprus Gazette No 63, 8th December 1880).
      He was later appointed Second-in-Command of the Force on 1st September 1881 (Cyprus Gazette No 78, 8th November 1881).

19.   Major Robert William Thew Gordon, 93rd (Sutherland Highlanders) Regiment.
      Monthly Army List, August 1880 page 338.
      Appointed Commissioner at Nicosia from 10th November 1879 (Cyprus Gazette No 38, 13th November 1879).
      He resigned from 1st January 1882 (Cyprus Gazette No 8l, 3lst January 1882).

20.   Charles Anthony King-Harmon. Private Secretary to the High Commissioner and Clerk to the Executive and Legislative Councils from 1st December 1879.
      (Cyprus Gazette No 4l, 8th December 1879).

21.   Lieutenant Andrew Scott-Stevenson, 42nd Highlanders(The Black Watch). Served as Assistant Commissioner and Local Commandant of Police, Kyrenia from 10th November 1878. (Cyprus Gazette No 3, 1st January 1879). Appointed Registrar of the High Court of Justice on 25th February 1879. (Cyprus Gazette No 11, 25th February 1879).
      Appointed Commissioner, Kyrenia on 27th February 1880. (Cyprus Gazette No 46, 1st March 1880).
      His wife was the author of the book 'Our Home in Cyprus' which was published in London during 1880.

22.   Hilgrove C. Nicolle, Assistant Auditor, appointed on 17th February 1880. (Cyprus Gazette No 47, 15th March 1880).

23.   Kophinou. Georghallides, op cit, page 14.

24.   Lieutenant Robert Edward Powell, 35th (Royal Sussex).

Monthly Army List, August, 1880, page 279.

25.   Captain Henry Grattan and Lieutenant Lionel J. Trafford. 35th (Royal Sussex).
      Monthly Army List, August 1880, page 279.

26.   During 1879 the British Government, under Disraeli, wished to reduce expenditure in Cyprus and in order to effect a reduction in the strength of the British Army garrison stationed on the island, paid for the raising of a Police and Pioneer Corps, the duties of which were of a semi-military nature. The formation of the Cyprus Police and Pioneer Corps was promulgated by the passing of the 'Cyprus Police Augmentation Ordnance, 1879'.
      In March 1881 the Cyprus Pioneer Corps, as it was known was disbanded by Gladstone's Government and the personnel absorbed into the Cyprus Military Police.
      The dress of the Cyprus Police and Pioneer Corps was as follows:
      Red fez with a black tassel at the back.
      White yemeni (handkerchief), worn wrapped around the fez.
      White kavushturma (shirt) without collar or cuffs, fastened down the front with buttons. Gold coloured edging around the neck of the shirt and a single row of braiding on either side of the buttons. A gold-coloured inverted stripe around the lower sleeve.
      Navy blue dizlik (Turkish trousers) with a single thin yellow stripe.
      Kushak (wool cummerbund) of yellow with a thin brown check pattern.
      Canvas gaiters (worn scrubbed).
      Black boots.
      NCOs wore gold-coloured chevrons and carried a cane.
      A Cepken or yelek (waistcoat) was sometimes worn. This was of a red material, open fronted with gold edging.

6   The Grand Tour

DONNE commenced his four and half month leave on the 17th April and as usual disliked the sea voyage. His journal for the leave period commences with his note on the voyage:

April 1881

17.   "We had a dogfish (sic) passage, the ship rolling all day & next night, getting into the Grand Harbour of Alexandria 6 a.m.

19.   19th and I was pretty thankful to land. Grattan[1] left by French Mail, Trafford[2] & self stopping at the Hotel D'Europe in the great square of the town. Alexandria is an unusual place to get in and out of, the rapacity of the boatmen for coin being unequalled anywhere. We went out to see Pompey's Pillar in the afternoon and made ourselves fairly acquainted with Alexandrian places of amusement in the evening. My time being limited and being anxious to see something of Cairo while in the land of Egypt I started early next a.m.

20.   Leaving Trafford to go to Malta. I did not get into Cairo till the afternoon, going to the Hotel Du Nil a very cool & pleasant place. As it was already late in the season here, it was beginning to get very hot, most of the tourists & 'Nile-ists' having already left. I secured my ticket at Cook's office for my voyage as far as Vienna, and made use of the rest of the day to visit the Citadel, Mosques, the Tombs of the Califs and the town. Everything in Cairo, the 'City of the Califs' is surprisingly interesting and the view over the Citadel of the town with the Great Pyramids rising in the distance, as they did in the days of (the) Pharaoh, (is) calculated to inspire one with the great antiquity of the surroundings. The Arab and Bazaar quarters of the town team with picturesque views, and oriental life, and the ride on one of the donkey's around the suburbs to the Tomb of the Califs exceedingly eastern.

Cairo would of course be incomplete without the Pyramids. So I left early next a.m. to inspect them closer. My donkey went well, and we arrived underneath these gigantic monuments of the past world in due time. I scrambled, or was rather assisted to the summit of the big one Cheops and even then it is difficult to take in all the gigantic proportions of these Tombs. It was stiff work getting down and I had evidently attempted the assent too rapidly. After trying to sketch the 'Sphynx' in a sand storm which came on I rode back to Cairo, but the ride was by no means pleasant, as the sandstorm battled hard against me, and soon converted my straw hat into chaff and what was eventually left of it eventually blew away.

I did the bazaar under the guidance of my rapacious Dragoman, and bought many bronze articles, and next day went to see the 'Dancing & Howling Dervishes' on a peaceful hot afternoon.

I returned to Alexandria late at night, ready to embark next afternoon on board the Khedive Steamer 'Fayoum'. She was a fine old roomy paddle boat, of a bygone type, and I had an excellent cabin on board for the trip to Constantinople.

When we left it was spendid weather and with 3 other English passengers on board, it was pleasant work. When off the north of Crete it came on to blow a bit, but we then began to sight the Island of the Cyclades. We were making for Santarino Island, which was straight

Santarino Island, Cyclades, April 1881.

Volcanic Island, 1881.

Above: Tayorsin, 1881.

Below: Island of Melos, April 1881.

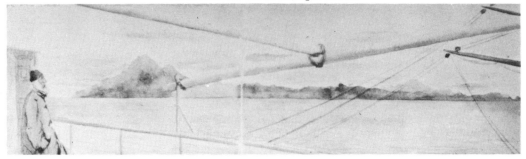

ahead, and at midday we were inside the curious volcanic anchorage. Three volcanic little Islands have been thrown up in the middle of the harbour at quite recent dates: one of them is active, and was smoking merrily away while we were there. We steamed away in the p.m. threading our way in and out between the Isles and when the sun set behind *Melos* (sic)[3] the spectacle was a very lovely one. There were islands looming up all round us and the sun tinged the sea with a golden & blooded hue, which was well passed off to the high mountain tops of Melos.

When I awoke next a.m. we were entering the harbour of Athens, the celebrated old Piroeus, (sic) and there in the distance stood the Acropolis of old with its world wide collection of ruins. It was Sunday, and the Greeks were in festa (sic) attire. I took a carriage with some Germans and started for Athens, and made straight for the Acropolis, and spent the a.m. looking about the ruins and sketching the *Parthenon,*[4] with the distant views of Piroeus and Salamis. After seeing the grand columns of Jupiter Olimpus, it was time to be leaving, so I hurried it back to the Piroeus in time to leave in the evening.

We passed along close to the shore till darkness hid the land from sight. Early next a.m. we were in the harbour of Syra, where we stopped some hours, and took on board a large party of refugees returning from Chios. They were a motley & poor looking crowd. Syra is a pretty little town as seen from the harbour, sloping up the hills in the form of two high pyramids. It is the principal port of call in the Aegean for steamers for all ports. We went on to the Island of *Tinos* (sic)[5] where we dropped anchor and landed. The celebrated Greek church of Evangheliotria, above the town is worth a visit, which is supposed to possess miraculous healing powers. The small town struck me as being very clean and nice. We did not call at *Andros* (sic),[6] a large Island to the north, but turned our course straight for *Chios* (sic).[7] It was nearly dark when we arrived off the port. We were anxious to see the ruin and desolation caused by the recent earthquake before dark so we went on shore as quick as possible.

The town was deserted and resembled Pompeii in the ruins and desolation. The people were encamped in large numbers of tents outside the town near the Fort, which was much shattered. 300 (sic) people had been killed there alone, and about 3000 perished altogether. We left late at night for *Smyrna,* and were steaming up the Gulf of Smyrna next morning. There was no time at Smyrna to go beyond the town, or to see the ruins at Epheus as we left again about 5 p.m. Late that night we called at *Mitclene* (sic),[8] but it was too dark to see anything more than the high outline of the Island. Coming on deck next morning we had already left *Jenedos* behind and were off *Besika Bay,* and the mouth of the Dardanelles. The plains of Troy were away to the south. The scenery going up the Hellespont was very interesting and later on we arrived off Galippoli (sic),[9] and then on to Chanak, on the Asiatic side, where there is a custom house & pratique[10] given for 'Stambul' (sic). While this was going on I went on shore and strolled about this rambling Turkish town, which is strongly fortified. We then steamed on and entered the Sea of Marmora.

Next morning we were in sight of the famous *Constantinople,* where the voyage was to end. We were however not destined to see it in all its glory, with sun shining on its minarets and domes, as it should be seen for the first time. On deck at 5 a.m. the next day broke cloudy and before we were in the *Golden Horn* it had broken into rain. We landed at the Galata Bridge and crossing over to the Pera side, after bidding adieu to the 'old Fayoum' and her officers, took up our quarters at the Royal Hotel. I called at the Embassy, and in the afternoon we went up the Golden Horn to the Sweetwaters in a ferry steamer. Capt Swayne[11] of the Embassy called next a.m.: he had been Comm[er] at Famagusta after the occupation and kindly offered his services. The next day was raining but did most of the sight seeing at Stambul (sic) marshalled about by a magnificent looking Croate with a big sword. We saw the St[n] Sophia mosque and wondered at it, and many others. After going to the Bazaar we took (a) steamer for Therapia in the Bosphorous (sic) on board I met Browne of old 'Simoom' days, and his wife, who were also going up to their Hotel at Therapia, and we spent a pleasant enough day there in the pretty Garden of the Khedive –

Entry of Captain Swaine into Levcarno, Cyprus, 1878.
From the Illustrated London News, July-December 1878.

we had a lovely passage back to Pera in the evening. One is not likely soon to forget the Great Cemetery at Scutara, and the lovely views from there of Constantinople and the Bosphorous. The miles and miles of tombs, the great Barracks where Miss Nightingale worked during the Crimean War and the peaceful little English Cemetery with its beautiful panorama of the Sea of Marmora & Stambul. We left Constantinople in the afternoon on board the Austrian Steamer for Varna. The voyage was enlivened by the presence of Baker Pasha on board, [12] who flew his flag at the fore, also of a band of Gazis tourists who had been gazing in the Holy Land. They afforded us much amusement, and all appeared utterly sick of the life they had been leading. They went with us most of the way up the Danube. As we steamed up the Bosphorous red with the 'Judas' trees in full blossom, the different forts saluted the flag of Baker Pasha. We also met a Queen's Messenger on his way back to England, and a young traveller of the name of Williams joined our party for the Danube. We entered the Black Sea at sundown, the sea perfectly calm. Next morning early we all scrambled on shore at Varna, in Bulgaria, and after long delays, were finally on our way north by train to *Ruschuck.* (sic)[13]

It took us most of the day to cross the Bulgarian plains. At last we arrived in sight of the Danube and were soon after on board our steamer for the five days trip to *Vienna.*

We managed (3 of us, Halton, Williams & self) to secure a berth to ourselves, which went by the name of a cabin and a very merry trip we had up the great river. We stopped one night at *Turna-Severin,* and went on shore and next morning early passed through the celebrated Rapids of the *Iron Gates.* The waters were high, as the steamer could do it easily. At *Orsova,* on the Hungarian frontier we had to land, and pass through the Austrian Custom House. We next passed through the beautiful *Defile of Kasan* through which the river rushes pent in by huge perpendicular cliffs. It is the finest river scenery I have ever seen, and well worth the trouble and money to see, near it is the old *Inscription of Trojan* which one can just catch a glimpse of as the steamer passes along. After this the river became flat, but not by any means uninteresting. The sunsets were lovely and made me "remember that month in May, on the Danube River". Halton and many others left us at *Bazias* to go by rail to Pest,[14] but Williams & self stuck to the boat. We passed *Belgrad* (sic) and the Battlefield of Petervardine, and after a long journey, arr[d] at *Budapeste* (sic) on Sunday the ... and went to the Hotel ... for a couple of days. Buda and Ofen are gay interesting cities, and we continued up the river by steamer to Vienna ..."

Donne quite obviously wrote his journal at a later date, probably after his return to Cyprus. The missing date and hotel name and the actual writing in the journal continue to indicate that he kept a day to day note of happenings and then periodically wrote his journal. During this first part of his leave he completed three water colours, these being titled 'Santorin Island, Cyclades, April 1881', 'Volcanic Island, Santorin harbour, 1881' and 'Island of Melos, April 1881'.

Donne continues his journal having reached Vienna:

"... *Vienna* It was a very cold day on the river when we arrived, and Vienna was all en fete, as it was the marriage day of Crown Prince Rudolph with Stephani (sic) of Belgium. The city was deserted. We put up at the Hotel Arch Duke Karl for two or 3 days, and did most of the sightseeing in Vienna. The weather was however cold and wet. I was in a hurry to get on, so saying goodbye to my companions in travel Halton & Williams, I left early on the ... for Heidelberg. Snow was lying deep on the line between *Salzburg* and *Linz* in the Salz cammergut. I did not stop at *Munich,* which I had passed two years before, but travelled through the night by *Augsburg* and *Ulm* to Heidelberg, arriving there about 3 a.m. To my great surprise I met my aunt Mrs. Barker on the platform. Not having seen her for more than 17 years this meeting was an unexpected surprise to both of us.

I put up at Mrs. Hoffman's pension and stayed nearly a week. It was just about six years since the old stay there, on my way home from Germany in '75.

A week in Heidelberg is easily spent. Pleasant walks, excursions on the river to Steinach, or an afternoon at the old castle are jolly enough. But a rolling stone gathers no moss, so I was off again to *Cologne* where I stopped for the night, and had time in the morning to look into the Dom Kirche, and to go and see some German troops drilling outside the town. I left at midday for Ostend. It was very hot and dusty travelling over this uninteresting corner of Europe, and when I got on board the steamer for Dover I found myself the only single passenger for London, it being Saturday. I landed at Dover and went to Town sleeping at the Cannon Street Hotel, where my months tour finishes.

May 1881

22. I took over lodgings the next day at No 4 Princes St, Hannover Square, which were not easy to obtain, London being very full. I occupied myself in Town till the 4th June holiday

Seen from the Orient Express – four studies of uniforms, 1881.

making. Saw the Academy, visited my Tailor, and lived a bachelor life at my club the Jun(ior) Army & Navy in Grafton St, which came in very handy. Also met the Markham's and looked up the Beatties, 2 of whom were home from different ends of the world and daughters still unwed. Our Regimental Dinner came off at the same time, at which there was a large and merry gathering and a hot debate whether the new link Batt[on] should be invited to dine or not. Not being in a very satisfactory state of health at this time, for a recurrence of my old Malta complaint, I cut my tour in Town as short as possible and ran down to Misterton Manor.

June 1881

4.   I found everything and everybody much as of yore in Haselbury days, and a tennis party going on. The day was lovely, but unhappily the British weather reigned supreme during the rest of my visit to Somersetshire, so there was not much getting about, so I lived a delightfully lazy tame cat life until the 1st July, and found myself much the better for it.
     As usual of course all the old Crewkerne Aunts and friends were hunted up, and duly passed in review – so much so that I was obliged to pass 3 terrible days under the same roof with my loquacious great Aunt Baker.

July 1881

1.   On the 1st July I packed up my traps once more, and after lunch said goodbye to many friends (and to no one with greater regret than Aunt Parsons what a perfect woman she is, and how few in this world so utterly unselfish) and soon found myself on the track once more, a rolling stone, my baggage & me, and Charing X Hotel by night. After one day in town, and a few parting commissions I was en route to Newhaven & the Continent once more. Two loquacious American officer companions enlivened the hot but calm passage across to Dieppe, and old England disappeared once more from my view, the Sussex downs wrapped in a thick fog which however soon lifted and we had a glass calm passage. *Paris* by night and Paris by day was stifling. I seldom recollect such heat, and wished for a helmet, and missing the morning train made it decidedly worse. However I used the shining hour by trotting half round Paris. I saw the British Flags at the Invalides, but failed to discover their Regiments, and saw also the great panorama for the sum of 2 fr at 7.30. I was packed into a stuffy 1st class carriage with many other unfortunate fellow voyagers, en route to Suisse (sic) but sleep & comfort were out of the question heat & dust reigning supreme. Next morning we were over the Swiss Frontier and on to Berne – old familiar haunts but I had not been at Berne since that great 1871 excursion which is not to be found in this book of cronikles (sic). Berne was a treat, especially the Restaurant, and the journey on to *Thun* through the cool Swiss lowlands a refresher after the last journey. At Thun came the delightful boat journey down to *Interlaken* – old hunting ground again ... up to the Old Staubach and here I met my Father as the dark was setting in, and we climbed up to the Wengen Alp chalet Pension where (there) was any amount of (rejoycing by all members of the family) ..."

Donne had, in fact, joined his family who were at that time residing in Switzerland. He then records in his journal the details of the reunion and other accounts of parties, picnics etc. He concludes his entry with a comment dealing with the 1881 Cardwell reform of the British Army:

"... On the 1st July there was a great Gazette. The 107th was incorporated with the 35th, and numbers ceased to exist in the British Infantry.
I was now 4th Senior Subaltern of the new two-Batt[n] Regt, with liability to be promoted into either Batt[on] ..."

The next entry in the journal is dated 29th July:

29. A letter arr(ive)d from Col Gordon CCMP, Cyprus[15] offering me the Post of Local Commandant Military Police at Larnaka (sic) which was about to become vacant, so I determined to throw up the remainder of my leave and return to Cyprus forthwith, so I

Mountain View, Switzerland, 1881.

The Breithorne, 1881.

went down to Lauterbrunnen and wired that I should be in Larnaka on the 12th Prox. Pleasant days at Wengen were therefore cut short suddenly as I should have to leave on the 1st Prox and travel hard to get down to Brindisi in time for the boat.

Mrs. Barker was also going back to England en route to America, so it was arranged for us to go together as far as Lucerne. After a farewell stroll up the valley I said goodbye to all once more, and we started off down to Lauterbrunnen early next morning.

August 1881

1. Father and Anna[16] wishing us goodbye at the Diligence Station.[17] From Interlaken we took steamer down Lake Brienz past the old Greisback fall, then a long hot diligence journey across the Brunig Pass to Alpuach on Lake Lucerne. Then over the lake to Lucerne itself, where we arrived at dusk and put up at the Rigi Hotel. We had time to see grand old Lion de Lucerne.

2. Next morn at 5 a.m. after bidding Aunt Mary god speed on her long journey we separated for our widely different destinations, and I was soon steaming away down the lake alone to Fluelen, and the lake looked grand as a thunderstorm gathered round. At Fluelen I took diligence to cross the Alps by the St. Gothard route into Italy. The long journey was intensely grand and interesting. Although I had to put up with an inside seat as far as Andermatt. We passed the celebrated Devil's Bridge and after a short halt at the small inn on the summit, commenced the descent into Italy. It was a long hot and terribly dusty journey but the changing scenery was very interesting. I had a seat in the Imperial behind. We did not arrive at the Railway terminus at Biasea before 8.30 p.m. and then on down to Locarno on *Lago Maggiore* late in the evening.

3. I put up at the Grand Hotel where my people had stayed the Spring before, and this patronage of ours had the effect of considerably reducing my 'note' next morning. From here I steamed away down lovely Maggiore passed Pal[1]anza and the Borrowmean Isles of Arona at the other end – a lovely day and the pleasant companionship of an American family from Chicago. We went on to Milan in company and after dinner strolled about the city.

4. Spent all next day in Milan leaving by the night train for Brindisi.

5. Passing Bologna, Ancona along the east coast line to Foggia. I got into Brindisi 10.30 the following night after a journey too hot to mention and went straight on board the Austrian steamer 'Forwarts' for *Corfu.*

6. The next a.m. we were out on a glassy sea in the Adriatic, no English on board. We were soon in sight of the Islands to the north of Corfu and soon after steamed in round the Straits and arr(ive)d off the town of *Corfu* at 2 p.m.

    I landed & put up at the Hotel St George a most comfortable English sort of Hotel, but no one was there at this hot season of the year. What a lovely place Corfu is! I went away with the impression it was the fairest place I had seen in the blue Mediterranean and with it the British Soldier had certainly lost the best station in the world. The 35th, my own Regt had been present at its capture. The views from the Citadel and the 'telegraph' are very fine and every where one sees traces of the British occupation. The Hospital, Officers Mess, and even the English names of the Batteries still remain 'to attest its old importance and lasting aspect for the British Lion'.

7. Next a.m. I drove out through the town to a place called the *'one gun battery'* from whence one has a superb view to the south, over a small Isle called the 'Ship of Ulysses'. I spent the morning sketching it ..."

The sketch of this island has not been found with the Donne papers, or with the collection of water colours and sketches and may well have been lost, or even given away by Donne himself at a later date.

He continues with his narrative of his return journey to Cyprus:

7. Unfortunately my steamer came in before her time, and I was obliged to up camp and get on board at 5 p.m. before I had half time to digest the place properly. We steamed away in the 'Saturno' as the sun went down over the mountains and citadel of Corfu, and a happy thunder storm came on to cool the air.

8. Coming on deck at 4.30 am next morning we were passing along the narrow strait between *Cephalonia* and *Ithaca* with S[an]ta Maura and the mainland in the blue distance beyond. The view was most lovely, and I remained all day sketching different points along our passage. After rounding the S. point of Cephalonia with the great Elato Vano or Black m[oun]t[ains] towering up we passed along Zante, where in former days the Regt had been in garrison, and had stormed the citadel. With a calm sea, we passed down close in shore, to the *Bay of Navarino* and *Sphacteria Island,* and then past the town and fortress of Niodon and steamed in through a cluster of small Isles to the S. Finally we lost sight of Greece by leaving Cape Gallo in a thunderstorm, and a most extra ordinary sunset effect.

9. At early morn. Crete was in sight in the hazy distance, and in a few hours time we were running close in under the rocky shore, with Mt Ida range standing up clear in the sun light.

11. Early in the morning we were inside the harbour of Alexandria after as calm a passage as one could wish for. The Cyprus Boat, that infamous old craft the 'Elpitha' was waiting with steam up to be off, so I made hasty tracks on board her, after being horribly fleeced by the rascally boatman, and found Leach[18] on board, looking over the side and laughing gayly at the volumes of expletives I had been heaping on the heads of these Alexandrian fiends.

12. 1 p.m. next day we were off Cyprus once more and soon at anchor off Limassol, after having been just twelve days out from Wengen Alp."

Donne had arrived in Cyprus on the 12th August as he had stated in his telegram to Colonel Gordon. He had made a number of sketches en route, none of which appear to have survived but two water colours do remain to illustrate his journey from Switzerland to Cyprus. One is entitled 'Sunset' and the other has a more detailed title being called 'Sunset off Crete, August 1881'.

Donne was now to resume duty but not with his regiment which was still stationed in Cyprus, he was to be seconded to the local unit 'Cyprus Military Police'.

Sunset, August 1881.

Sunset off Crete, August 1881.

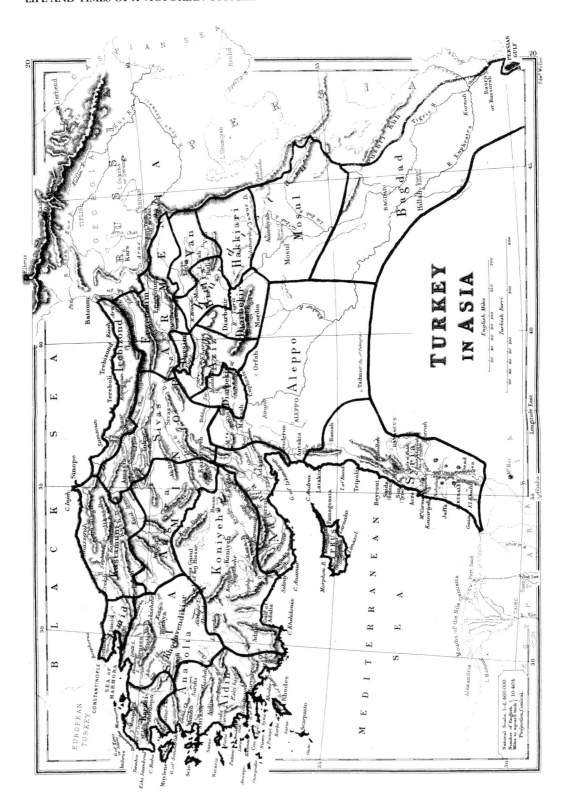

Notes to Chapter Six

1. Major Henry Grattan, The Royal Sussex Regiment,
   Monthly Army List, August 1881, 363.
2. Lieutenant Lionel J Trafford, The Royal Sussex Regiment,
   Monthly Army List, August 1881, 364.
3. *Melos* – refers to the Island of Milo
   The Public School Atlas by The Rev. George Butler,
   Published by Longmans, Green & Co., 1894, Map 19.
   Currently known as Milos.
4. There is no trace of the sketch of the Parthenon by Donne. Donne however did return to
   Greece in May 1883 and sketched the Acropolis at that time.
5. *Tinos* – refers to the Island of Tino.
   Butler, op cit, Map 19.
   Currently known as Tinos.
6. *Andros* – refers to the Island of Andro
   Butler, op cit, Map 19.
   Currently known as Andros.
7. *Chios* – The island was also known by the name of Scio and is four and a half miles west of
   Smyrna (now known as Izmir) in the Aegean Sea. The island was devastated by an
   earthquake during 1881.
   The island is currently known as Khios.
8. *Mitclene* – this refers to the Island of Mitylene.
   Butler, op cit, Maps 19 and 20.
   This island is currently known as Lesvos with the principal town being Mitilini.
9. *Galippoli* – the correct spelling of the area is Gallipoli.
10. Practique – a licence granted to a ship after quarantine, or on showing a clean bill of
    health.
11. Donne for some reason used this officers previous rank in his journal, probably because he
    had known him in his former rank in Cyprus. He also spelt the name incorrectly. At the
    time of the meeting Swaine (not Swayne) was shown in the Monthly Army List as being:
    "Swaine, Major L. V. Rif Brig ... Military Attache, Constantinople ..."
12. Baker Pasha – Valentine Baker, born 1827, was known as 'Baker Pasha'. He was the brother
    of Sir Samual White Baker, one-time Governor General of the Equatorial Provinces in the
    Service of the Khedive.
    Valentine Baker joined the British army in 1848 and served in the 10th (Prince of Wales'
    Own) Royal Hussars. Commissioned by purchase in the rank of Cornet on 1 August 1848,
    became Lieutenant on 29 July 1853 and became Captain, by purchase, on 1 August 1856.
    He served in the Kaffir War (1852-1853), in India and in the Crimea. In 1855 he was
    present at the siege of Sebastopol, and was on the escort to the Commander-in-Chief on
    the final assault and the capture of the town, and at the Battle of Tchernaya. Received
    Crimea Medal and clasp, and Turkish Medal. He became Major on 14 June 1859,
    Lieutenant Colonel on 30 March 1860 and Colonel on 30 March 1865.
    He became a Major-General in the Turkish army in 1877, and served in the Russo-Turkish
    war. He organised and commanded (1882-1887) the Egyptian gendarmerie for the
    Khedive, and was disastrously routed at the first battle of El Teb (1884) by the tribesmen
    of Osman Digna. He was author of *'Clouds in the East'* published in 1876 and *'War in
    Bulgaria'* published in 1879. He died in 1887.
13. *Ruschuck* – this refers to Rustchuk.
    Butler, op cit, Map 19.
14. *Pest* – Donne refers to *Pesth* the town on the right bank of the River Danube which,
    combined with the town of Buda on the left bank of the river, formed the city of Budapest.
15. Major A. H. A. Gordon, 65th Regiment. Was appointed first Commandant of the Cyprus

Police and Pioneer Force on 29th November 1879 (Cyprus Gazette No 39 of 29th November 1879). He was promoted to Lieutenant Colonel and appointed Chief Commandant of the Cyprus Military Police and held the combined command of the two existing Police Corps – The Cyprus Military Police and the Cyprus Police and Pioneer Force, under the provisions of 'The Cyprus Ordnance, 1880' dated 1st December 1880 and promulgated by the Cyprus Gazette No 62 of 26th November 1880.

16. Donne refers here to his elder sister Anna Jane Merifield Donne who was born in 1855 and who was, like Donne and his younger brother, Henry Richard Beadon Donne, a talented water colour artist.

17. Diligence – a continental public stage coach.

18. Donne refers to Assistant Commissary General (with ranking of Major) C. F. Leach who was holding the appointment of Senior Commissariat Officer, Cyprus Garrison. Monthly Army List, August 1881, 31 and 548.

Gates to home: Merefield House, Crewkerne, Somerset. 1948.

7   The Cyprus Military Police

DONNE RECORDED his arrival back in Cyprus as follows:

August 1881

12.   "I went on to Larnaca in the 'Elphitha' and happily met Colonel Gordon[1] at the Club who informed me that I was destined to take the Limassol police and not the Larnaca as I had thought, and Gilmore[2] was to come to Larnaca instead. This change of course suited me well. I therefore remained at Larnaca.

13.   Dined with Cobham[3] the Commissioner on the 13th inst.

14.   Returned to Limassol with the Colonel on the 14th inst. per SS 'Cymiote'.
      Limassol Being unable to take over the duties for some days, until orders were received I started off for the Camp on Mount Troodos about 5 p.m.

15.   Having nothing but a miserable screw to ride the result was disastrous for I spent most of the night on the road, only arriving dead tired out at the Platres Hotel at 1 a.m. After a nap and a 'cooler' I rode on to the camp on the top, my wretched screw more dead than alive, and which I vowed I would never ride down again.

16.   *Mount Troodos* After the scorching heat of the plains the air was delightfully refreshing and cool, and the water like ice. I rode over in the afternoon to call on the Warrens[4] at their house above Platres. I stayed on the hill till the 18th living at our mess 'in civilian', Colonel Hackett at the time being Acting High Commissioner of Cyprus.[5]

18.   On my way down to Platres I called at Colonel Warren's, the Chief Secretary, for orders (this time on a good mule).

19.   Got into Limassol again at 7.30 and put up at the Club.

20.   On the 20th order came for me to take over the duties of Local Commandant of Military Police from Gilmore, and the next four days we were busy taking and handing over the many and laborious duties of the Command.

Donisthorpe Donne sketched by
Lieutenant Allan Gilmore, Limassol, 1881.

24.   On the 24th I found myself properly installed as L.C.M.P. and Governor of Limassol Prison with 60 jail birds to be responsible for inside. It took me some time to get into the swing of the work which embraced all police duties in the Town and District of Limassol, the management of the Prison, and prosecutions at the Daavi Court,[6] to say nothing of payments and accounts and book keeping. There were about 100 zaptiehs[7] all told, of which 30 were mounted (including prison wardens). Lieutenant Mustafa Shafki was native officer to the force, Dayan interpreter and De Yough police inspector.

26.   On the 26th I took over Gilmore's Qtrs in Albert Street at Hedji Nicola's house, and engaged John Houlihun a Corfu lad as servant and groom. A short time after I bought Lieutenant Mustafa's pony, a nice looking grey, and which suited me very well, for £19. During the last week in August the heat was very trying. Bairam Festival was on and the men as usual had a holiday. Mitchell[8] the Commissioner was away on leave in the Lebanon, Thompson[9] doing the work. The most disagreeable part of my work was visiting the Prison and town at night.

September 1881

5.   Colonel Gordon[10] came down on quarterly inspection and inspected the Detachment and Prison: and again on the 9th Sir R Biddulph the High Commissioner returned from England and I had a zaptieh Guard of Honor (sic) on the pier.

10.   Started off on my first district tour with Dayan and 3 zaptiehs and rode up to Selico[11] and investigated a peculiar case of theft. Then over the hills to Kilani the chief village of the Nahieh,[12] and put up there for the night. The next a.m. we went on to Malia the centre of a very lawless district near the Papho boundary. Chiefly Turkish inhabitants and much given to raiding and cattle lifting it being my special object to try and capture some of the men who had been long wanted by the Authorities. However although many complaints of theft were brought forward no information was obtainable, the people being very unwilling or unable to give information.

11.   So after waiting till dark I rode on to Pahna to try and capture a man named Andoni Nicola, a notorious ruffian who with several others was the Scourge of the district. He however had flown having apparently got wind of our being in the neighbourhood, and as I afterwards found out had been warned from Malia by his confederates and had ridden off that evening, armed, on a donkey, no one professed to know where.
So this expedition was so far a failure, and we put up for the night in the best house we could find, a wretched Greek hotel, full of wine chatties and dirt, but the inmates did their best and cleared out for our reception. I have often since had to put up in as bad, and even worse places. The next morning we left Pahna at daybreak and set out for Limassol over the mountains, Pahna being in the midst of very rough country on the top of a hill.
We rode back through Khandu and other villages and got into Limassol again about midday, after a very hot ride.

15.   A few days afterwards a report came down that a soldier had been shot at on Mount Troodos so I hastened off along the long and dusty road to Platres to find that the case had been settled by De Yough who had gone up the day before. So I slept at Letts Hotel at Platres and came back the next day.

18.   H. M. S. 'Hecla' came in and curiously enough I found a connection on board. Naval Lieutenant Bradley, who knew that I was in Cyprus.

October 1881

6.   Today the new pier[13] was opened by the High Comm(ission)er with great festivities; a guard of honor (sic) of the Reg[t] and most of the Officers and Island officials were present, and the ceremony was followed by a Banquet to everyone and much speech making. About 70 persons sat down in the new Konak buildings.

10.   Left Limassol on a round of Inspection in the District in the Limassol Nahieh, riding to Gelagi[14] village and on to Heftagonia[15] for the night. The scenery in the valleys and mountains round was very fine, and this part of the Island had been little visited before by

Limassol Bay, 1881.

anyone. We rode up a very fine valley to Aracapa,[16] Atracko[17] and Collochaco[18] to Zobie[19] where we rested. The Bishop of Kition was also here inspecting but I did not see his holiness as he was taking his siesta. The village was in gala, and the little church was flying the white church flag in honor (sic) of the occasion. After a short rest for ourselves and the ponies we had to be up and off over the long and very mountainous road to Agro.[20] We passed over a very breakneck road and had to lead our ponies most of the way to Ayayanni[21] a picturesque little vine-growing village in a dell, and at last arrived at Agro the highest village in the mountains of Limassol. There is a Monastery[22] here which is disused apparently, as we could find none at home but a decrepid old monk, who informed us that there was no bedding or food to be got, and that we had better go to the village the other side of the ravine. I shall always remember Agro village as being the worst place I have ever found Qtrs in. It would be difficult indeed to find a place more primitive or more cut off from the outer world. But there are many such in Cyprus high up in the mountains, where one would least expect to find them.

12.   Leaving early the following morning we arrested a man in his vineyard who had been reported by the Muchtar as a villain of the deepest dye. He drew a knife and ran at first, but the Zaptieh appearing over the crest of the hill with a rifle, he was brought to his senses and surrendered to the call. He was soon in tow of the Zaptieh and we proceeded down the valley and passed through Potamnitza[23] and then crossed over a mountain range to Palendria[24] a large vine-growing village. Here I released the man thinking the lesson would be a warning to him and seeing the impossibility of getting back that night if we kept him with us.

The vintage was in full swing here as everywhere else and we lunched accordingly on some magnificent bunches of grapes, the finest I recollect having ever seen. From here we rode over hill and dale to Hia Mania,[25] an incident occurring on the way which I first thought was going to be a great catch. A man sitting down at the bend of the road a short distance in front suddenly sprang up when he saw me and bolted out of sight, a companion who was with him remaining. I immediately thought of the men who were 'wanted' and followed hard. Not until the interpreter came up however could I gain any information from the old man, whom in my eagerness I had seized and was about to beat to make him speak.

It turned out however, instead of the runaway being a murderer or such like as I suspected, he had runaway from fear, and looking up we saw him standing on a hill above. He came down on his father's summons and we could then see that the poor boy was shaking from some imaginable fear and was too much afraid to speak. Having therefore assured ourselves that their errand was an honest one and having searched them, we proceeded, thinking the boy at least to be crazy.

At Hia Mania a murder had been committed a short time before, so after having collected some necessary evidence and lunched in a very clean little house, owned by the muchtar's son, we rode back to Limassol through Gabellu[26] and Corfi.[27]

Passing Corfi we were caught in a heavy shower the 1st of the season, and a prelude of the coming winter weather, or should I say the break up of the hot weather.

25.   Rode out round the Salt Lake to see the ruins of an old Monastery[28] from whence a picturesque view of the Salt Lake and hills beyond.

26.   The next day the 'Tyne' Troopship[29] came in with a large draft for the Regiment under Campbell and Ramus,[30] and the latter who was evidently very ill with consumption put up with me for a week.

November 1881

3.   The 3rd Nov, being a 'Bairam' holiday for the men, I issued the new police clothing to the whole force in the afternoon the old red jacket being discarded for a blue uniform with red braid.[31]

6.   On the 6th Colonel Gordon came down and inspected the Detachment again, heavy rain falling overnight and Troodos being covered with snow for the 1st time this winter. The Zapt(ieh)s and Troopers were paraded next day.

11.   Left again for the district of Evdimu,[32] acts of violence becoming more numerous every day. I rode out with 5 troopers along the coast through Episcopi arriving at Evdimu at dusk. After a long rest we started again up country for Pahna[33] to try and surprise Andoni by night this time. We surprised some donkey stealers on the road who, seeing the party coming along left the path and fled to the bush. After a wild scurry through the bush by moonlight over rocks and stones and bushes, it ended by the principal thief getting away; however we got one man, and the stolen convoy and took them on to Prassiu[34] with us where they were indentified by the village priest as his property. So we bound the captured culprit up, and sent him back to the Konak at Evdimu.

We arrived before Pahna about 3 a.m. and after picqueting the horses separated into two parties for the attack. With two Zapt(ieh)s I crept up to the suspected man's house, the other making a detour to prevent his possible escape in the other direction. Placing one man on the roof with a Martini Rifle ready loaded, I went to the door with revolver ready cocked, but we eventually found he was not 'at home' that night, his Lady love being the only occupant. After searching several other houses we were forced to give up the search and, having gathered the villagers together and warned them on the subject of harbouring the criminal, we rode back again to Evdimu in the morning.

12.   After the fatigues of the night we were glad to stop at Evdimu and in the evening I rode down to the shore and had a dip.

13.   On my way back to Limassol next day I found the ruins of the Temple of Apollo Hylates near Curium. It occupies a commanding position not far from the promontory and a few 100 yds from the road to Paphos. There is a jumble of ruins and fallen columns and the foundations can all be traced and in one place I observed a fine piece of Greek inscription bearing the word 'Apollo' on it. At Episkopi the black Muchtar gave me a very good dinner a la' Turk. After which I summoned the principal villagers to a meeting on the subject of theft, etc. We also called on the Lord of Colossi Tower[35] on our way back.

Gilmore[36] arrived in the evening on board the Mail en route to England, and after dinner at the Hackett's, I bade him farewell from the pier. He had worked hard in the Police for more than 3 years.

24.   I made another excursion into the Evdimu Nahieh sleeping as usual at the Mudir's[37] house.

25.   And the next day visited Prassiu, Platanissia[38] and Electora[39] riding through a fine country with charming views seaward. We put up for the night at Pissouri and had a long discussion with the native magnates on the subject of theft in general but like all Cypriots they were free enough to complain, but not to assist the police in the apprehension of offenders.

26.   The next a.m. the sky was black and rain coming down hard, making it impossible for us to proceed as Pissouri is on top of a high hill with steep roads leading to the plain. From Cape Blanko near there is a splendid view along the coast.

It cleared up about midday however, and as the roads were in consequence execrable, we

Zaptieh on Patrol, 1881.

did not get into Limassol before evening.
27.   HMS 'Superb' came in next day and lunches and cricket matches were enlivening topics of
       the day, and also an inspection of the ship."

During the three and half months that Donne had been back in Cyprus he had been
very busy taking over his new duties and in patrolling the large area under his
command. He did, however, complete two water colours and one black and white
sketch during that time. The water colours were of Limassol Bay and a Zaptieh on
horseback wearing the old scarlet tunic. The black and white sketch was entitled
'Zaptieh on patrol – 1881' and is now hanging in the Cyprus Police Officers Mess at
Limassol.[40]

Notes to Chapter Seven

1. Lieutenant Colonel Alex Herman Adam Gordon.
    (See also Note 15, Chapter 6).

2. Lieutenant Allan Gilmore, 61st Regiment.
    Appointed Local Commandant Military Police, Nicosia 28 August 1878 (Cyprus Gazette No 1, 5th November 1878).
    Appointed Local Commandant Military Police, Limassol 8 August 1879 (Cyprus Gazette No 33, 8th August 1879).

3. C. D. Cobham, Assistant Commissioner, Larnaca 1st October 1878 (Cyprus Gazette No 1, 5th November 1878.
    Appointed Registrar of the High Court of Justice, 25th February, 1879 (Cyprus Gazette No 11, 25th February 1879).
    Appointed Commissioner, Larnaca from 18th March 1879. (Cyprus Gazette No 15, 18th March 1879).

4. Lieutenant Colonel F. G. E. Warren, Royal Artillery.
    Appointed Commissioner, Limassol from 1st October 1878 (Cyprus Gazette No 1, 5th November 1878).
    Appointed Chief Secretary to Government; member of the Executive and provisionally member of the Legislative Council from 1 August 1879 (Cyprus Gazette No 32, 3lst July 1879).
    Georghallides, op cit, page 46.
    Georghallides records that "... When serving as Commissioner of Limassol Warren had quarrelled with Kyprianos the Bishop of Kition concerning the rights of the Church and other questions of local administration. The Bishop accused Warren of an arbitrary and oppressive management of public affairs and of prejudice against both the Church and the Greek Cypriots ..."

5. Lieutenant Colonel Simpson Hackett held the post of Acting High Commissioner of Cyprus from 11th July 1881 until 9th September 1881.
    See Chapter 5, Note 8.

6. Georghallides, op cit, page 46.
    "... At the time of the British occupation the Law (Nizam) Courts in existence were –
    a Daavi (Pleas) Court in each of the six Qazas (districts), and a Temyiz (Appeal) Court in Nicosia and a Tijaret (Commercial) Court at Larnaca; and there were also tribunals called the Mahkemeh-i-sheri, which had jurisdiction in religious and domestic matters between Moslems. But all the above Courts, except the Mahkemeh-i-sheri, have been superseded by the Courts constituted by the 'Cyprus Courts of Justice Order, 1882' ..."

7. The Cyprus Military Police force was formed largely from the old force of Turkish Zaptiehs (Police).

8. Ronald L. N. Mitchell, Commissioner of Limassol from 1st August 1879 (Cyprus Gazette No 34, 21st August 1879).

9. Assistant Paymaster H. L. Thompson, Army Pay Department.
    Appointed Civil Treasurer 31st August 1878 (Cyprus Gazette No 1, 5th November 1878).
    Appointed Assistant Commissioner, Paphos from 1st September 1879 (Cyprus Gazette No 36, 6th September 1879).
    Acting Commissioner during the absence on leave of R. L. N. Mitchell from 21st June 1881 (Cyprus Gazette No 76, 20th August 1881.

10. See note 1.

11. Georghallides, op cit, page 47.
    Donne is referring to the mixed Greek and Turkish village of Silikou. (This annotation by Georghallides was made before the partitioning of Cyprus in 1974).

12. Georghallides, op cit, page 47.
    "... The casa (district) of Limassol comprised the following nahiehs (sub-districts):

Limassol, Episkopi, Evdim (Evdimou), Kilani (C. G. *No 82, 3 March 1882).
Note* – Cyprus Gazette.

13. Donne refers here to a new pier that had been constructed at Limassol port.
14. The village of Kellaki.
    Georghallides, op cit, page 16.
15. The village of Eptagonia.
    Georghallides, op cit, page 16.
16. The village of Aracapas.
    Ibid.
17. The village of Athrakos.
    Ibid.
18. The village of Kalokhorio.
    Ibid.
19. The village of Zoopiyi.
    Ibid.
20. The village of Agros.
    Ibid.
21. The village of Ayios Ioannis.
    Ibid.
22. Georghallides refers to this monastery as "... the Great Monastery of Agros, a ninth century foundation which after the 1770's was overcome by debts. By the nineteenth century it was practically derelict.
23. The village of Potamitissa.
    Georghallides, op cit, page 17.
24. The Greek village of Pelendria.
    Georghallides, op cit, page 47.
25. The village of Ayios Mamas.
    Georghallides, op cit, page 17.
26. The village of Kalilio.
    Georghallides, op cit, page 17.
27. The village of Korphi.
    Ibid.
28. Donne refers to the monastery 'St Nicolas of the Cats' which is reputed to be one of the earliest monasteries to be founded on the island of Cyprus. According to legend it was built by the rebel Calogaerus in the reign of Constantine the Great. It was he, as the founder of the monastery, who introduced cats in order to destroy the large number of serpents found in the Akrotiri area.
29. The reinforcements would have been posted to Cyprus from the Royal Sussex Regiment Depot at Chichester.
30. Captain Francis Selwyn Campbell,
    Lieutenant Charles L. A. Ramus of The Royal Sussex Regiment.
    Monthly Army List, August 1881, 363 and 364.
31. The first issue of clothing for the Cyprus Military Police Zaptieh consisted of the following:
    Red fez with a black tassel
    White yemeni (handkerchief) wrapped around the fez (turban style)
    Red Chepken or Telek (waistcoat), this was fastened at the top and cut-away at the waist.
    There was an edging of light blue to the coat, with zig-zag braiding on either side of dark blue.
    The top of the sleeve had a decoration of narrow light blue braiding and the lower sleeve a decoration of an inverted stripe, also of light blue, with a dark blue cuff.
    Red kavushturma (shirt) was worn under the Cepken. The shirt was collarless with light blue braiding at the neck band which continued down the front of the shirt on either side of the buttons.
    Dark blue dizlik (trousers).

Chizme (long boots) of black leather.

Kushak (wool cummerbund) of blue.

The identification of these items was provided by Mr. Asim Ali Refki, of the Turkish Museum, Nicosia during 1975 and was confirmed by Major Muftizades OBE, the Turkish Liaison Officer at Episkopi at that time.

The records of the Royal Army Clothing Depot, Pimlico reveal that the clothing authorities in the United Kingdom had decided that the dress of the West India Regiment and the Cyprus Military Police should be identical, except of course, for local embellishments. Although the dress details were given in English terminology at the RACD the contractor producing the uniforms in Cyprus used 'local' names for the various garments.

Donne refers to the change-over of uniforms during 1881 but the actual entry in the RACD Form 66 is dated September 1885 and gives the following information (in English terminology):

"... Cyprus Police

(Discontinued)	11/8/85	*(Substituted)*
No Designation		*No Designation*
7027 Jacket without sleeves scarlet cloth		P415 Jacket tweed without sleeves
7028 Waistcoat with sleeves scarlet cloth		P416 Waistcoat serge with sleeves
7029 Breeches, Blue Tweed Mounted Men		P417 Breeches Blue Tweed
7030 Breeches, Blue Tweed Dismounted Men		P418 Breeches Blue Serge
		P419 Sash Turkey Red
		P420 Stockings

and Pattern Nos 7033 Boots Knee & 7031 Army Badge are to be retained as patterns ..."
The above information was kindly supplied by the National Army Museum, London.

32. The village of Evdhimou.
     Georghallides, op cit, page 18.
33. The village of Pakna
     Ibid
34. The village of Prastio.
     Ibid.
35. Colossi Castle was built in 1454 by the Knights of St John of Jerusalem and in the sixteenth century it became the property of the Cornaro family. After the Turkish occupation the ownership is obscure.
36. See note 2.
37. After the Tanzimat of 1839 Cyprus was divided into cazas administered by a Kaimmakam and into nahiehs administered by a mudir.
     Georghallides, op cit, page 47.
38. The village of Plataniska.
     Georghallides, op cit, page 19.
39. The village of Alekhtora.
     Ibid.
40. The black and white sketch 'Zaptieh on Patrol' was presented to the Officers Mess, Limassol by Donne's grandson Lieutenant Colonel William Donisthorpe Shaw.

8   The Cyprus Bandit Hunt

ONE OF the officers serving in Cyprus during the latter part of 1881 was Lieutenant H. H. Kitchener, later to become Lord Kitchener of Khartoum, who was at that time employed as the Director of Revenue Survey. Kitchener assumed this appointment on 15th March 1880, under the authority of the Cyprus Gazette No 47 dated 15th March 1880, and was based in Limassol. Kitchener's house, which Donne must have visited on many occasions, was located at Limassol but was demolished to make way for the a rebuilding programme after the end of World War 2.

Lieutenant Kitchener was working in the Pissouri area when he was shot at and it was on the following day that Donne left Limassol to lead the man hunt for Kitchener's attacker. He records the events in his journal as follows:

December 1881

7.   "Today I started on a very memorable excursion to my usual hunting ground, a report having come in overnight that Kitchener, the Government Surveyor, who was surveying round Pissouri had been shot at near Platanissia by a man unknown. We saddled early next morning and rode off to Pissouri with a force of Troopers and arriving there in the afternoon I had time to ride over to Platanissia with Kitchener himself, and examine the ground. We also examined the natives in the village but could get no information of the man in particular. Having therefore returned to Pissouri I put up for the night. After having retired to bed, my servant Yanni came in with a shepherd, who volunteered information against a man who was in hiding in a mandra (sheepfold) a little distance off. Having therefore got two Troopers together with their rifles and borrowing Kitchener's shotgun myself, we proceeded to the place on foot with the shepherd as a guide and Yanni as interpreter.

Kitchener's house at Limassol. By courtesy of H. M. Williamson.

After an hour's walk we were indicated the fold by the shepherd, who however refused to go further not relishing the chances of being 'potted' as he informed us the man was armed. Having made my disposals to surround the place as well as possible, and guided by the moonlight, and the barking of sheepdogs, who had already taken the alarm, we advanced to the Attack at a smart pace in order if possible to get up before the dogs woke the inmates. I missed the entrance myself and before I was aware found myself looking down on the sheepfold from some rocks above, and the two Zapt(ieh)s creeping outside with their rifles ready. I soon discovered my error and was down in a minute beside them and clearing the fence outside with as little noise as possible, got at the entrance of the cave inside the fold. At the further end a fire was smouldering beside which sat a shepherd who had apparently just roused himself to the fact someone was at the entrance. The nearest Zaptieh and myself then ran and saw at the same time that another man was also lying on the ground near, with a pile of arms near him. Before we had time to do anything or to take in the situation, he leapt up with a howl and attempted to catch the arms near him. The Zaptieh and myself however were on him in a moment, and after a struggle that lasted for a few seconds, pinioned him on the ground. The other Zaptieh who was guarding the entrance then came in, and after a short time, we soon had both men securely bound up. On searching the cave which was a spacious one, and ran back some way, we found a considerable store of arms, consisting of 2 large knives or yatagans, carried by the Turks in their belts, two flintlock pistols loaded with ball, and two double barrel fowling pieces, also loaded with shot and slugs. One of the knives we found drawn in the shepherd's bed. One of the men also wore a large sporting belt well stocked with powder, ball, shot and slugs. In fact had we not surprised them in time, they might have kept any number of men at bay at the narrow entrance of their cave. Having secured the arms and the men, and ransacked the cave, we marched them back to Pissouri about 1 a.m.

8.   Instead of being a murderer, however as I had expected, I found that the younger man was one Salih Bobi a notorious ruffian and an escaped convict from Nicosia, who had long defied the Paphos police and been fired at in that district once by the L. C. M. P. It was also clearly established that he was actually the man who had fired at Lieut Kitchener. So thus far our raid was an entire success. The other man was a shepherd who had knowingly harboured the convict and was in consequence sentenced to Limassol jail for 6 months. Salih Bobi was sent in the next a.m. to Limassol. I rode to the cave again next a.m. to examine it by daylight but could gain no information of the murderer, whom I afterwards ascertained from my informant, had actually been there in Salih's company that night! But by some accident or other he had left the cave a short time before we entered it. (This was proved by the fact that one of the guns was his, also that he had but one boot on, we having found the other odd one in the cave). His brother was there in morning but would vouchsafe no information. I rode on to Platanissia again and back to Pissouri, dining with Kitchener and on to Evdimu to sleep at the Konak.[1]

9.   I prepared next morning to ride up country to Pahna and Malia to try to gain some news of the wanted Andoni who had again been heard of in the vicinity. We started for Pahna accordingly but getting scanty news pushed on to visit a village called Chissousa[2] en route to Malia. Having entered the village and perceiving a large mandra just above it, I called for the commission to enquire for my 'wanted' friends, but as usual no information was forthcoming. They knew nothing of any of them. Retracing our steps therefore I was in the act of riding up to the mandra where several men were loitering, when my leading Zaptieh Mouslu Osman, shouted out loudly that Molla Tahir, a notorious ruffian and long wanted by the police, was in a ruin in front. Almost at the same moment I saw him running across the front of the Zaptieh, down the steep hill towards the river. He carried a gun and a long knife in his belt. Another moment and he would have disappeared, so, in the excitement and fear that the man would escape us, I shouted down to Mouslu to fire. Mouslu carried one of the fowling pieces we had captured the day before, and which was loaded, but no one knew with what sort of ammunition. Mouslu turned his horse and raising the gun, fired at the man about 20 paces off, who was running across him. Molla Tahir then

disappeared behind a wall and was lost to our view, no one knowing at the moment whether he was hit or not. I fancied he had made for the river bed and would escape on the opposite side, so in great anxiety lest he should after all elude us, I rode as fast as the ground would allow down to the river directing Dayan the interpreter and the other Zaptieh to ride through the village and cut him off. Mouslu rode to the other side of the river where the ground was rough and rocky.

Finding no traces of the man in the river bed, about 5 minutes later as I was turning my pony to ride towards the village again I saw him emerge from a house facing the river and run towards the Zaptieh on the opposite side with his gun raised to fire. Mouslu, who from his position had seen the man in the house before me, was shouting wildly to the other Zaptieh, who was now standing on the flat roof of one of the houses close by. At the same moment he raised his rifle and fired at Molla Tahir, 2O or 3O paces off. I thought that the bullet had again missed its mark as Tahir ran on, and disappeared again round some walls.

I rushed up and dismounted taking the rifle from the Zaptieh who was very excited, and followed in the direction I had seen the man go. Blood marks on the ground a little further on however soon told me that the ball had told but too truly, and meeting the interpreter at the entrance of the village, I asked him hurriedly where the man had gone. "He's lying round the corner of the road there, Sir, and must be dying" was his answer. Dayan was trembling with evident fear, and excitement. When I came up with this ill-fated highwayman, robber and thief, one could see at a glance that he was fast dying. He was lying in the arms of a villager, his life blood ebbing out on the stones, and the palor of death on his rough countenance. His unhappy wife, a Turkish woman with her white yashmak all bathed in blood, was hanging round his neck uttering wild exclamations of anguish, terror and vengeance against the Zaptieh who had shot her husband, and several other Turkish women who had gathered round joined in the dismal wail making a scene I shall not soon forget. Molla's gun, yatagan and belt were lying round dripping with blood and we could do nothing but stand round as spectators to the scene, the women being far too frantic and violent to permit anyone to interfere. Turning my back therefore on this terrible picture I took out my pocket book to make the necessary entries and to note the names of those standing round. These craven-hearted fellows (for they were the ones who had been in the mandra with the deceased, and whom I had questioned before in the village as to Molla's whereabouts) tried to slip away seeing my object, and I had even to send the Zaptiehs for some in their houses.

Molla Tahir breathed his last about 10 minutes after I came up, having been shot right through the body; he had gone a considerable distance after receiving the fatal bullet, and had even attempted to shoot the interpreter, the latter (being unarmed) having taken refuge in the nearest place, and barred himself in.

Molla was a man notorious throughout the Island as a desperate ruffian, and the terror of the country round for years past. He was a great cattle stealer, as well as having committed many highway robberies. I flattered myself on having done a great stroke of business in having rid the district of such a pest, and congratulated the Zaptieh Ahmet warmly on having shot the poor fellow, Ahmet being in a great state of mind from fear of the consequences, and the execrations heaped on him by the wailing women. Nothing would comfort him, so I sent him straight off to Limassol, where he arrived I believe the same night without stopping a moment on the way such was the man's terror of vengeance from Molla's relatives. Nothing more remaining to be done at Chissusa, I rode on to Malia to inform the man's relatives of his death, and also to show the villagers here that the police meant work, and to hold up Molla's fate as a warning to his confederates. Having accordingly gathered the villagers together in the Square I informed them that Molla Tahir, one of their own number, had been shot dead at Chissusa for refusing to surrender himself to me when called on, and added that I meant to hunt out the rest of his associates and treat them in the same way if they did not give themselves up. This had an astonishing effect on the hitherto indifferent crowd amongst whom were two of Molla's brothers, and many relations, and men women and children all set out for Chissusa as fast as they could

go to verify with their own eyes if the astonishing news was really true.

It being necessary for me to return forthwith again to Limassol to report these circumstances and to send the D^r out to make a post-mortem exam, we lost no time in turning our backs on Malia to get over the long ride back to Evdimu before nightfall, where we arrived about 6 p.m.

10.   I got into Limassol again next midday where I found greatly exaggerated accounts of the case had preceeded us. The Konak was besieged, and when we arrived with such an array of knives, pistols and guns etc stuck about us, everyone thought that at least we had had a desperate fight for it. I telegraphed the circumstances to the C. C. M. P.[3] at Nicosia who in his turn hardly knew how H. E. the 'Vali'[4] would take it.

11.   However all's well that ends well, and when my detailed report in writing went in, it was generally accepted at H^{d}Q^{trs} that nothing better could have happened. Many of the villagers who had suffered by this man's depredations afterwards came in to thank me for the service that had been rendered them and to express their joy at his death. As the result of this energy on the part of the police, Molla's brother, one of the gang, gave himself up shortly after, and the notorious Andoni of Pahna who had all along evaded all attempts to capture him, was taken by the Zaptiehs at Nicosia".

As a result of these activities during the early part of the month of December Donne did not complete any further water colours during 1881, he did, however, complete two sketches depicting the events leading up to the capture of Salih Bobi.

The fight in the Cave, December 1881.

Opposite: Approaching the Cave.

Notes to Chapter Eight

1. The newspaper *'Cyprus Herald'* carried a number of reports covering the events from the attempted killing of Lieutenant Kitchener to the apprehension of the bandit Salih Bobi, of which the following are extracts:

    December 7th

    "... Information was received in Limassol yesterday evening to the effect that Lieutenant Kitchener R.E., Director of Survey, had been shot at near the village of Pissouri: it appears that seeing a man near where he was at work, Mr. Kitchener approached him to ask for some information, when the man levelled a gun at him, and kept moving about still keeping the gun in a threatening position. Mr. Kitchener then went some distance to fetch a native to interpret for him, and on returning to the spot the man again levelled his piece, and eventually fired a shot at Mr. Kitchener, but fortunately without hitting him. The native with him bolted, and Mr. Kitchener was unable to capture the miscreant. Lieutenant Donne with two of the police started for Pissouri this morning ..."

    December 14th

    "... Following the outrage attemped on Lieutenant Kitchener, R.E. which was reported by us last week, the police have had a very busy time of it in the district, resulting in the capture of an escaped convict named Salih Bobi, who is supposed to be the man who fired at Lieutenant Kitchener, and in the death of another named Molla Tahir, who was shot by a Zaptieh while in the act of levelling his gun at another Zaptieh.

    Considering the arsenal with which Salih Bobi had surrounded himself, his character and the state of the neighbourhood, we think that Mr Donne deserves high praise and commendation for the energy, zeal and courage displayed by him in the capture of one who for so long had been able to defy the law.

    The man Molla Tahir whom we have already alluded to as having been shot by a Zaptieh, is said to have been the terror of the district; and was wanted by the police as an escaped prisoner on charges of rape, theft and highway robbery: the police were in reality searching for one Andoni an escaped prisoner.

    Since writing the above we learn from different sources that the inhabitants of Episcopi and the Circassian Village near the Salt-Lake, have expressed their satisfaction at the death of Molla Tahir of whom they have been in constant terror: several of his late comrades have fled from the district, in the direction of Papho, with the intention of embarking from thence in a caroub ship ..."

    December 21st

    "... From every village in the neighbourhood, we hear nothing but expressions of satisfaction at the death of Molla Tahir, who has been a terror to all the inhabitants of the district ..."

    In respect of Andoni the following report in the *'Cyprus Herald'* closed that particular case as far as Donne was concerned:

    "... We have received news of the capture of Andoni Nicola, an inhabitant of Pahna, near Nicosia where he had gone with several members of his family with the intention it is said, of treating with the authorities for his surrender. It appears that for some months past Lieutenant Donne, our energetic L. C. M. P. has so harrassed Andoni and kept him on the move, that he at last came to the conclusion that liberty under such circumstances was scarcely worth having ..."

2. The village of Kissousa.
    Georghallides, op cit, page 21.

3. C. C. M. P. – Commandant, Cyprus Military Police.

4. A Turkish administrative rank roughly equivalent to Governor-General. Before the British occupation the Mutessarif (Governor) of Cyprus was under the authority of the Vali of the Vilayet of Rhodes. (Georghallides, op cit, page 47).
    Within the context of the journal Donne means the 'High Commissioner'.

9 Nicosia and the Locust Destruction

DONNE CONCLUDES his entries for the year 1881 with a postscript:

December 1881

13. "The French gunvessel (sic) 'Voltigeur' paid us a visit and we entertained the officers at the Club. Fairfield[1] of the Colonial office came down to overhaul government affairs.
23. Olive,[2] L. C. M. P. Papho, came up and next night being Christmas Eve, we entertained the English married people at the Club at dinner with a very small hop afterwards.
25. Being Xmas (sic) Day I had my Parade of the Zaptieh and visited the prison in the morning, and in the afternoon entertained Hedji Emmanueli's family and some --- friends at my lodgings, and rode out to Polymedia to dine with the Regt in the evening. It was a warm fine day.
    1881 being well nigh run out I may safely say that I have seen and done more during the last twelve months than in any previous year.
    "Non numero horas nisi serenas".
    and I cannot resist this little quotation dedicated respectfully to the year passing away:-
    "yet I leave, as waves leave their Treasures of coral and shell,
    a gift passing sorrows and pleasures, our friendship to tell." ... "

Donne was destined to leave Cyprus before the end of the following year, and during his final eight months of service with the Cyprus Military Police he was to have the opportunity to serve in Nicosia as well as Limassol. His diary for the year 1882 commences:

January 1882

1. "... 1882 Limassol Cyprus – Most of my time during the 1st half of January was occupied in making up the Annual Police and Prison reports. I had but little time to go into the district myself. To my disgust Andrea the Corfi[3] murderer was again captured by Zaptiehs but succeeded in escaping from them, and the loss of a rifle by one of the Zaptiehs on duty at Pahna led to an enquiry on the subject.
20. About the 20th the weather became unusually severe, and the hills round Silico[4] were covered with snow.
27. On the 27th I rode round to Fassoula,[5] Palodia,[6] and several other villages within a day's ride to inspect.
    About this time I was ordered to relieve Bor[7] L. C. M. P. at Nicosia whilst he was employed superintending the Locust Destruction.

February 1882

3. I accordingly handed over the Limassol Command & Prison to Powell[8] 35th, as a temporary measure during my absence at Nicosia and started for the Capital on the 5th. Having packed up my traps and sent them on ahead, I said goodbye to Hedji Emmanueli's family (amongst whom were not a few moist eyes) and left Limassol on a very cold morning for Cofinu.[9] Later on it commenced snowing and when I arrived at Cofinu under the shadow of the great Stavrovouni Mount I was not sorry to take shelter in the little house of --- Effendi, a very hospitable old Turkish gentleman.
6. Continuing the road next morning I covered 25 miles in time for lunch with Bor and Inglis[10] at the Commissioner's house Nicosia, after which I went out to stop with Col Gordon[11] at his new house outside the walls – until I could find lodgings in town. The country all round was looking very fine and wintry with the Troodos Mountains completely wrapped in snow away in the distance and the fine northern range looking strangely near in its covering of snow.
7. The next day I took over command of the Nicosia Police from Lt Bor – a large force of over 300 men of which 70 were Suwaris, or mounted men.

8.   Having found suitable rooms in town in the Bashmahallak Quarter[12] I shifted into them
     and settled down for a few months. I also got over several calls on the English of Nicosia
     and H. E. the Gov[or] at the Tepe.[13] Harden was commanding a Dett[ment] of 50 men of the
     Regt[14] at the staff huts with Thornton[15] under him. A burst of gaiety seemed to have
     possessed Nicosia, at this time, a farewell dance to Mr. and Mrs. March,[16] the retiring
     Auditor General, and several others of minor importance among the smaller officials. I

Entrance to the Nicosia Mosque, 1882, courtesy Mrs Michelle Cooper.

Macheras Monastery, 1882, courtesy Mrs Michelle Cooper.

dined with Seager,[17] an old Wellingtonian, and Deputy Commissioner on the 12th, the cold still continuing and even running up to 7 degrees of frost.

15. The Nicosia Harriers[18] were also in full swing and the season ended by a big field on the 15th in the Larnaca direction, but unfortunately I was too late to take part in the run. Nicosia life was exceedingly pleasant, albeit quiet, and to my liking. Numerous dinner parties were the order of the Day. It was impossible to be living in Nicosia without enjoying the lovely scenery of the surroundings, and the innumerable picturesque bits which every turn and corner of this old Turkish Capital afforded.

21. Parsons[19] and I rode out together on the 21st to a village called Kaimakli to take sworn evidence on a murder case which he followed up by riding on to Voni and from there home through the pretty village of Kitherea,[20] under the Pentadactylon Mountain. Without a doubt a murder under peculiar circumstances had taken place some time since at Chrisostomo Monastery and the monks had heavily bribed those cognizant of the facts to keep what they knew to themselves. The case however when brought to court fell through. It was a mystery that will never be solved now, and when I think of Chrisostomo and its monks I cannot help bracketing them with the murder mystery.

22. The Molla Tahir shooting case as heard by Themez Court[21] on the 22nd which ended, as I have already recorded, in the police being honourably acquitted of all blame in the man's death.

March 1882

4. Col Gordon came down to inspect the force which was drawn up in the Courtyard of the Buyuk Hahn.[22] about 200 strong.

8. Today I took a holiday and made one of those rare excursions which one is not always in a hurry to forget. Harden, Dr. Johnstone[23] and myself started off early for Chrisostomo Monastery and the Castle of Buffavento, perched on one of the highest peaks of the Northern Range. We galloped away through the Kyrenia Gate with a Zaptieh to show us the way and were soon across the Messaria plain and among the Hummucks (sic). After another hour's scrambling we arrived at Chrisostomo Monastery (alias the White Monastery) most picturesquely situated at the foot of the mountains. The monks received us with great hospitality as usual and as we were picknicing (sic) I did not introduce myself as the Commandant of the District which in fact is not in Nicosia but Kyrenia, so I

The Quarter at Limassol, 1882.

actually had no jurisdiction there, although the murder mystery rather tempted me to have a look round.

We left our ponies behind and scrambled up to the summit on foot and I seldom recollect having been up a more breakneck place. When we arrived at the fork of the hill just below the summit, a most glorious panorama burst on our view. The Northern shore lay at our feet 3000 feet below and behind us the whole of the Messaria Plains with the Troodos range like a massive wall in the blue distance topped with snow, and away to the North across the deep blue straits that intervened were the Taurus Mountains with a similar night cap on. I have always considered it to be one of the finest panoramic view in Cyprus. The beautiful soft colouring of the hills with the azure sky above and intense blue of the sea at one's feet combine to produce a lovely effect. We scrambled about and explored our mountain eyries which indeed must have been a strong place in the days of King Richard of England who reduced it.[24]

Away in the midst of the great brown Messaria Plain was Nicosia like a round spot in the distance with its minarets sticking up like slender sticks in the hazy distance. I was glad to have time to get a sketch as a memento of this most wonderful view, as well as another small one from Chrisostomo ..."

Unfortunately neither of the two sketches mentioned in the journal have been traced. However during his tour of duty at Nicosia Donne did paint a water colour entitled 'Entrance to Nicosia Mosque' which is dated 1882. The only other paintings dating from his tour of duty in Cyprus are of the 'Macheras Monastery' and of the view from his quarters at Limassol.

Donne was soon brought back to his police duties when a problem arose at Kyrenia. The journal reads:

10. "Revenant a nos moutons, however, the alarming news came in from Kyrenia on the 10th

that 5 convicts had broken loose from there, having taken with them rifles and ammunition. This demanded immediate measures being taken for their recapture, and in an hour's time I was galloping out of the Kyrenia Gate with a Dett[ment] of 8 armed Troopers.

In two hours' time we were at the foot of the Agurda Pass leading over to Kyrenia and, detaching 4 of them to watch the pass and the village of Pano Dicomo[25] near there and two others to watch another mountain path I took the remainder with me along the Northern slope of the mountains to see if I could gain any intelligence of the runaways.

After riding a considerable distance and passing several villages the evening began to draw on, so we made for a large village named Hia Mola[26] a short distance ahead. An extraordinary scene presented itself on my arrival. A number of villagers rushed up to us, shouting and crying and gesticulating in every imaginable tone, and one man was bleeding profusely from a wound in the head. Further on were lying what appeared to be dead or dying corpses, some moaning and howling in a piteous way. I first of all imagined that the convicts had been there and sacked the village and that we had arrived in the nick of time, and I instinctively drew my revolver as a precautionary measure. We were soon however undeceived for when something like order had been restored and we could hear each other speak my interpreter extracted the truth from the villagers. It appears there had been a free fight between the villagers and a band of strange gipsies (sic) who were from "across the sea" and the latter having been followed up from Morfou[27] and other villages by their creditors, the minds of the peaceful men of Hia Mola had been prejudiced against the intruders, and Hia Mola had in consequence become the theatre of a desultory warfare which had thus far been going on all day. Our opportune arrival happily put an end to hostilities, and we therefore set to work to collect the casualties. There they lay like so many logs in the street, who seemed incapable of moving, but after a bit we managed to drag them all into the nearest 'Caffeeniss', and set about to patch up their wounds. The men were nothing like as bad as they appeared to be at 1st sight: their wounds consisted of cuts and bruises and contusions, which my interpreter, Theodore Mavrogordato[28] very cleverly overhauled. The only serious cases appeared to be two women one of whom appeared to have a broken thigh and the other a fractured skull. I therefore despatched a messenger across the mountains to Kyrenia for a surgeon, and a report of the case to the Commissioner of the District. We then set to work to take evidence as to the Causus belli which occupied us till midnight when we went to roost in the most decent looking hut we could find.

Scott-Stevenson[29] with his medical officer, Interpreter and Prison Sergt turned up about 4 a.m. having been out all night, and in a short time the casualties were again overhauled and the whole gang of gipsies (sic) bundled off to Kyrenia, some as prisoners, some as patients, and I have never seen a motley utterly miserable looking troop in my life as they collected their wretched traps and decamped, leaving the villagers once more to resume the even tenor of their everyday life – .

During this little bit of excitement we had almost forgotten the convicts of whom Stevenson informed me 3 had already been recaptured, it being most probable that the remaining two had got well away over night. It was therefore hardly necessary for me to remain in the Kyrenia District any longer, so after a hearty laugh with Stevenson over the amusing little incident, my party saddled up and rode back to Nicosia in the afternoon.

11.   I was called up to a fire that night which soon burnt itself out, fires in Cypriot towns being of rare occurrence owing to the mud and stone construction of the houses.

12.   Several of our fellows and the band[30] came up from Polymedia for the race week and during the week the townspeople were treated to some good music.

17.   The race meeting was a great success. The numbers of Turkish women & harems who turned out to see the fun and settled themselves down in a great cluster opposite the Stand all clothed in their picturesque dress and white yashmaks, gave the prettily situated course a most unusual and oriental appearance.

Nicosia was very gay all the week and the festivities wound up with a bachelors' ball at the

Government offices outside the town. Morton won the handsome cup given by the Regiment.

I rode over to Kyrenia on the 14th with Campbell and Ashurst[31] where we had a look round the fort and lunch at the Stevensons.

22. Being anxious to make a more extended tour of the Nicosia District whilst the weather seemed favourable, I started with my interpreter on 22nd to inspect the Morfou and Lefka nehiehs.[32] The locusts had begun to appear in large quantities and most of the traps for their destruction were already in working order. In order to visit them therefore, we rode cross country via Gonelli[33] and found Naim Eff, the Lefka Mudir and Chief Superintendent Locust Destruction at work there. We joined the road again to the north of Yerollaka[34] and shortly before sunset arrived in sight of Morphu.[35] The Bay of Morfu was beyond with the bold Troodos Range and Lefka hills springing up from the sea in fine cliffs, and Cape Kokkino the west point of the bay, jutting out into the sea, was growing very dark with the sea glittering all round as the sun went down. Morfu itself is a mile or so from the sea in the midst of the great plain. It is essentially a Greek town, just as Lefka is Turkish. We put up at the Monastery[36] which in the matter of interior economy and hospitality is rather behind most of the Cypriot Ecclesiastical Establishments of the sort. However as long as I was in the Nicosia District I always took care to steer for one of them if within a Sabbath day's journey.

Lefka is situated at the foot of one of the finest valleys of Troodos and is one of the happy lands of Cyprus watered by unfailing streams from the great, as Sir S Baker says.[37]

23. Lefka is not a long journey from Morfu so we rode to Caravastasi next a.m. visiting a string of villages on the way. The former is the sea port & custom house of Morfu Bay, and on a hill to the west once stood the ancient Athenian city of Soli, of which nothing now remains but a mass of scattered stones and broken pottery, precisely like Amathus ..."

There is, unfortunately, no record of Donne ever having sketched any scenes from this area of Cyprus, nor is there any record of any of his watercolours. His journal continues with his description of Lefka:

"The valley is filled with innumerable fruit trees, and the houses are almost hidden by the luxurious foliage that surrounds them. It is a great place for lemons. The little mosque with its minaret, surrounded by fruit, olives and caroub trees, makes a very pretty picture with the snowy tops of Troodos for a background.

Having inspected the Police Dett^{ment}, and slept at the little Konak, we started next a.m. for the Marathasa Valley.

24. It is a good eight hours ride to Ghikko[38] Monastery but through some of the finest and wildest scenery in Cyprus. The bridlepath is rough and steep continually crossing and re-crossing the stream until one at length arrives at the quaint old village of Kampos.[39] Lunching here at a very clean and respectable little dwelling where our hostess was busy weaving, we continued our journey up the steep hill sides to Ghikko and after innumerable twisting and turnings round the hilltops, at length sited this greatest and most important of Cyprian Monasteries. It was a massive looking building under the brow of a hill to protect it from the west, with a fine view of Troodos opposite.

The Monastery is very rich with a staff of about 80 monks so needless to state we were regally entertained. The Agumenos[40] was a grand old veteran and showed us all over the curious and unique old Chapel. I also tasted the Ghikko 'red mastic' for the 1st time.

My excuse for coming to Ghikko was to try to find a murderer who was supposed to frequent the place at times, but our errand was fruitless. There was still snow lying about the vicinity in patches and the nights were very cold at this altitude so early in the year. Having written our names in the visitors' book which Sir R. Biddulph had given to the Monastery the summer before we said good(bye) to our kind hosts and got on our way to Everico.[41] It was over one of the most abominable tracks I know in the island and we had to dismount and lead our ponies down most of the steep descents. It was a wild and lonely part of the Island, and the haunt of the Moufflon some say, but I never saw any of those

Kykko (Ghikko) Monastery, photographed by June Harfield, 1983.

'spectre animals'. After riding down a steep and difficult gorge we reached Kalapaniotissa[42] one of the largest and certainly the most curious Cypriot villages I had seen. The houses were built in tiers in the side of the hill, one above the other, and one had to ride over the flat mud roofs to reach beyond. This is likewise a Greek colony and we lunched at the little 'Jack of all trades' shop. The villagers had their usual complaints to make and after noting them, we got on our journey again down the valley, and did not arrive at Everico until after sundown at 7 p.m., having been nearly 10 hours in the saddle.

Everico is an important place in the fertile Everico Valley and, like Lefka, rejoicing in a bounteous supply of water from Troodos which renders its valley nearly the most prolific in the Island. We put up in a very superior 2 storyed (sic) house rejoicing in a superior iron bedstead to have a good sleep on, but although our hostess emphatically denied their absence I was nevertheless able to undeceive her the next a.m. by showing a goodly number of slaughtered 'Bugbears' which thanks to Keating, I had netted.

A deputation awaited me in the morning on the subject of the never-ending water disputes, so we did not get on our homeward road to Nicosia before 10.30. It is a long journey across the plains. We arrived in the afternoon at Peristerona where owing to the indisposition of my interpreter we were delayed an hour or two. Calling at Akakie and Tremitia[43] on our way in we finally passed through the Baffo Gate at 7 p.m. after 5 days' hard riding.

April 1882.

5.   I was ordered to Morfu again a few days afterwards on Locust Inspection. After zig zagging across country visiting the different Traps and screens about Gonelli, Yerollako and Akakie we were caught in a regular Cyprus downpour before reaching Morfu, and it rained hard most of the night 'thru the roof of the old Monastery over our heads being little better than a seive.

6.   In the morning it brightened up, so crossing the limestone hills and sand ridges to the east, we rode to Aya Marina, and visited all the traps on the way back to Nicosia by Aya Vasili[44] and Gonelli, reaching home at even.

9.   Being Easter Sunday and the great Greek festival of the year, feasting and holiday-making was the order of the day with the Greeks.

16.   On the 16th I rode over to Kyrenia to see Houston the Stevensons being away at the time. I was induced by Houston to remain overnight, and such has always been my admiration

of this fairy land that the more I saw of it the more it stamped its rare beauties in my mind. Can it be wondered that a man like Houston, possessing an independent property as he did of his own in Scotland and having travelled all over the World should in visiting Kyrenia last of all determined to buy land there and settle. He too no doubt saw its exceptional beauty and advantages.

After trying to sketch the harbour and hills we dined together at Law's,[45] the Assistant Commissioner's and an old Wellingtonian friend of mine, and had a good talk over Cypriot affairs in general, Dr. Carlotti[46] the D. M. O.[47] also joining us. I don't think any poet has ever yet visited this out of the way spot otherwise we should have heard its praise chronicled in verse before now. I got back to Nicosia early next a.m. and luckily in time to install myself in office, as the High Commissioner inspected the Buyuk Hahn and Prison that morning.

The locust campaign was now fairly well started and these pestivorous insects were now appearing in alarming quantities and every day increasing in size and developing their destructive qualities.

21.   I was ordered out again on the 21st by the Commissioner on a round of inspection embracing all the Traps in the Nicosia District which took me a week riding round. Throughout the Messaria plains stretching from the Carpas to Morfu on the north there were altogether in use upwards of 140 miles of Traps and Screens! This astonishing length will give some idea of the work in hand.

The Screens were of canvas bound with oil cloth at the top, and about 3 ft high, the oil cloth over which the animals could not crawl obliging them to crawl along the canvas until they hopped into the pits dug for their reception. These pits were dug at right angles to the Screens at intervals of about 20 yds, being likewise lined with zinc, preventing the locusts from climbing out again. In whatever direction the locusts appeared to be advancing therefore, were the Traps and Screens erected to intercept them. In this manner vast multitudes were destroyed, so many labourers being detailed to watch a certain length of trapping.

The whole of the Messaria was in this manner spread over with long lines of Screens, sometimes a mile or more in length, according as they were more or less required in any particular locality.

22.   I started in the Kyrenia direction and after a hard day's riding visited all the traps in that direction, and put up for the night at a very comfortable little place in Kitherea.[48] We were off again early next a.m. in a westerly direction passing by Timbo,[49] Margo and Piroi. Here the locusts were passing the Larnaca road in countless myriads, filling the traps to overflowing. The streams were all full of them; the country was all black with them, such an extraordinary sight did they present.

The labour and the Screens seemed indeed utterly inadequate to entrap a hundredth part of their number. Here I met Col Gordon on his way to Nicosia by Diligence with a friend fresh arrived from England, and they were looking in amazement at the extraordinary procession of these insects – all treading in one direction, and hopping into the traps as if despising the puny efforts of man to diminish their numbers.

We continued our ride to Dali the ancient Delium, where Chesnola excavated so successfully, and put up for the night. Dali is the chief town of the Mudirate,[50] and an important one for Cyprus. It has a Christian and Mussulman population and we found a very intelligent schoolmaster there, with a considerable flock under his command. Close by there to the little Greek church is the grave of an English Soldier who belonged to the 71st Highland Regiment in the days of the occupation.[51] A curious place quoth I, to find a British Grave, but then the British soldiers never can reckon where their mortal clay will rest – the whole of this wide world is his burial ground.

In the village great matrimonial preparations were going forward; the belle of the village was about to be given in marriage and it was amusing to watch all the buxom females of the place, Turk and Greek alike, busily beating up the nuptial bed to the sound of dance music. It was a curious Levantine scene. As I desired to see the bride, she was in due course

The church at Dali (Dhali), photographed by June Harfield, 1983.

brought forth and presented to me, and, indeed, for a Cypriot woman very good looking in truth she was. On the strength of my arrival in the Town the musicians came down and serenaded us at meal time. The accommodation at Dali was exceptionally good.

23. We left for Latchia[52] next a.m. and were drenched by a heavy hail storm on the road. We continued cross country to Deftera[53] and the sun which had again appeared soon dried us off. The Mudir of the Dagh nahieh gave us a feed at Deftera and hungry enough we were. On the road across the hills to Yerollako we passed large quantities of locusts moving in the Deftera direction. At Yerollako we arranged to stop for the night at the Muchtar's house, tempted by its clean and neat appearance from proceeding further that day. The Muchtar and his family (and he had two pretty daughters) served us with a most excellent supper.

24. From Yerollako to Peristerona is not a heavy day's journey but as we moved about in all manner of directions to inspect the various traps we did not get to our night's resting place till evening. Passing through Acachie[54] and Tremithia we rode to Meniko in which direction the locusts were marching in hosts, and the river brown with them. They made no difficulty of crossing it, taking their chance of being washed up on the opposite side and then proceeding to attack the crops. Naim Eff., the energetic Mudir of Lefka, was here running up screens in all directions to intercept their march. Meniko is a quaint little Greek village, after the usual pattern. We got down to Peristerona towards evening and I took a drawing of the extremely curious Greek church,[55] which is of great antiquity and has three or four domes springing from the roof. Being on the high road to Troodos, Peristerona is accustomed to see strangers passing through and an old Turkish lady offers excellent accommodation in a superior 2d story old house with a well furnished divaned room for travellers. The wall there which was scratched over with the names of those who had found shelter there, acted as a visitors book.

25. Next day, Tuesday, we crossed the Messaria to Panteleimon Monastery in the Kyrenia District near Cape Kormakiti. We rode through Potamie and Astromeriti where the

locusts were in millions, and the work of destruction progressing well. Then on to Gira, Chrisoliou[56] and Caouti where we got some food at the Priest's miserable little den. Two hours' ride over a rugged uncultivated succession of rocky hills and valleys zigzagging up and down over a surface of white marl overgrown with stunted myrtle bushes, we at length arrived at Myrtu village, close to which is Panteleimon Monastery. The Bishop was here at the time and everything about the place betokened an unusual advance in civilisation one is hardly accustomed to find outside the big towns. In the little house I put up in at Myrtu Village everything was as clean and comfortable as one could wish for a week's stay, and my kind hosts and their grown up daughters were as kind as they could be, refusing to let me pay anything for my board when I left next morning.

26. From just beyond the Monastery on the brink of a steep precipice looking down a 1000 ft into the sea is a splendid view across to Asia Minor, a reminiscence of which I managed to secure before it was too dark to draw. We rode in next day along the Northern Range to Aya Marina, Shillura[57] Ay Vasili,[58] and Gonelli[59] visiting traps all the way, and got home at 4 p.m. having had six day's continuous riding.

May 1882.

10. Col Gordon inspected my detachment again on the 10th May at which I had but about 70 men – and having a day or two's leave, I started on the 11th May for Famagusta.

11. I broke the long and monotonous journey across the parched up Messaria plain to Eshia[60] where there is a very decent resting place, and got into Varosia, a large village outside Famagusta walls where the officials and most of the inhabitants live. Famagusta itself is a wonderful mass of ruined churches and palaces and I walked through with Buchan, an architect, and brother-in-law of Col Gordon who was staying there. There is nothing in Cyprus that impresses me more vividly than this once important fortress. The old Cathedral of St Nicholas, now a mosque, is a grand specimen of a Gothic church and presents a much finer appearance than even Santa Sophia at Nicosia. Inside the great walls which are for the most part dug out of the solid rock all is abomination and ruin, with the exception of the Government offices, a small bazaar and the Zaptieh Konak. It has remained in this ruined state ever since it was sacked and ruined by the Turks after the memorable siege of 1571. The walls are still in almost perfect condition which illustrates the massive construction of the Venetians. The Venetian Lion and Coat of Arms is still affixed to all the principal bastions. The subterranean works and magazines would from the massiveness and durability of their construction have afforded an admirable lesson to many an architect. I made several sketches of these interesting and picturesque old ruins with the silted up harbour and Carpas M^{ts} beyond running out until they lost themselves in the regions of Cape St Andrea.

12. Young[61] the commissioner being away with his family on tour to Cape St Andrea, I put up with Capt Gordon[62] the A^t Comm^er who also had the Bishop of Gibraltar as a guest, and Mr Spencer[63] our Nicosia Chaplain.

13. I rode out to the site of ancient Salamis on the 13th where many of the foundations of this ancient Capital can be traced. Excavations for the London Museums were being carried on, and a fine piece of mosaic pavement just brought to light. In the days of St. Paul's visit this was the most important town, and the place where he landed. A mile and a half inland is the Church of St. Barnabas, supposed to mark the spot where the Saint's body was found, with the Gospel of St Matthew. An ancient Cyclopean Mausoleum called the Tomb of St Catherine is almost the only ancient monument now visible of the Necropolis of Salamis.

14. I rode back to Nicosia on Sunday 14th, Gordon keeping me company for a few miles, but he was driven back by a heavy storm that overtook us. I took a different route as far as Esher[64] and after a long and lonely ride of 35 miles entered the old familiar Larnaka Gate of Nicosia at sundown ..."

Unfortunately the sketches made by Donne at Famagusta have either been lost or he may even have given them away during the remainder of his tour in Cyprus.

Notes to Chapter Nine

1. Mr Fairfield was engaged in writing a report on the island's administration which was published in *Finance and Administration*, London 1883.
2. Laurence Olive appointed Adjutant Military Police on 1 October 1878 (Cyprus Gazette No l dated 5 November 1878.
   Acting Assistant Commissioner at Nicosia from 21 August 1879 (Cyprus Gazette No 34 dated 21 August 1879).
   Registrar of the High Court of Justice on 6 September 1879 (Cyprus Gazette No 36 dated 6 September 1879).
   Acting Police Magistrate at Larnaca on 8 December 1879 (Cyprus Gazette No 40 dated 8 December 1879) and
   Local Commandant of Military Police, Paphos on 23 April 1880 (Cyprus Gazette No 49 dated 23 April 1880).
3. The village of Korphi.
   Georghallides, op cit, page 23.
4. The village of Silikhou.
   Georghallides, op cit, page 24.
5. The village of Phasoula.
   Georghallides, op cit, page 24.
6. The village of Palodhia.
   Georghallides, op cit, page 24.
7. Lieutenant James Henry Bor, Royal Marine Artillery.
   Appointed Local Commandant Military Police, Paphos on 28 August 1878 (Cyprus Gazette No 1 dated 5 November 1878).
   Local Commandant Military Police and Governor of the Prison at Nicosia on 8 August 1879 (Cyprus Gazette No 33, dated 8 August 1879).
8. Lieutenant R. E. Powell, Royal Sussex Regiment.
   Monthly Army List, April 1881, 410.
9. The village of Kophinou.
   Georghallides, op cit, page 24.
10. Captain James Argyll Spalding Inglis, 71st Highland Light Infantry.
    Appointed Assistant Commissioner at Famagusta on 1 August 1878 (Cyprus Gazette No 1 dated 5 November 1878).
    Commissioner at Famagusta on 13 October 1878 (Cyprus Gazette No 6 dated 11 February 1879).
    Acting Commissioner at Nicosia from 4 to 31 December 1881 (Cyprus Gazette No 80 dated 19 December 1881).
    Commissioner at Nicosia on 1 January 1882 (Cyprus Gazette No 81 dated 31 January 1882).
    He died whilst still serving in that appointment on 1 April 1883. A brass plaque in memory of 'Major' Inglis is in the Anglican Church at Nicosia. (Inglis was buried in the Christian Cemetary at Famagusta).
11. Colonel A. H. A. Gordon, Chief Commandant of the Cyprus Military Police.
12. Georghallides notes that this was the principal quarter of the town, around the present Ataturk Square.
13. The low hill on which the Government House was built.
14. Captain G. Harden, Royal Sussex Regiment. The detachment was provided by the Royal Sussex Regiment which were, at that time, the Garrison troops.
15. Lieutenant F. G., Todd-Thornton, Royal Sussex Regiment.
    Monthly Army List, April 1882, 410.
16. W. H. Marsh. Acting Auditor and Accountant-General and member of the Executive Council and provisionally of the Legislative Council.

Appointed 1 September 1880 (Cyprus Gazette No 59 dated 13 October 1880) and resigned on 14 February 1882 (Cyprus Gazette No 82 dated 3 March 1882).

17. Lieutenant M. B. Seager, Royal Marine Light Infantry.
Appointed Assistant Commissioner at Nicosia on 7 August 1878 (Cyprus Gazette No 1 dated 5 November 1878).
Registrar of the High Court of Justice on 25 February 1879 (Cyprus Gazette No 11 dated 25 February 1879).
Commissioner at Kyrenia from 1 July 1879 (Cyprus Gazette No 31 dated 28 June 1879).
Acting Commissioner Nicosia from 19 August until 10 November 1879 (Cyprus Gazette No 38 dated 13 November 1879).
Police Magistrate and Deputy Commissioner at Nicosia from 27 February 1880 (Cyprus Gazette No 46 dated 1 March 1880).

18. The British official in Cyprus organised a pack of harriers for hunting hare. The Master of the Hunt was Major Luttman-Johnstone, of the York and Lancaster Regiment, who was at the time serving as the Brigade Major, Cyprus.

19. John Parsons Inspector of Police.
Appointed on 1 August 1881 (Cyprus Gazette No 79 dated 26 November 1881).

20. The village of Kythrea.
Georghallides, op cit, page 25.

21. See Chapter 7, note 6.

22. Georghallides notes that the Great Khan (inn) of Nicosia which was built soon after the Turkish conquest of Cyprus was used, together with the Konak as prisons by the British authorities.

23. Surgeon W. M. Johnston MD., the Civil Surgeon at Kyrenia from 30 December 1879 until 2 April 1880. (Cyprus Gazette No 41 dated 30 December 1879 and No 56 of 7 July 1880).

24. The Castle at Buffavento surrendered to King Richard when Isaac surrendered to Richard. The Castle was in fact not taken by storm.

25. The village of Pano Dhikamo.
Georghallides, op cit, page 26.

26. The village of Ay Ermolaos.
Ibid.

27. The village of Morphou.
Ibid.

28. Theodore E. Mavrogordato was appointed Interpreter to the Police on 1 February 1882 under authority of Cyprus Gazette No 85 dated 23 May 1882.

29. See Chapter 5 note 21.

30. Donne refers to the officers and the regimental band of the Royal Sussex Regiment who were, at the time, the Garrison troops.

31. Captain F. S. Campbell and Lieutenant C. H. Ashurst, both of the Royal Sussex Regiment Monthly Army List, April 1882.

32. The sub-districts of Nicosia were:
Nicosia, Dagh (Orini), Morphou and Lefka. These Divisions were promulgated in the Cyprus Gazette No 82 dated 3 March 1882.
The High Commissioner exercised his authority on 8 December 1880 and having been granted suitable authority under the 'Administrative Divisions Ordinance, 1878' abolished the old Turkish caza of Deyrmanlik and replaced it with the casa of Nicosia.
Georghallides, op cit, page 49.

33. The village of Geunyely.
Georghallides, op cit, page 27.

34. The village of Yerrolakkas.
Ibid.

35. The village of Morphou.
Ibid.

36. The monastery of Ayios Manas was founded at the end of the twelfth century.

37. Cyprus as I saw it by Sir S Baker.
     Published London 1879.
38. Donne refers to the Monastery of Kykko. The name of the monastery is pronounced 'Jicko' by the local inhabitants.
     It was founded about 1100 AD in the reign of the Byzantine Emperor Alexios Kommenos who gave it a picture of the Virgin Mary and Child believed to have been painted by St Luke, and a great icon which has survived several fires that have, in the past, destroyed the monastery.
39. The village of Kambos. Georghallides, op cit, page 28.
40. Hegoumenos, the abbot.
41. The village of Evrykhou.
     Ibid.
42. The village of Kalopanayiotis.
     Georghallides, op cit, page 29.
43. The village of Trimithia.
     Ibid.
44. The village of Ay Vasilios.
     Georghallides, op cit, page 30.
45. Archibald FitzGerald Law was appointed Assistant Commissioner of Nicosia on 4 February 1880 (Cyprus Gazette No 45 dated 7 February 1880).
     Assistant Commissioner, Kyrenia on 1 March 1880 (Cyprus Gazette No 46 dated 1 March 1880). and
     Registrar of the High Court of Justice on 11 September 1880 (Cyprus Gazette No 58 dated 11 September 1880).
46. Doctor Clement Carletti was appointed Civil Surgeon and Health Officer for Kyrenia on 2 April 1880. (Cyprus Gazette No 56 dated 7 July 1880).
47. District Medical Officer.
48. The village of Kythrea.
     Georghallides, op cit, page 30.
49. The village of Tymbou.
     Ibid.
50. Prior to 8 December 1880 Dali belonged to the old nahieh of Deyrmanlik. It subsequently came under the nahieh of Nicosia and it, and Kythrea, were the two most important villages in the sub-district.
51. The manuscript Record of Service of the 71st Foot records that the regiment arrived at 'Camp Dalli' (sic) on 29 August 1878 having disembarked from Larnaca on the 24 July. The one known soldier who died in Cyprus, belonging to the 71st Foot was Private James Hewitt. An old photograph, taken prior to the occupation of Cyprus has a note on the reverse which reads
     "... Born in 71st Regt.
         James died at Cyprus
         Charlie, Bandmaster 35th Regiment ..."
     The photograph is of the two Hewitt brothers and was probably taken after the return of the 71st Foot from India in 1865.
     Correspondecne between author and Major D. I. A. Mack, Assistant Regimental Secretary of the Royal Highland Fusiliers of 1983.
     It is probable that as the surviving brother was the Bandmaster of the 35th Regiment, by then the Royal Sussex Regiment, that Donne would have known that his brother had died and was buried at Dali and had intentionally looked for the grave.
52. The village of Laxia,
     Georghallides, op cit, page 31.
53. The village of Dheftera.
     Ibid.
54. The village of Akaki.

Ibid.

55. The church of St Barnabas and St Hilarion which was built in the early eleventh century.
56. The village of Khrysiliou.
    Georghallides, op cit, page 32.
57. The village of Skylloura.
    Ibid.
58. The village of Ay Vasilios.
    Ibid.
59. The village of Geunyely.
    Ibid.
60. The village of Asha.
    Ibid.
61. Lieutenant Arthur Henderson Young, 27th Foot.
    Appointed Local Commandant, Military Police Kyrenia on 28 August 1878 (Cyprus Gazette No 1 dated 5 November 1878).
    Assistant Commissioner at Paphos on 20 November 1878 (Cyprus Gazette No 3 dated 1 January 1879).
    Registrar of the High Court of Justice on 25 February 1879 (Cyprus Gazette No 11 dated 25 February 1879).
    Commissioner at Paphos on 1 September 1879 (Cyprus Gazette No 36 dated 6 September 1879).
    Commissioner Famagusta on 1 January 1882 (Cyprus Gazette No 81 dated 31 January 1882).
62. Captain W. H. Gordon, Royal Welsh Fusiliers.
    Appointed Assistant Commissioner on 5 January 1879 (Cyprus Gazette No 6 dated 11 February 1879).
    Registrar of the High Court of Justice on 25 February 1879 (Cyprus Gazette No 11 dated 25 February 1879).
    Assistant Commissioner Famagusta on 2 June 1880 (Cyprus Gazette No 53 dated 4 June 1880).
63. The Reverend Josiah Spencer, BA., was appointed Director of Education on 3 December 1880 under authority of Cyprus Gazette No 64 dated 24 December 1880.
64. Georghallides thinks that Donne is referring to the village of Asha.

10   Farewell to Cyprus

AFTER DONNE'S return to Nicosia from his short holiday in Famagusta he was soon involved in another chase after a criminal and was soon to return to his normal duties as L. C. M. P. at Limassol. His journal for the 20th May reads:

May 1882

20. "A man having stabbed another at Ay Vasili we had an exciting chase after him but he had too good a start of us to come up with him, so I secured his house with a Zaptieh guard, as well as some weapons we found in his house. One was a fine long yatagan which I annexed, as also a remarkable old blunderbuss bearing the date 1765 with a muzzle as big as a railway bell.

 We did not get back to Nicosia till after midnight. The gentleman in question was brought in a few days after.

24. The next great event at Nicosia was the Queen's Birthday, for which the Zaptiehs and Troopers had to be drilled up a day or two in advance. I had about 30 Troopers as escort to the Vali, and 2 Comp^y of Infantry as a guard in front of the Konak. I rode out with the Comm^{er} & Bor[1] in full uniform to meet H. E. outside the Papho Gate and quite a procession was formed to the Konak. After a reception of the Greeks and Turks the proceedings terminated. I dined with Bor and rode out afterwards to the Reception at Government house which like most of its kind was a very stiff affair.

27. I rode over to Kyrenia on the 27th to spend Sunday with Law, spending a few hours at St Hillarion on the way. As I was entering the stable at Law's house I was kicked in the face by one of the ponies, which knocked me over insensible, nor did I recover till next a.m., when I found my head tied up in a bundle.

28. Happily the consequences were no worse than a severe headache for the rest of the day, and a plaster patch over my left eye for a fortnight after.

29. I got back to Nicosia midday on Monday meeting Barry[2] and Colonel Melville[3] who had come over to have a sniff at the Kyrenia scenery. Nothing much else happened until the time came for me to hand over my stewardship to Bor again, the locust campaign being now over. It was getting very hot and stifling inside the walls of Nicosia, so after bidding adieu to many kind friends there I started for Limassol again on the 14th June.

June 1882.

14. It was a terribly hot day the sun glaring down on the parched-brown plains like a furnace. I struck out a new route from the ordinary road by Corfinu in order to cross the Macheras[4] Mountains. We rode through Somiloff[5] and struck up the Mountains to Macheras Monastery, arriving there in the afternoon.

 It was without exception the most curious old place in Cyprus and well worth seeing, seldom however visited owing to its out of the way situation.

 There were a goodly No. of Monks here, and they kept a visitors' book in which however there were but few English names. But every entry testified in warm terms to the hospitality of Macheara. The old Agoumenos and his mirmidons danced continual attendance on me and I had an excellent appartment to sleep in. Even up here in this mountain retreat it was very hot and I found afterwards the glass had registered 103 in the shade that day at Nicosia.

15. The good monks complained much of the Common Enemy, the Locust, which eat up everything in their well stocked garden.

16. The old court and the buildings round offered a heap of picturesque study, but I had to be off at 5.30 a.m. next morning on our long journey to Limassol. After missing the way once or twice (for in many places there was no road at all) and riding up and down innumerable hills and valleys, we arrived at last on the highest ridge, saw the Southern Coast down below like a map and commenced the precipitous descent to Oron[6] in the Larnaka District – and from there on to Heftagonia[7] and had a good rest. I was so thirsty that I drank

A picnic at Troodos, photographed in June 1882.

the whole contents of a pannikan of cocoa. We got into Limassol at 6 p.m. that evening. Limassol – Refugees were pouring in from Alexandria in numbers, every sailing & steam ship being full of them, and until the Bombardment of Alexandria on the 11th July they continued to arrive every day in large numbers. So after taking over the Police again from Powell,[8] we had our work considerably increased in registering their names and nationalities.

24. I took a run up to Troodos on the 24th for a day or two holiday. Starting at Daybreak I rode up to Platres in 5 hours and from there on to the camp at the top, finding a rest in Keay's[9] tent. What a glorious place Troodos is to enjoy a few days' cool rest after the hot plains, and who could describe the wonderful panorama view from the top! It is second only in extent to Etna that I have seen in the Mediterranean. The sea vanishes into the sky all round except in the Karamanian[10] direction where the opposite M(oun)t(ains)s stand out grander and golder than ever as if disputing the sovereignty of the seas with old Olympus. The rocky ridges of Troodos spring up all round and away in the west is Chrisofou Bay[11] and the fine promontary of Arnauti. Limassol can be seen with a glass and on a fine day even the Towers of the Cathedral at Famagusta. It is the favourite promenade of Troodos Society to walk to the Summit of an evening.

28. I rode down again on the 28th in time for dinner.

July 1882

Events were now rapidly culminating in Egypt and numbers of refugees continued to arrive in port. One ship had left so hastily that she had been two days without water, and on board another from Damietta two of the crew had been killed by the mutineers before leaving harbour there.

11. On the 11th Alexandria was bombarded and given over to fire and pillage, the telegrams causing immense sensation in Limassol. The rebellion[12] had commenced and Troops

were already on the move from Malta and Gibraltar, and our own men were itching up in Troodos to be off to the scene of operations.

13. Part of the Channel Squadron arrived on the 13th

14. and 14th with General Sir A. Allison and troops for the front, who sailed again the next morning.

After this Limassol became a very active little base of operations, ship after ship with either troops or stores arriving for the war. Our own half Battalion at Malta under Col Vandeleur[13] was also on its way to Egypt, the H^{d}Q^{trs} being also placed under orders of readiness. But although they were every inch ready to march down from Troodos and equipped for the campaign, for nearly two months had they to remain in this state of expectancy and excitement, without being allowed to go, nor was it until the whole army of Sir G. Wolseley had been concentrated in Egypt that our unfortunate selves were given final orders to march.

About this time I was obliged to prosecute my Greek servant Yanni Holihun for stealing a cheque. He had been behaving very unsatisfactorily of late and it ended in his being convicted and sentenced to Limassol jail for a year. I was sorry for the boy, because he was very smart and intelligent. I replaced him by another Greek from Papho.

26. Hake,[14] having come down from Salamis was excavating near Curium for the S Kensington Museum about now, and some highly interesting tombs were opened near the road between the old acropolis and Episkopi. I rode out on the 26th and was present when the best find of all was opened. It was Phoenician and its contents were as they had been left some two thousand odd years before. Mixed up with the crumbling bones of the deceased were a fine collection of glass and pottery – the irridescence of the glass being unusually brilliant. They had to be taken great care of as the action of the air speedily impaired them. Some of the vases too were fine, with the usual description of ring ornamentation on them. As the deposit was carefully brought to light and sifted several gold earrings, rings etc were found. This tomb was about 18 ft under the present level of the road and, unlike many others had never been despoiled.

We lunched under the shade of some fine caroub trees with the glass and pottery lying around us – the spoils of the dead. I wonder what aspect that bit of country with Curium and the sea for a background, presented so many years ago, when the dead were brought there for internment! In those days Curium must have been a flourishing little city.

The results of the excavations were afterwards collected at the Limassol Konak, to be packed up for transport to South Kensington, and a goodly collection they made.

I still held on in the Police Force but had signified my intention to H^{d}Q^{rs} of rejoining my Regt when ordered away, in order to take my chance of active service with the rest.

August 1882

6. Campbell[15] came down on the 6th and put up with me, and Hadfield[16] of the Comm^t also did the same on many occasions when down from Troodos. Ponies and mules were being collected at Limassol for the Egyptian campaign and I had the care and shipping of a good many of them.

19. I was appointed Acting Staff Officer on the 19th for the Superintendance of Embarkation etc, pending the arrival of an officer from England.

21. Law who was doing duty from Kyrenia vice Thompson[17] rode with me to the Quarantine ground and the next evening I took a farewell ride round the Akrotiri Bay (which proved (to be) my last).

25. Croker[18] came down to inspect my Dett(ach)ment on the 25th and Col Gordon returned off leave by the mail the same day.

26. The next day definite orders at length arrived from England for the Royal Sussex to embark on board the 'Navarino' expected on the 6th Prox for Ismailia the new base of operations. So at last our suspense was likely to be at an end, and our hopes of active service realised. I sold my old pony 'Sali Bobi' to Tolson who intended to take him to Egypt.

September 1882.

4.   On the 4th Sept I handed over Command of the Police and Prison to Thompson, Asst
      Comm(ission)er, on which my brief period of Civil Service in Cyprus ended, and I again
      became a soldier. Between that and the 9th, on which we embarked, I was employed on
      Transport duty at the wharf. Having packed up and bid adieu to the scene of my labours,
      the Regt marched on to the pier in the evening from Troodos in Service marching order,
      and I found my old (H) Company there under Capt Kelly.[19] Ammunition was here served
      out and we got on board the Steam Tug 'Cephalonia' to put us on board the Transport.
      Crowds had assembled to bid us goodbye and God Speed on our warlike errand. As the
      Tug cast off the band struck up 'Old Lang Syne' and hearty cheers were raised from the
      crowds on the pier and responded to by all on the Tug. It was almost dark when we got on
      board, so we soon lost sight (of) the shores of old Cyprus.
      'Though lost to sight, to Memory dear',
      and although there were not a few among us who were not heartily glad to be under weigh
      at last, yet I must own to a pang of regret on my own part to be cast adrift from the old place
      which I had learnt to like like a second Jamaica, and only those who have had an interest in
      the Island can know how to appreciate its best qualities and resources. Hard work and
      occupation for the mind is more condusive to happiness than life in a mess-room, where
      one cannot but reflect on the amount of one's time lost in idleness and good living.
      So we sailed away from the Isle of Venus, and the next evening were off Port Said and the
      entrance to the Canal ..."

Notes to Chapter Ten

1.   Chapter 9, note 7.
2.   F. W. Barry, MD. Appointed Sanitary Commissioner of Cyprus on 23 April 1880 under
      authority of Cyprus Gazette No 49 dated 23 April 1880. He resigned from the post on 10
      July 1882.
3.   Lieutenant Colonel H. B. Melville, Corps of Royal Engineers.
4.   Also spelt as Makheras.
      The Travellers Guide to Cyprus,
      by H. Thurston,
      Jonathan Cape, London 1967.
5.   The village of Psomolophou.
      Georghallides, op cit, page 34.
6.   The village of Ora.
      Ibid.
7.   The village of Ephtagonia
      Ibid.
8.   Lieut. R. E. Powell, Royal Sussex Regiment.
      Monthly Army List, April 1882.
9.   Surgeon (Ranking as Captain) W. Keays, Medical Department.
      Monthly Army List, April 1882.
10.   Georghallides annotates this as referring to 'Taurus'.
11.   This refers to Khrysokhou Bay.
      Thurston, op cit.
      Map on end papers.
12.   By the middle of May 1882 a number of military demonstrations had taken place in Egypt
      and a Colonel of the Egyptian Army, named Arabi, had virtually taken control of the
      executive power in the country.
      Thewfik, who had been appointed Khedive of Egypt by the European Powers had retained

little more than his title. Ninety thousand Europeans, the majority of whom were French and English, were engaged in commercial business in Egypt at this time and therefore there was wide spread concern over their own safety and that of the businesses.

The English and French Governments gave, on 6 January 1882, the Khedive assurance that they would support him and help him maintain law and order within his country.

On 20 May 1882 an allied English and French fleet sailed into Alexandria Harbour to protect the interest of those nations in that area. Serious riots broke out at Alexandria on 11 June 1882 between Mohammedan and Christian factions. The unrest spread throughout the country and within the following weeks it was estimated that two-thirds of the European population had fled the country leaving many of the businesses closed and with the Egyptian workers without means of work.

A Conference of six European countries was held at Constantinople on 24 June to discuss the problem of Egypt. Turkey refused to send a representative.

At this time it was seen that with the unrest spreading in Egypt there was a definite threat to the Suez Canal and that to merely occupy the canal area was not an answer. It was therefore necessary to bring a stable Government back to Egypt.

13.   Lieutenant Colonel J. O. Vandeleur.
      Royal Sussex Regiment.
      Monthly Army List, April 1882.
14.   George Gordon Hake. Appointed Chief Clerk in the Chief Secretary's Office on 14 April 1879 under authority of Cyprus Gazette No 26 dated 20 May 1879.
15.   Captain F. S. Campbell, Royal Sussex Regiment.
      Monthly Army List, April 1882.
16.   Lieutenant Charles Arthur Hadfield, Commissariat and Transport Staff.
      Appointed Lieutenant in the Police and Pioneer Force and Acting Local Commandant Military Police at Famagusta on 1 March 1880. (Cyprus Gazette No 46 dated 1 March 1880).
17.   See Chapter 9, note 45 and Chapter 7 note 9.
18.   See Chapter 5, note 18.
19.   Captain W. F. Kelly, Royal Sussex Regiment.
      Monthly Army List, April 1882.

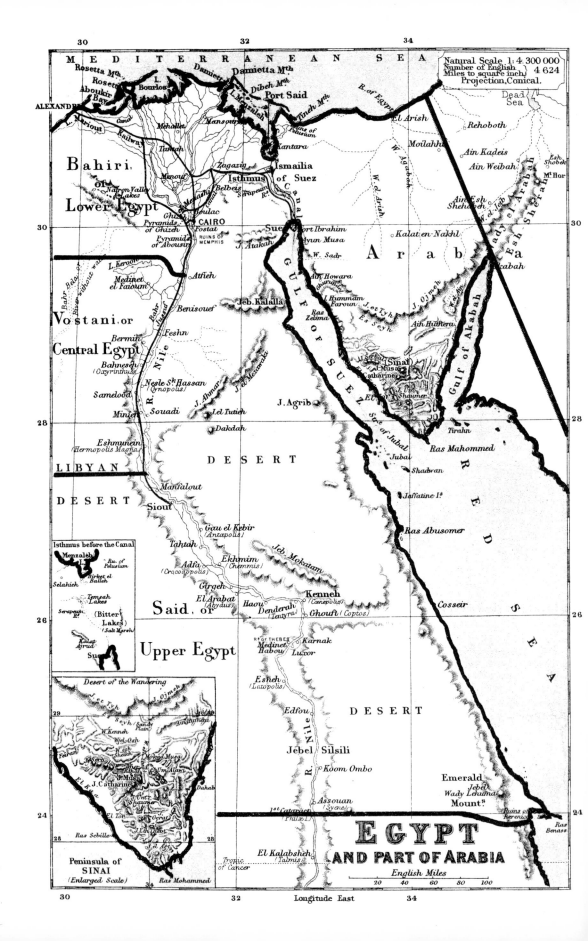

EGYPT AND PART OF ARABIA

11   Eygpt 1882

DONNE AND his regiment arrived in Egypt too late to take part in the Battle of Tel El Kebir on 12 September, and on arrival in that country joined 4th Brigade at Cairo on 29th September. Donne describes the arrival in his journal as follows:

September 1882

10.   "The sea was calm and the air hot as we steamed in by the fleet of British Ironclads laying off.
We anchored off Port Said for the night, just astern of the French flag ship 'Gallisonierre' and ahead of the 'Iris'. There was a double line of Foreign men of war in port, who seem to have been attracted like vultures to the scene of action.

11.   Port Said was occupied by a Marine Garr^n. We moved off next a.m. with the band playing "La Marseillaise" as a compl(iment) to our french (sic) neighbours, who returned it with cheers, also the men of the 'Monarch' to our "Rule Brittania" as we proceeded all the crews of the merchantmen in port took up the cheering – and then we entered the canal – we only got as far as Cantara Station that night, where the 'Carysfort' & 'Don' were stationed with their guns bearing on the surrounding country. I went ashore with some others to see the little Naval guard house, which was occupied with a force of blue jackets.

12.   We arr(ive)d at Lake Timsah & Ismailia about 10 a.m. next day. The whole lake was crowded with transports, men of war and shipping. The Regt landed in the aft.
I following at sundown with the horses, etc We bivouacked (sic) that night under the trees in the public gardens of the town. That night Kelly[1] & myself were called out for outpost duty in front of Ismailia with the Company. Not having seen anything of the country by day light we had some little difficulty in getting to the place assigned for our Picquet. So having marched up the railway and round the Naval batteries & Picquets we hit the Canal (dry) indicated. It happened to be the night of the storming of Tel El Kebir and as we were waiting there in the sand for day light to dawn, our Army in front was storming Arab entrenchments. The object in keeping picquets round Ismailia was to prevent a flank attack from Salahia where some troops were centred, as the dawn broke we began to see better where we were. Nothing but desert in front, and Ismailia behind us. Close to us were some dead carcasses of mules, horses etc that had been cast out in the desert and the scent of them was not over lovely. After the sun had risen we marched back to camp again being no longer required out.
There was lots of work to be done at Ismailia and no sooner had I got back and expected some rest, than I had to mount on main guard at 9 a.m.

13.   It was anything but a pleasant place to spend 24 hours in. The heat and dust, & the flies especially, being almost unbearable. But there was lots going on outside, the roadway being thronged with passengers of all sorts, and trucks full of stores for the army in front were being hauled up & down the incline from the pier to the railway all day long. I managed to get fed from the Hotel near the pier. Our men were mostly employed on Fatigue parties all day long, and everybody felt the excessive heat considerably.

14.   The flies which settled upon everything in swarming blackness like the Egyptian plague of old, were our worst enemies. The sick & wounded from the front were being brought down in large numbers by train, which conveyed them straight to the Palace, which had been converted into a big hospital, or to the wharf for shipment.
From sunrise to nightfall Ismailia was full of bustle & activity the heat being quite a secondary consideration to the necessity of the hour.
Altogether this 'Base of Operations Garrison' consisted of about 3000 men, chiefly composed of ourselves and the 63rd Regt[2] from India. Whilst on bathing parade one morning a fine young Corporal of ours was drowned in his depth, in Lake Timsah. He appears to have had a fit, and although unceasing efforts for two hours were used to try and restore life, it was useless. Sick and wounded continued to arrive in large numbers, and

Portrait of Donne by his elder sister Anna. It is probable that the title was added later as the rank shown is not contemporary with the painting, which is dated 1882.

Colonel D.B.A. Donne.
1882. by Anna Donne.

then the news came down that the Cavalry had taken Cairo, and that Arabi was a prisoner. The Railway was also opened to Cairo. The campaign was thus virtually over and we had arrived too late to take any very active part in it.

A General Order was shortly issued by Sir G. Wolseley, expatiating on the glory of the brilliant campaign etc, and fixing the 14th as the termination of the war. So at all advents we could console ourselves with being entitled to the War medal.

21.   Harden[3] being invalided about this time, I took over command of 'B' Company. It was sometimes very pleasant work getting a sail on Lake Timsah when one had time, and a relief from the dry heat of the Desert.

27.   A draft of 150 Reserve men under three officers had also joined us, and raised our strength
       to about 500.
       We were ordered up to Cairo on the 27th.
       So striking our camp in the Gardens at daylight we intrained (sic) at 9 a.m., and rattled
       away for the City of the Califs, where the army was being assembled.
       We passed through the scene of the whole operations on our way up, Kassasin, Tel el
       Kebir, etc. At the latter place we stopped a couple of hours – arriving at Cairo about 6 p.m.
       We slept at the Station as best we could the men piling arms and sleeping outside.
       Cairo was en fete in honor (sic) of the arrival of the Khedive, and as a small token of the joy
       of the European inhabitants at having been spared the fate of Alexandria. The streets were
       gay with coloured lamps and a grand display of fireworks was going on in the Esbekiah
       Gardens – some of us dined at the New Hotel where about 200 British Officers sat down to
       Dinner.

28.   We marched off at 5 a.m. next morning to go to Geziret Island where a large number of
       troops were already encamped. There we found Col Vandeleur[4] with the left wing of the
       Regt already encamped (in the 4th Brigade lines) the Regt being thus reunited 'under the
       Pyramids' after being divided for more than two years. Those who had served before
       Alexandria had all bushy beards by this time and in consequence hardly recognisable to
       their Cyprus comrades.
       We pitched our Camp on the hot sandy island of Geziret not far from the road to Gizeh,
       and within view of the Pyramids. The Marines, 2^d and 3^d Brigades were also encamped
       there probably in all about 12000 men. In fact the island was crammed with troops, and
       one heard nothing but the rattle of Drums and highland pipes going on from sunrise to
       sunset. It was intensely hot in the day time. Altogether there were about 25000 British
       Troops in and around Cairo.
       Before dawn on the 29th we were ordered off to the Station Depot where a fire was raging
       that had been illuminating the heavens all that night.
       Several men had been killed by the explosion of gunpowder & shells which were stored in
       trucks there. We relieved another Regt at Picquet Duty and fatigue, and after several hours
       work at the fire, by which time it had become exceedingly hot, we were thankful to be
       relieved by the 50th Foot[5] and get home to some breakfast. These early morning
       excursions revealed the great Comet at its best, it used to rise at about 2 a.m. from the
       Eastern horizon – a grand and wonderful object in the starry heavens, and one of those
       Solar wonders so rarely seen.

30.   The next great event in our now very military lives was the great march past of Wolseley's
       victorious troops before the Khedive in the Abdin Square on Saturday 30th. Nearly 20,000
       men were on parade, horse, foot, guns and Indian troops. They must have presented a gay
       and solid appearance, these veterans and pick of the British Army. I think everyone felt
       proud as he marched past the General and all the foreign officials in the Grand Stand –
       proud of the position he found himself in, of his own Corps and the grand old Army to
       which he belonged. We trotted back to Camp directly it was over, passing the Brigade of
       Guards on the way shoulder to shoulder.
       In these times, when we had no mess in particular, fellows used to go generally into town
       to one of the Hotels to get a good square meal, and on Sunday Divisional Church parades
       were the order of the day.

October 1882

2.   On Oct(ob)er the 2nd the Khedive gave a splendid and most brilliant fete to the Officers
       of the British Army at his palace at Geziret.
       Hundreds of Officers were present, and all the great Generals of the day. Everything was
       brilliantly illuminated even the steamers & Dahabeahs on the Nile, and refreshments and
       supper were served on such a sumptuous scale that every one was loud in the Khedives
       praise.

5.   The 'sacred' carpet started about this time on the Mecca pilgrimage whose departure is

kept as a feast day in Cairo. In default of Egyptian Troops to line the way, and to do homage to the sacred emblem as it passed on its way the British troops were ordered out to present arms and to me individually it appeared a most ludicrous affair for Christian troops to engage in. Some awkward questions were afterwards asked in Parliament on the subject.

8.   Sunday we made up a party for the Pyramids but having been up to the top on my former visit in 1881 I explored the inside this time, but having once done it, I cannot say I should care about trying the experiment again.

12.   On the 12th the 49th Regt[6] marched in and camped on our Right, thus completing Sir E. Wood's[7] brigade which now consisted of 5 Batt^{ons}, (35, 38, 49, 53 & 1/60th).[8]

14.   On the 14th the Brigade was formed up at 6 a.m. near Geziret Place for the inspection of Sir G. Wolseley which occupied nearly an hour, went off very successfully.
Not long after when the army commenced to be broken up, Sir E. Wood gave up command of the 4th Brigade which in the reduced state of the command became the 1st Brigade under Gen[l] Earle.[9]

17.   On the 17th our camp was broken up at Geziret Island, and we marched at 5 a.m. through Cairo to Abasseyeh, 3 miles the other side and pitched the camp there near the old Egyptian Barracks. The rest of the Brigade followed soon after. About this time Baker Pasha[10] arr(ive)d in Cairo to remodel the grand armies etc. Whilst camped at Abasseyeh a good number of our officers & men went sick, and the Hospitals were crowded. At one time the mortality was unusually heavy and I buried as many as 5 men in one week. It was miserable work trudging down to the Cemetery about 5 miles off.
In about the space of two months about 150 British soliders were buried there.
What with sickness, drills, inspections, examinations, etc the routine of duty became unusually hard and monotonous.

28.   Trafford[11] & myself went up the River by steamer on Saturday 28th to visit Saquarah. After landing at Bedreshim, we mounted donkeys and rode off to the Great Step Pyramid of Sakkara, after which we visited Serapeum and other highly interesting tombs of the very early Dynasties. We passed over the sight of Memphis on our return. Memphis is the Noph of the Bible, about whom Jeremiah (xlvi – 19) prophecys "Noph shall be waste and desolate without an inhabitant". There is no remnant of that mighty City left now. After a pleasant outing, and return trip down the river, we got back to the Kasi el Nil at evening.

November 1882

7.   Col Hackett took the Regt out route marching to the Virgins Tree and Heliopolis. The latter is one of the most celebrated cities of ancient Egypt and a solitary obelisk is still standing as if to attest its ancient importance. All other evidences of its site had disappeared long since.
Heliopolis was the 'On' and Bethshemesh of the Bible, of which Jeremiah says "He shall wreak the Images of Bathshemesh that is in the land of Egypt".
For the remainder of 1882 I have but little to write down. I met my old 'Fayoum' friend Halton several times, he lunching with me, and I dining with him at Shepherds.
Sir C. Allison, now Com(man)ding the troops in Egypt also reviewed the Brigade in the desert near Abasseyeh. I dined with Rees[12] one night at the Royal Hotel and saw Hake[13] for the last time, he had been very seedy, and was just off for England.
Inspector Parsons also turned up from Cyprus with Col Gordon[14] for a few days.

December 1882

15.   On the 15th Dec(emb)er our existence under canvas came to an end, the men shifting into the Infantry Bks near, and we Officers getting very luxuriously fitted up Qtrs in the Zafferen Palace nearbye (sic). Our mess establishment was a very fine suite of rooms.

25.   Our Xmas Day in Egypt brought cold and wet with it, but I spent the afternoon very profitably with Keays at the Bonlak Museum of Egyptology. In the evening the usual revelry and frivolity was carried on.

28.   I walked into Cairo on the 28th to see the Highland Sports in the Abdin Square, and I think

I now have nothing left to chronicle for 1882.

My journal is also completed for 10 years and if not particularly interesting to others, is to myself at least the valuable record of several years spent in knocking about the world ...”

Although Donne implied that this was the close of the Journal there are in fact another thirteen pages which were written by him, after the events, but cover the period 1 January 1883 until 25th December of that year.

Notes to Chapter Eleven

1.   Captain W. F. Kelly, Royal Sussex Regiment.
     Monthly Army List, April 1882.
2.   Donne is referring to the 1st Battalion, The Manchester Regiment (formerly the 63rd Foot), who embarked from Bombay and arrived in Egypt on 6 September 1882.
3.   Captain G. Harden, Royal Sussex Regiment.
     Monthly Army List, April 1882.
4.   Lieutenant Colonel J. O. Vandeleur. Royal Sussex Regiment.
     Monthly Army List, April 1882.
5.   Donne refers to 1st Battalion, The Queen's Own Royal West Kent Regiment (formerly the 50th Foot) who had moved from Aldershot.
6.   Donne refers to the 1st Battalion, Princess Charlotte of Wales's (Berkshire Regiment) who moved from Malta and arrived in Egypt on 27 July 1882.
7.   Major General Sir H. E. Wood, Commanding 4th Brigade, 2nd Division.
     The Campaign of 1882 in Egypt.
     Colonel J. E. Maurice,
     Published by J. B. Hayward & Son, London, 1973, page 193.
8.   Donne continues to use the old pre-1881 titles.
     The units he refers to are:
     1st Royal Sussex Regiment
     1st South Staffordshire Regiment
     1st Berkshire Regiment
     1st King's (Shropshire Light Infantry)
     3rd Kings Royal Rifle Corps (not 1st/60th as shown).
9.   Major General W. Earle.
     Initially in command of base and lines of communication.
     Maurice, op cit, page 142.
10. See Chapter 6, note 12.
11. Lieutenant L. J. Trafford, Royal Sussex Regiment.
     Monthly Army List, April 1882.
12. Donne probably refers to Lieutenant E. M. Reed, Royal Sussex Regiment, who was serving in Egypt at this time and who qualified for the medal.
13. George Gordon Hake. See Chapter 10, note 14.
14. Lieutenant Colonel A. H. A. Gordon,
     The York and Lancaster Regiment serving in Cyprus in the Cyprus Military Police.

Donne photographed in 1883.

Opposite: The Cyprus Pioneer Corps, Limassol, February 1881.

Above: After The Battle of Tel el Kebir, September 1882.

Opposite: Turkish Zaptieh, 1881.

Below: Camp of the Egyptian troops at Asssouan, under Colonel Duncan, March 1884.

Above: Donne's tent at Korosko, "120° in the shade", 18 June 1884.

Opposite: The Egyptian Camel Corps, 1883.

Above: The Nile expedition, 1885.

**Opposite: The Nile expedition – conveying stores to the front along the Abu Fakmak.
Dongola Reach, 1885.**

Above: Types of the Egyptian Army by R Simkin.
Print kindly loaned by Mr W Y Carman FRS FR Hist S.

Opposite: Cairo, a street scene, 1892.

**The Taj Mahal,
1897.**

**The Taj Mahal in early morning mist, painted by Donnisthorpe Donne's younger brother
Henry Beadon Donne.**

Above: HMS Implacable, 1904.

Opposite: Donisthorpe Donne – a portrait by Mary Donne, 1889.

Above: The colours of the 35th Regiment of Foot.

Opposite: The colours of the 107th Regiment of Foot.

No. 69573
5

It is requested that in any further communication on this subject, the above Number may be quoted; and the Letter addressed to—
The Under Secretary of State for War,
War Office, Pall Mall,
London, (S.W.)

WAR OFFICE,

14th March 1883.

Sir,

With reference to your letter of the 16th ultimo, forwarding an application from Lieutenant B. D. A. Donne, of the Battalion under your command, that his service in a civil appointment in Cyprus might be credited to him as Staff Service in the official (Quarterly) Army List, I am directed by the Secretary of State for War to request that you will be good enough to inform that officer that, as nothing is known in this Department of his being so employed, no reference to it can be inserted in the above publication.

I have the honor to be,

Sir,

Your obedient Servant,

H. G. Deedes

12 Egypt 1883

DONNE'S RECORD of the year 1883, which appears to have been penned at the close of the year, is brief and covers only essential information and was probably written as a mere aide memoir with the intention of amplifying it at a later date. The first entry commences on 1st January and reads:

January 1883

1. *"Abasseyeh, Cairo, Egypt*
    I have now a years record to write up, and as I have seen and done much in that space of time, I shall have to condense it from my Diary notes into a few remaining pages. The beginning of the year was busy with Musketry, Exams, brigade parades on the desert etc.

4. I was anxious to join the new Egyptian army being formed under Sir E Wood who dined with us on the 4th, but as all appointments were filled up, there appeared to be little chance for me.

13. The Regt was inspected on 13th by Gen[l] Earle.
    On the 12th the sports of the 53rd Regt[1], at which Mitchell[2] turned up from Cyprus.

18. And our own sports on the 18th, which the Khedive and all Cairo patronized.

21. I handed over B Coy to Harden[3] on the 21st and went on leave to the Nile and Upper Egypt on 22nd, for 3 weeks to see all the wonders of Carnak[4] & Thebes. I went by Train to Sioot[5] and took the postal str 'Boulak' for Luxor.

24. Passed Souhag and arr(ive)d at Girgeh for the night then the next day on to Farshoot and got to Kench[6] at night time, which I explored in the dark with 2 French fellow voyageurs, who were bound for Luxor. On the 25th we passed the great pylons of Karnak at midday, and were soon landed opposite the Temple of Luxor.

25. I put up at Hotel Luxor, a very comfortable place where I stopped ten days. Very few visitors were up the river this year, and the place was nearly empty, but I enjoyed the solitude of exploring all the splendid remains of ancient Thebes, and sketching bits that took my fancy from among this world of wonders. It was a real treat after the last six months' hard work! I visited the aged Mustpha Aga, the British Consul, renowned as a local celebrity, and next day commenced ruin hunting on farside of the 'Bahr', visiting in succession The Tombs of the Kings, Mussee, the Rammeseum, Gourna & Medinet Heboo all of which are equally wonderous reserving my visit to Karnak on the Luxor side till last, whose colossal ruins dwarf all the rest into apparent nothingness.
    I spent several whole day at Karnak, and each day found new wonders. Of course I saw a 'Fantasia' at the Consul's and dined there also one evening a' l'arabe with Mr. Villiers Stuart who was up in a Dahabieh, Mr. Loret, the young Frenchman was also very entertaining, and a Skotch (sic) architect named Ross.

February 1883

1. Started for Assouan[7] with two Englishmen named Pengelly and Arthur, and saw the Temple at Esneh the same day.

2. On to Edfou next day, and visited the great Temple there and arr(ive)d at Silsilis[8] at night time.

3. Midday the 3[d] arr(ive)d at Assouan, the limit of Egypt Proper, and next a.m. early we visited Phylae --- picnic and commenced our return journey to Luxor the same day, visiting Kom Ombos on the way down. I stopped here again until the 8th, meeting Halton who was up in a Cooks Str (steamer). After another Fantasia at old Aga's and a visit to Mr Chester at H(otel) Karnak, I embarked for Sioot again, and saw Denderah next day. On the

Opposite: Letter from the War Office of 14 March 1883, to the officer commanding 1st Battalion Royal Sussex Regiment in Cairo, rejecting Donne's request for "his service in a civil appointment in Cyprus" to be listed as "Staff Service" on the ground it was activity unknown to the Department.

eve of 12th I was at Abasseyeh again and found Vandeleur[9] Com[ding] the Regt. I had said goodbye to my old Chief before leaving and I heard that his farewell dinner was a very pathetic affair, and I was glad to have been away ..."

During the early part of 1883 and during his leave Donne completed a number of water colours including the following titles:

Looking across the Nile valley from the Great Pyramid, 1883;

Valley, after the rains, 1883;

Going up-stream – three masted Nile craft;

Entrance to the small Temple of Thotmes, 1883;

Portion of the Rammesseum, Thebes, January 1883;

View of the Temple of Luxor, January 1883;

Statue at Luxor, January 1883;

The Ptolemaic Temple of Edfou from the Nile, January 1883;

and after his return from leave:

The Sphinx, 1883, and
The Sphinx from the rear, 1883.

The Nile Valley, after the rains, 1883.

Entrance to the small Temple of Thotmes, 1883.

Looking across the Nile Valley
from the Great Pyramid, 1883.

Going up stream – three masted Nile craft, 1883.

Above, left: View of the Temple of Luxor,
January 1883.

Above, right: Portion of the Rammeseum,
Thebes, January 1883.

Below: The Ptolemaic Temple of Edfou
from the Nile, January 1883.

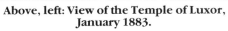

Statue at Luxor, 1883.

Above: The Sphinx, 1883.

Opposite:
View of the Pyramids,
1883.

Left: The Sphinx from the rear, 1883.

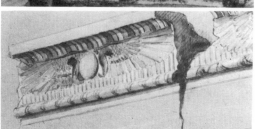

Left: Two winged globes over the entrance
of the temple at Kom Ombos, 1883.

Below: Nile craft, 1883.

Donne continues his narrative on 2nd March:

March 1883

2. "Egyptian War Medals were issued to the Regt on 2nd March.[10] Went out with Bent of 38th[11] to see (the) school at Goobeh and review of Egyptian troops.

23. Poor Chapman died at Algiers on the 23[d] followed not long after by Ramus, both of consumption.[12] My old Chief Inglis died also suddenly at Nicosia.[13]

April 1883

11. Took over the duties of Adjutant from Thornton[14] on the 11th which I held for a month until Pierson[15] the new Adjt came out, who arr(ive)d with (a) draft on 10th May and drove the same day with Hardin & Miss Hardy to see Old Cairo and (the) Nilometer.

May 1883

13. Saw Sir E Wood on the 13th who held out hopes of taking me into (the) Egyptian Army.

14. Got leave of Absence to England on 14th and left next day for Alexandria.

15. Put up with Halton and Royle,[16] and drove round to see the Forts.

16. Left in SS 'Dakalieh' for Athens, with a Mr & Mrs Barr for fellow passengers. We passed off the last of Crete next evening, and were all among the Greek islands next a.m. and arr(ive)d Pireus after a calm passage. I put up at H(otel) Angleterre, & stopped till (the) 22nd.
   On the 22nd I drove to Eleusis with the Barr's and an anglo Greek family named Notarra, where we had a pleasant picnic ..."

It was during this short stay at Athens that Donne completed a sketch of the Acropolis. Later on the 22nd May he continued his journey noting in his record:

22. "Started for Kalamaki and the Isthmus of Corinth by steamer and cross the Isthmus by carriage to New Corinth, and embarked on board the S.S. 'Akrene' down the Gulf of

**On the Acropolis, Athens,
a working sketch, May 1883.**

Corinth & Patras. Lovely scenery all round, with the rugged ranges of Parnassus on the right. We got into Patras after nightfall.

23.   Arr(ive)d next a.m. at Zante. Then on to Argostoli the port of Cephalonia and found a heavy head sea off of Sta Maura.

24.   At day break I was for the 2nd time off Corfu, "the fairest of all the Isles of Greece". I lunched at the Hotel with my fellow voyagers the Philps and the Dixon family, a merry party. I took in a sketch from the Citadel, and at noon the English fleet under Lord J. Hay fired a royal salute in honor of H. M.'s Birthday. We left in the evening for Brindisi, passing the fleet on their way up the Adriatic.

25.   We were in at Brindisi early next a.m. and after a long days railway journey across Italy got into Naples at 10 p.m. and went to (the) H(otel) Rome, just as the moon was guilding (sic) the Bay in the most tipical (sic) manner possible.

27.   Drove to Pozzuloi in the morning and left for Rome having 3 38th Fellows from Malta for companions. Took the night train to Florence, and on to Bologna and Milan, and after a nights rest there, got into Stresa on Lago Maggiore, as evening was settling down. After a pleasant day's rest at Stresa, I took the Diligence (the last time it ran from Arona) at 6 a.m. for the Simpton. It was raining heavily but cleared off as day wore on, and the cloudied effects generally added to the grand scenery of the route. Passed D'Omo d'Ossola & the Hospice, and got down to Brigue[17] and arr(ive)d at last at Hotel D'Angleterre Vevey, on old Lac Leman[18] again, which I had not seen for 10 years. I found our old friends the Priors still there, and as hospitable as ever.

June 1883

3.   On Sunday the 3rd June I was once more in town via Dover & Calais, and home at 31 Campden Grove, and found everything up-side down in consequence of house changing. I remained in London till the 2nd July spending a good deal of my time in the Library of the British Museum collecting records on the Conquest of Cyprus etc. Met Travers in town who was on leave from India.[19]
       Was also a good deal at the Exhibition with my own people, and Hake who was Superintendent of the Exhibition.

July 1883

2.   Went down to Exmouth in a.m. (Monday) to stay with the Strongs once more, and remained there until the 17th, amusing myself in a very quiet way. Met the Pollocks and other friends of yore and some tennis at the lawn (at) Exmouth.

17.   I returned on the 17th calling at Crewkerne on the way, lunching at Misterton and came on to London with Kate Parsons, in time for our house warming at home in the evening which was crowded.

18.   Down to the Park in a.m. with A & Miss Fife and called at (the) War Office.

19.   Saw Rose[20] off at Charing Cross for the Tirol & Miss Fife off at Paddington. I rec(eive)d a W.O. letter on the 21st ordering me to rejoin my Regt in Egypt by the 8th August, my leave being cancelled on account of the Cholera epidemic out there, and I accordingly arrange(d) to leave on the 31st, and travel straight through. This gave me 10 more days in London.

24.   I rec(eive)d a letter from Vandeleur on the 24th saying Sir E Wood had offered me an appointment in the Egyptian Army if I returned, with my expenses paid out. So in any case I should have left England speedily irrespectively of my cancelled leave. I had also previously written to the Colonial Office authorities to have my name recorded for re-employment in Cyprus should occasion offer, having made up my mind not to serve any more as a Subaltern if I could help it.

25.   On the 25th I met Kelly and Cobham,[21] and heard that the Regt was moved to Ismailia on account of the heavy mortality from cholera at Cairo, where the panic was great.

28.   I completed my kit at the A & N Stores and spent the eve with a party at the S. K. Museum. Next p.m. I spent with P & M for a farewell stroll in the Park.

31.   And the following evening found myself once more en route to Egypt, via Dover &

Outward bound from Naples, 1883.

Marseilles there were about 15 others on board also going back. Met Col Grattan[22] at Paris, and travelled with him.

August 1883

2.   We embarked on the M. S. 'Tage' passed (the) Straits of Bonifacis, touched at Naples where Ischia had just been destroyed by (an) earthquake ..."

Donne took this opportunity to paint another water colour which he entitled 'Outward bound from Naples, 1883'.

8.   "Arrived at Alexandria on the 8th after a splendid passage.

9.   Went up to Cairo next day, and reported myself to Gen[l] Grenfell of the Egyptian Army, and found myself posted as Major, and to command the Camel Corps, with a salary of £450 a year.
      I took over Quarters and Command of the Camel Corps next day at the Polygou Abasseyeh. I was in Army orders as appointed Supernumary Major to 1st Brigade. The cholera had greatly diminished, and the 35th at Ismailia had lost upwards of 35 men. I signed a contract with the Egyptian Minister of War to serve for two years.

September 1883

I held command of the Camel Corps for over two months, until Turner[23] came back, when I was posted to the 4th Batt[on] under Col Wynne[24] at the Polygon.
Although in the Egyptian Army I had considerable hopes about this time of being reappointed to (the) Cyprus civil service, and Sir R. Biddulph telegraphed home for my services – after considerable delay however the C.O.[25] decided to bring in a civilian.

October 1883

6.   I was presented to the Khedive in private audience.

12.   On the 12th marched past in Abdin Square with the Camel Co(r)p(s). On handing over to Turner I was thanked by Gen[l] Grenfell for commanding them.
      Dr Acland, our energetic P. M. O. left for England on the 13th and I saw him off.

November 1883

13.   I was promoted Captain in the Royal Sussex vice Purvis,[26] in the Gazette of 13th November, and was thus transferred to the 2nd Batt[n] (107th) at Malta. I was however seconded in the Gazette of 23rd Nov[er] for service in the Egyptian army.

      26.   Was employed at Maussurah in the Delta for a few days where there is a small English Colony, and on the 10th Dec(e)m(be)r was a week at Fautah conscripting.

December 1883

17.   On the 17th and 20th I passed the preliminary Arabic exam.

25.   Spent part of Xmas day on the Ranges with Zobher Pasha's black troops, and dined with
       Kelly at the Sussex Mess.
       News of Gordon Hake's engagement to R came soon after but 1883 closes with a football
       match at Geziret which also completes this record of eleven years of Diary ..."

The final page in Donne's journal gives details of his Promotions and appointments
which he listed as follows:

"Appointed Sub Lieut Unattd	10.9.75
Appointed Sub Lieut 35th Foot	9.76
Promoted Lieut 35th Foot with antidate	10.9.75
Instructor of Signalling	24.11.79
Appointed to Command Cyprus Pioneers (Dett)	6.1.81
Appointed Local Com^{dant} Cyprus	20.8.81
Acting D. A. and Q. M. G. Limassol	8.82
Acting Adjt R Sussex	11.3.83
Appointed Major Egyptian Army	9.8.83
Promoted Captain R Suss Regt	20.10.83"

Donne completed one water colour during his short tour of attachment to the
Egyptian Camel Corps and the painting is dated as being 1883.

In support of the rather meagre entries in the Journal for 1883 there are five letters in
the Donne collection which amplify the comments in the Journal. The first of these is
dated 3 August 1883 and was written to his parents:

"... We are a very jolly party of 15 British Officers on board (the Tage); hardly any other
passengers, as you can easily imagine.
     Cols Ardagh & Gordon[27] of the Staff and 6 officers of the Gordon Highlanders stationed
at Cairo are among the number. Col Gratton is the only other officer of ours. The rest have
taken some other route. We expect to get into Naples tomorrow morning where we shall
get a run on shore, but shall pass Ischia too early to see much of it. We passed the Straits of
Bonifacio early this morning.
     There is hardly a ripple on the water, so locomotion is exceedingly pleasant, and I have
the best cabin in the ship to myself. No one seems to care or think much of cholera, and the
Gordon Sub^{tns} are banging away at a piano now.
     Lt Col Hallam Parr[28] of the Egyptian Infantry is also on board and as all the Egyptians are
located at Abasseyeh I suppose I shall go up to Cairo.
6th Aug – Things are going on swimmingly so far – especially in respect of locomotion, as
the rapid increase in temperature makes our southing (sic) all the more apparent. It is too
hot to stop below for pleasure, but very pleasant on deck under the awning. I have never
travelled on a Messagerie boat before: they feed and look after us extremely well: in fact
we seem to eat all day long. Several of us were poisoned by something we ate the day
before yesterday, and the nausea lasted for two days, but every one is right again now I
think. The sea remains calm as ever. We all had a run on shore at Napoli and saw Ischia in
the distance but nothing of the earthquake havoc. We passed the Straits of Messina early
Sunday morning but Etna was very hazy, and we soon lost sight of land round Calabria. Col
Ardagh of the Staff does a power of sketching, and has a large collection, and is always at it
below or on deck. I managed a couple of small ones of Naples. We expect to get into
Alexandria early on Wednesday.
Cairo, Saturday 11th – I must write you what I can in the little time at my disposal, and
have not written before because there is no mail before tomorrow. You see I have
arr(ive)d at the Plague stricken city all right after stopping a day en route at Alexandria
with an old friend named Donald, and came on here on the 9th. The place looks very dried
up of course with but few people stirring and I put up at one of the town hotels and shifted
out to Abasseyeh yesterday and am now somewhat recovering from the horrid confusion
of changing without servants etc. When I arr(ive)d here I found myself in General Orders

as transferred to the Egyptian Army – curiously enough the same day I arr(ive)d in Cairo as follows: "H. R. H. has approved of the services of Lieut B. Donne, 1st R Sussex R being placed at the disposal of the Foreign Office with a view to his employment with the Egyptian Army". So you see I have regularly become an Egyptian, – well, on arrival here I reported myself to General Grenfell.[29] and was quite scared as you can imagine on being told off Command the Camel Corps! Being absolutely ignorant of such animals to say nothing of their Drill, organisation, etc., you can believe that this was rather a smasher. I have however had to take it over this morning nolens volens, and this is my first introduction to the Egyptian Army, and I hardly know my head from my heels, or where on earth to begin or end. Major Turner[30] who commanded them has gone home sick, and the whole thing seems left in confusion no one seemingly knowing anything about the business, and I of course know less than any one.

There are about 103 camels, who can make a good noise between them, and perform marvellous evolutions in the desert. It is very hot and glary (sic) here of course and we are out in the desert beyond Abasseyeh at a place called the Polygon. I have a great barnlike room to fix up in which is by no means tempting, as it is on a level with the ground, and swarms with ants etc.

The cholera seems diminishing fast, but I have as yet had no time to think of it much. They keep up their spirits in Cairo with bands of an evening in the Gardens. The Sussex have lost upwards of 30 men, and insubordination seems at one time to have been rife down at Ismalia and Col Vandeleur is reported to have quite lost his head. There are two officers up here still with one company.

Address me – Egyptian Army
        Abasseyeh.

for the present. I have no time for more now, as I must call on Sir E Wood this p.m. He is just off to England. I must also buy a Fez and other things ..."

The next letter was written from Abasseyeh to his Father and was dated 10 September 1883 and reads:

"... This is my anniversary today (10th Sept[er]): 8 years ago I was commissioned Sub Lieut in H. M. Forces, and although not having had the luck to obtain my company yet, I have this day rec(eive)d my commission from the Khedive as a Major in the Khedival Army, thus being spared the necessity of signing my name as "Cap[t]".

Bathurst,[31] the fellow above me who was promoted the other day provisionally has failed him exam and of the alternative given him of reverting to Lieut or resigning his commission, has chosen the latter, and will shortly be gazetted out.

Most of the troops are back in Cairo again, and old Vandeleur with his Regt among them. They seem very chirpy, and camel rides are the order of the day. Trafford,[32] and two R. E. fellows & self have been out today to the 1st station on the Suez Road – about 6 miles and came back in 45 minutes. They were highly amused with the new mode of transit.

The Corps of Dromidaires is getting on first class, and the original overwhelming importance has died off. I make them drill now like smoke, and they are quite the wonder and admiration of the British troops, and a British General Officer who was looking on one morning was quite dumb-founded at the way they can wheel and charge. Its quite like a circus performance on a large scale! This is a fighting Corps and not a baggage train by any means. I may as well mention here that I've been offered an L. C. M. P.-ship (sic) in Cyprus again, or rather a resume of the old business but I think I shall stick to Egypt now. In fact I'm in lucks way for a change, as you perceive. I must say I have a hankering after Cyprus but I do not think it would be quite as good there as here although the climate is better. I wrote to say I would accept nothing indefinite, i.e. that I should like the salary and District specified before going back. If they had offered me the Police Adjutancy at H[d]Q[rs] I would have accepted it. I had my tableau taken the other day in the Govt of Egypt and enclose a copy. It is good one for me. I'm glad to hear you have been having a nice time of it in Suisse. I should also like a sniff of the Laces (sic) air. I get the 'Overland Mail' sent weekly now.

**Donne as a Major
in the Egyptian
Army, 1883;
the photograph
was sent to his
elder sister,
Anna.**

... What do you think of the Egyptian kit, very flashy isn't it – how the girls would like it!
... During the last few days the heat has perceptibly decreased and Cairo with the English
troops back is looking itself again.
... I am looking about for a suitable horse which are difficult to get, as well as expensive,
about £30 seems the lowest order ..."

Donne's next letter to his parents was again from Abasseyeh and was written on 14
November. In this letter he again comments on his new Egyptian Army uniform and
gives further details of it:

"... White, my dear people, white, white, is what you see on the photos and it all washes.
Please inform everyone of this most important fact. Your letters are to hand and
appreciated as usual. Dyke of 5 Princes St, Hannover Square, is sending me out some of the
new uniform requisite. I also want a pair of Infantry Officers brass dress spurs for boxes.
(i.e. spurs with things like sixpences instead of spikes) brass – not steel. Perhaps you can
get them at the Cop, and let Dyke know by post card that they must be included in his box.
I have told him to send the things as soon as possible, so they might be nearly ready now.
Orders have come for the British troops to evacuate Cairo, so we shall soon have the
whole place to ourselves, and be able to see how things work without the protecting army
of England round our waists as at present. The 35th are under orders for 'Home sweet
Home' but I shall be non est at Portsmouth. There ought to be a big gazette out soon as
there are actually as many as five Companies going begging, so I shall soon be well up the
Captains list. Before you get this I ought to be both Promoted and Seconded.
The climate here now is lovely, and the Nile running down. We are getting into our winter
uniform – black with gold lacing. Sir E Wood has come back and assumed command, and
we expect a tremendous burst of drill soon. I am gradually picking up the infantry drill (in
Turkish), but find myself tremendously handicapped by those who have been here all
along. As far as the language goes, I am about quits with the worst of them. There is a
colloquial exam coming off on the 17th December, but I don't think I shall be up to the

task, as I learn very slowly.

There are no tourists here this season – cholera has choked them all off – so the Hotel keepers are gasping. Why don't you try and come out in January, and then we will have a spree up the Nile or in Syria, Cyprus etc. I told the Hotel keeper of the 'Nile' you were coming, so now he is disappointed!

Dr Acland, our late bn Dr left yesterday on return to England much regretted by all who knew him. He is a capital little chap, and a great curio hunter. I gave him your address, and he is going to look you up when he has time. The Khedive gave him the 4th class Order of the Majedie the day he left, which all say he well earned, having worked hard on the organisation of our hospital ..."

The letter closed with a page of comments dealing with family events and personalities. His next letter dated 24 November was written to his Father, and comments on the situation in the Soudan.

"... Great excitement has been the order of the day in Cairo on the bad news from the Soudan. Hicks Pasha and the whole of his army appear to have perished. The Mahdi having by all accounts literally cut them to pieces. They don't seem to know what they are going to do now, but presumably Kartoum will have to be relieved. Such a Victory will no doubt have given the Mahdi tremendous prestige up there, and he will now require a large army to lick him. But everyone asks where are the men to come from? It would require an army three times as numerous as ours (the Egypt^n) which consist of but 6000 all told. But there is at present no talk of sending us up, although we have been frightening the native officers nearly out of their wits by telling them we are off in a few days, and that they had better make their wills! They all have a wholesome dread of the Soudan.

You see they have given me my Company at last, but swindled me out of three months back pay by dating only from 20th October. I shall be seconded by now I suppose, and next four subs will also be promoted, or ought to be. The Regiment is under orders for England, and I belong until seconded, to the 107th at Malta. I suppose you see the movements and gazettes in the papers and of course the Soudan disaster has been placarded up everywhere.

The weather we are having now is simply perfect. I am getting on with the new infantry drill with the 4th Batt^{on} under Col Wynne Bey.[33] As far as drill does this new army will be everything that can be expected, but whether its fighting qualities will ever be improved is extremely doubtful. The officers are of the worst description and no amount of licking into shape seems to improve them.

Have just rec(eive)d your letters about my promotion – thanks – I got these letters by the mail, one addressed to Lieut: one Captain, and one Major, so its rather mixing presumably! 2000 of the Gendarmerie are just off for Souakim, and I am going down to Mansourah[34] in the Delta to take over from them and arrange transfers etc. There is awful disgust among the British Officers of the E. A. at their being cut out by the Gendarmes and being sent to do their work in the provinces. But there appears no chance of the Regular Army being sent off, as Sir E Wood says they are not yet fit, but time if it improves discipline will never improve their courage. So you see we Britishers are disgusted and the native officers intensely relieved! There are still many who doubt the Soudan business: if true in all details it must be very bad. As I am ordered away tomorrow morning early I cannot wait to answer your letters in details: I shall be back in two or 3 days when the relief is completed. I was rather hoping to inform you I was off to Souakim with the troops! ..."

Donne's last letter written in 1883 was written on Christmas day and addressed to "My Dear Family".

"... Once more this very festive season comes round, and I suppose you are all having a jolly fine time of it round your blazing coals. We are having an unusually cold time of it, with none of the usual appliances for heat. This makes my eighth consecutive Xmas in furrin (sic) parts.

1. Barbados	2. Jamaica
1. Malta	2. Cyprus
2. Egypt	

I have finished my conscripting work at Fautah, and came back again, and today we have been most of us enjoying an arabic exam, and exciting our intellects frightfully. I have no reason to suppose I did a particularly bad one, but d'ont think I was worse than many others. In fact we were all bad. I have still the viva voce to go through with Sir E Wood who tells one to ask most diabolical questions of a soldier brought in for the purpose. If I pass this preliminary exam, I shall be to a certain extent in front of those who have not been up. On Xmas night I am dining with Capt Kelly[35] of my old company, on the strength of which I have been nominally borne since I joined. I think I answered your last letter in my last. Soudan affairs do not seem much more settled since my last. You see the latest news I suppose in the London papers long before we do here, and can judge accordingly. Sir E Wood has just 'cash' (sic) one officer of this army for not having paid his Tailors bill, which has excited indignation and mistrust among the rest of us. This is what we call the 'high moral tone'.

I had a letter from Beadon[36] a few days since who seems festive enough with orders for England. Cook is just starting a party for the Nile, so you need not imagine there is much apprehension of danger out here. People at home do not realise the 'Gulf that is fixed' between Egypt and the Soudan. I hope, if they send Indian troops here, that an Egyptian Brigade will go with them. ...

Cholera has appeared again in one or two places seemingly, so it seems hopeless to think of getting out of this endless quarantine. The 35th have had their orders for England cancelled: and will have now to spin out the winter here ..."

Donne concluded his final letter of 1883 with festive greetings to various members of his family.

Notes to Chapter Twelve

1. Donne again refers to the pre-1881 title but is, in fact, referring to the 1st King's (Shropshire Light Infantry).
2. Ronald L. N. Mitchell, Commissioner at Limassol from 1 August 1879.
3. Captain G. Harden, Royal Sussex Regiment,
    Monthly Army List, April 1882.
4. Donne refers to 'Karnak'
    The Public Schools Atlas.
    by The Rev George Butler, DD.,
    Published by Longmans, Green & Co, London 1894. Map 22.
5. Siout.
    Butler, op cit, Map 22.
6. Kenneh.
    Ibid.
7. Assouan.
    Ibid.
8. Silsili.
    Ibid.
9. Lieutenant Colonel J. O. Vandeleur. Royal Sussex Regiment,
    Monthly Army List, April 1882.

10. Donne is shown as having been awarded the Egypt Medal, with bronze star.
    Maurice, op cit, page 140.
11. Lieutenant W. H. M. Bent, The South Staffordshire Regiment.
    Monthly Army List, April 1882.
12. Captain A. T. Chapman and Lieutenant C. L. A. Ramus, both of the Royal Sussex Regiment.
    Monthly Army List, April 1882.
13. See Chapter 9, note 10.
14. Donne refers to Lieutenant F. G. Todd-Thornton who was acting as Adjutant at that time.
15. Lieutenant J. E. Pierson, Royal Sussex Regiment.
    Monthly Army List, April 1882.
16. Assistant Surgeon M. C. Halton. There is no officer by name of 'Royle' in the Army Lists of 1882-1884.
    He may have been a civilian doctor working with Assistant Surgeon Halton.
17. Brieg.
    Butler, op cit, Map 15.
18. Lake Geneva.
    Ibid.
19. Lieutenant E. A. Travers, Bengal Staff Corps.
    Army List, 1883.
20. He refers to his younger sister, Mary Rose Donisthorpe Donne, who was born 1859 and lived until 1952.
21. Captain W. F. Kelly, Royal Sussex Regiment.
    There is no trace of any officer by the name of 'Cobham' in the Army List for 1883. As Donne wrote his Journal at this stage, a year at a time from his Daily Diary he may well have made a mistake in the name.
22. Lieutenant Colonel H. Grattan, Royal Sussex Regiment.
    Army List, 1883.
23. Major A. E. Turner, Royal Artillery.
    Army List, 1883.
24. Donne refers to Major A. S. Wynne, of the King's Own Light Infantry (South Yorkshire Regiment) who was at that time serving with the Egyptian Army as a Lt Col.
25. Colonial Office.
26. Captain A. K. Purvis, Royal Sussex Regiment.
    Army List, 1883.
27. Brevet Lieutenant Colonel J. C. Ardagh, Royal Engineers and Brevet Lieutenant Colonel R. W. T. Gordon, Argyll and Sutherland Highlanders.
28. Brevet Lieutenant Colonel H. Hallam Parr, Somersetshire Light Infantry.
    Maurice, op cit, page 172.
29. Brigadier General F. W. Grenfell employed on Line of Communication Staff.
    History of the Sudan Campaign, Part I.
    by Colonel H. E. Colville, CB.
    published by HMSO, 1889., page 272.
30. Major A. E. Turner, Royal Artillery.
31. Lieutenant A. C. H. Bathurst, Royal Sussex Regiment.
    Monthly Army List, April 1883.
32. Lieutenant L. J. Trafford, Royal Sussex Regiment.
    Monthly Army List, April 1884.
33. See note 24.
34. Donne refers to the town now known as El Mansura.
35. Captain W. F. Kelly, Royal Sussex Regiment.
    Monthly Army List, April 1884.
36. Donne's brother was at this time serving as Lieutenant Henry Richard Beadon Donne of the Norfolk Regiment.

13 Egypt 1 January to 9 November 1884

DONNE'S SECOND journal commences in September 1884 but fortunately there are a number of letters that have survived covering the first eight months of the year. These have, generally, been written to his parents. The first letter of 1884 was written from Cairo and dated 4th January:

"... One of our number has just gone over to Cyprus to buy up mules for a new battery, and has to undergo 14 days quarantine, otherwise I should have gone too I think. Is it not absurd that such should be still considered necessary! We in Cairo are on the qui vive for some great news before long – there are all sorts of rumours flying about and we are especially anxious to know what is really to be done as regards the Soudan. The Regt^s are now raised to 700 each there is also an intention to increase the No of Batt^{ons} and they are engaging fresh British Officers. Still however there are no signs of a move on our part: indeed we lack every kind of transport.

I may tell you here that I have just been removed from the 4th Batt^{on} here in the Polygon to the 3rd Batt^{on} at Abasseyeh, which will necessitate my moving my belongings down there. Genl Grenfell told me today that I shall be on a kind of probation for the 2nd in command of that Reg^t, and if I suit, I shall most probably be permanently posted to the 2nd in commandship of that Batt^{on}. This is owing to the pleasing discovery I made a few days back that I ranked according to British Seniority and not (from the) date of joining the E. Army, which puts me above all Sub^{trns} serving. He also told me he was pushing my case with the Sirdar to get me the appointment, as he seems to have been quite fetched with my command of the Camel Corps. So this will be a good shunt up, and the prospect of commanding a Reg^t in the field is already a castle in the air! The 3rd Reg^t was raised and commanded by Lt Col Hallam Parr CMG, a smart officer and a Somersetshire man, who has relatives near Chard, so we shall be the Somersetshire Batt^{on}! You see by being the 2nd in command of a Regt in the absence or sickness of the Lt Col one gets the Command of the Reg^t! Not a bad thing for a youth of 8 years service! The Reg^t has already been told off as the (one) to go to Assouam if any go. I have been cantering about this a.m. at Sir E Woods heels at the Holy Carpet Ceremony, which has just made its entry into Cairo from Mecca. The Khedive was there, but looking very dejected, and rumours of his resignation have been flying about. Whatever is happening you will hear just as much as we do by keeping a good look out on the morning papers, and you will generally find more detail in the Standard etc, than the Times.

... Tell Anna^1 I have not yet rec(eive)d my diary, which I am rather in want of. I will keep you informed of my movements

... I have at last also rec(eive)d Dykes box today with your things in it. The spurs are just what I wanted and suit very well, as well as the uniform ... I enclose you another Photo in full uniform, or as we call it in Arabic Tesherifa is very pretty, very dark, with gold lines. ...

I have passed the Arabic exam all right: ... I did not pass last, nor do I rank last, as you might be led to suppose.

I have just heard that the Ministry have resigned, and that we are all going up the Nile. Firm or not we shall no doubt have our work cut out. It has been awfully cold here of late, but better today. ..."

The next letter, again from Cairo, was dated 20th January and written to his parents commenced with family social gossip and then turned to events in Egypt:

"... Things are rolling along here in an element of fits and starts – 8 hours all day long of what is going to be but what is never done. No signs of a start yet in the Assouan direction. They have taken off the quarantine at last, that is the best news going. I told you I suppose in my last that I had received the box from Dykes. So I can now array myself something like a peacock in evening costume.

I have been hard at work at musketry of late to get 'em ready for any emergency. I am still

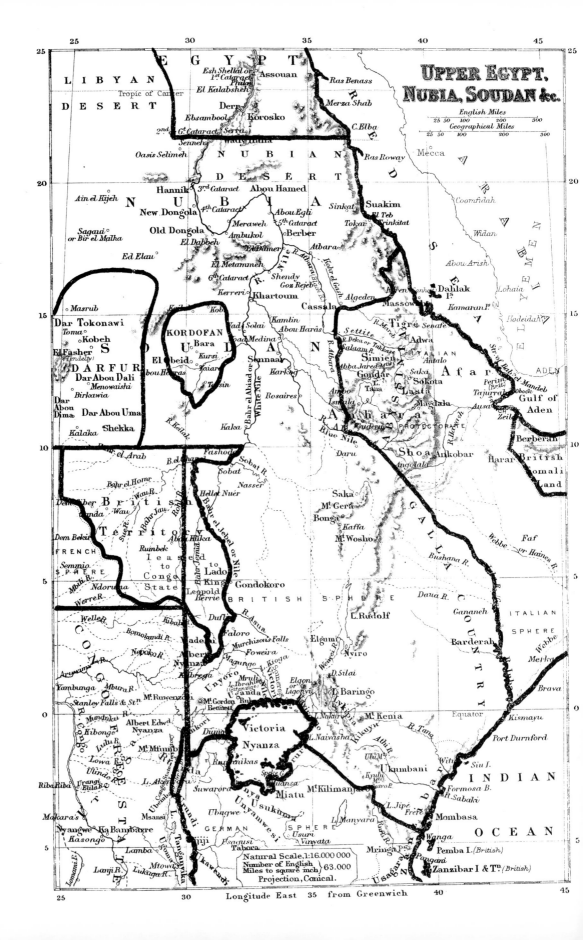

in my old diggings not having yet made a move. They are gong to raise some Turkish Regt[s] at once officered by English Officers of the Regular army, but I can predict that they will have much harder work to lick them into soldiers than they perhaps contemplate. They will get all the riff raff of the Levant. ...

I am thinking of getting a Winchester Repeater rifle out, and am going to ask you to go down to the agency in Victoria St and look one up, and get them to forward it out here. I will attach directions further down. It will be a useful thing to have for sport or war purposes. ..."

There was a P.S. to this letter concerning the purchase of the rifle which was merely a note saying:

"... In case I want a Repeater sent out I will send you directions by post card ..."

Unfortunately the post card does not seem to have survived.

On the 2nd February 1884 Donne wrote two letters from Cairo, one to his Father and the other to his Mother. The letter to his Father mainly deals with the handling of family deeds. The only military matters contained in that letter is a brief reference to the Soudan which reads:

"... We are not going up country as you will have learned by my last letter. The Soudan would not have been a bad place to leave ones bones in but we may go there yet. That of course depends on the outcome of Gordon's[2] mission and he is timed to reach Kartoum on the 17th ..."

At this stage Donne makes a rare comment on his Father's painting ability and says in his letter:

"... I am glad to hear of the excellent way your paintings have been criticized, and hope next to hear that you belong to the Royal Society ..."

His letter to his Mother at this time is mainly dealing with family matters, wedding etc but he does note that he has changed quarters:

"... I have changed my quarters lately, and have much better rooms than before although not in such a good locality ..."

The next letter was eight days later and showed that Donne was still in Cairo:

"...   Feb[y] 10th, 1884.

Your London news must have been decidedly spicey last week – more in sorrow than in anger I write to let you know that I am still in Cairo and, as before, likely to be.

Another crushing slaughter has no doubt convinced you that the fellah is no use to fight with, and I suppose all England is cursing the qualities of the Egyptian Army, and advocating its disbandment. Even the impression here is that we are worse than useless, and the Egyptian uniform is becoming a laughing stock. But not one man of the last 'smash up' belonged to Wood's army, and I have been maintaining all day long that there is no comparison between the two forces. The new army has in fact been condemned without a chance of vindicating itself, or the new qualities it may have generated under British Commanders. Disgust reigns supreme among us, as even now we are not going down. Parr, my CO has gone off to take command at Souakim, with several of the men and officers, all Volunteers. In fact, half the Batt[on] volunteered to go too. What do you say to that! I am now temporarily in command, but not for long as a new Col is to be appointed.

... Everybody of course talks of Baker Pasha and we saw the officers of our Army off for Souakim yesterday admist ringing cheers and hopes we should be soon after them, and that they would "leave some for us" etc., etc. There is anxiety about Gordon of course ..."

Donne concluded his letter with a short postscript:

"... Troops are going to Assouan but not my Batt[on], the 3rd to which I am now 2nd in Com[d] and temporarily Commanding.

D. D. ..."

The next letter was dated 1st March and was to his parents from 'The Nile' showing that his unit had at last moved out of Cairo.

"... I am glad to say we are well on our way up the river now, and clear of all the worry and hurry of departure, and surprizing to say we got away the moment we were timed to be off. I only had three days to do all the preparations necessary for the Batt^{on}, which were by no means few, and to get on board the ships was an intense relief. We marched out of Abasseyeh nearly 1400 strong headed by all the bands in the place, and filed past Sir E Wood at the Arsenal Bowlak, who with many others was there to see us off. As we passed the Karr el Nil bridge Col Vandeleur[3] and the Sussex officers were there to see us pass up and say goodbye, and probably this is the last I may see of the old Corps for some time. The field force consists of two Batt^{ons} and a battery, with 12 guns and gatlings: the whole in three steamers and five barges, so the procession up the river is quite imposing. There are four English officers with the force – Lt Col Smith Com^{ding} 2nd Batt^{on} and the whole force: self commanding the 3rd Batt^{on}, Major Shakespeare 2nd Batt^{on} and a young officer just arr(ive)d from England named Eagar, whom they have given to me, but of course he is absolutely useless at present knowing nothing of the country or work.[4] We mess together on one of the Steamers of Cook & Son. We get along very slowly, and hardly expect to arrive at Assouan in less than three weeks! If as soon, and as a sort of commencement we stuck on a bank three hours today.

March 3rd. We are progressing slowly, the steamers often getting on the mud banks and taking some time to get off. We have passed the Pyramid region and are about halfway to Sioot,[5] the railway terminus. Calculating our present rate I don't think we shall get to Assouan before 25 days more. I have directed the Cairo post authorities to send on my letters to Luxor and Assouan. I have got a very comfortable cabin on board, so life is pleasant and the varying river scenes so often described tempt one to take up sketching again, which I hope to do when I have cleared off a lot of office work.

We expect to hear of great doings from Souakim when we get within reach of news whenever that will be – ..."

Donne's next letter to his parents was dated 15th March and was written from Edfou[6]

"... I found two letters and Gordon's book waiting for me at Luxor (the) day before yesterday. We passed the Propylous of Karnak about sundown, which tower up like great barracks walls from near the river, and moored at Luxor on the 13th.

They have been digging out more of the Luxor temple since I was there last. I found "little Ahmet" the protege of Lady Duff Gordon in his exile and who is mentioned in "A 1000 miles up the Nile", the son of old Mustapha Aqa the Consul was very glad to see me and he came and dined on board. Old Aqa and his sons are quite celebrities. Every Britisher who has been at Luxor since 1856 is written in his books including, as you may imagine, all the celebrities of the day. We were only at Thebes for the night as usual, but, as the morn was well up, a dancing entertainment, we rode out to see Karnak which I had not seen before at night. I was a little disappointed I confess but having been there so often before perhaps took the wonder off. We left early next morning, and got a couple of peeps of the renowned Erment on our way up. We were at Esneh[7] this morning, and are now about halfway to Edfou. We expect to get into Assouan in 3 days time, where Col Duncan[8] has preceded us to make preparations.

The temperature is gradually changing, flies are increasing and no doubt white cloths will be acceptable there. Thank you for your letters and especially for the book, which promises to be interesting. Sir R. Biddulph[9] asked me over to Cyprus for the races on the 20th, but I am afraid I shall be a good way off at that time. There appears to have been more fighting at Souakim which makes us jealous of other people. I do not quite understand the correspondence you alude to on my part, but as I have never seen or heard anything else of it, it is perhaps as wise to say nothing about it. They are talking of sending a Steamer up to Assouan for us to Mess on board but unless it is done at a moderate rate, I shall be much more inclined to pig it under my own canvas. ...

Gordon seems (to be) getting on allright (sic) in the Soudan. They are sending down the Khartoum Garrison to be disbanded at Assouan. We are most of us growing beards now, but just at present look in a very half fledged state. The attractions of their native homes has proved too much for some of our men, as 20 have deserted on the way up. But this is really a very small number considering the force. When they are caught they will be made an example of by 2 years and sent to Souakim "never to see their 'appy 'omes no more", as the British recruiting Serg[t] said. I am afraid my poor old 3rd Batt[on] will be very much changed with all these new officers in it, and they have imported an English Serg[t] from England which I am totally against. Rather than see a red coat anywhere near I should prefer to do his work myself. Our young officers on board (who have been given the rank of Capt[n] in the E.A.) rather fancied themselves in red coats, but don't go in for it quite so much since we gave them a hint. Smith and self have unfortunately taken a dislike to 2 of the 3. Perhaps I am wrong, but I would much rather get on with one other English officer and the native officers ..."

Donne's next letter was dated 24th March, and was to his sister Anna, and was written at 'Camp Assouan':

"... We arr(ive)d here on the 18th and after making use of the ship as long as possible are now under canvas on top of the hills over looking the 1st Cateracts. There is not a vestige of anything green near so the heat is already excessive. The tents are pitched whereever we can get flat spaces sufficient. They have been having some hard fighting round Souakim as we all thought would happen, and I suppose there will be decorations & honours flying round again. The unmentionable disgust of being stuck out to grill in this unholy place instead is better less talked of. A certain Major Trotter of the 93rd[10] has been appointed Lt Col of my Batt[on]. He seems a very good fellow. I have been over to Phyla[11] once or twice where it is very hot.

People coming down from Kartoum that way in numbers. Heard from Beadon who says he's going home now.[12] ...

Nothing else particular to talk of. This is 7 a.m. and the granite rocks all round are beginning to look hot already. We are employing the men making roads and setting the camp up in general. They have lately inundated the E. Army with new officers, to the disgust of the old lot, who are in many cases superseeded (sic) by them.

A picture paper now and then would be amusing here ..."

At this time Donne painted a small picture which he entitled "The camp of Egyptian troops at Assouan under Colonel Duncan, March 1884'. This appears to be the only painting that has survived from that camp. His next letter was to his Father and was dated 31 March:

"... We are getting on middling as far as the temperature is concerned which is already somewhat severe. Our camp is considerably divided – perched about on the tops of these rocks like so many rookeries and to get on level ground for parade purposes we shall have to go down to the plain below. Col Duncan is Comd[ing] here, and there are now 8 British Officers with the force, and we have dragged the guns up and put them in position. Lt Col Trotter of the 93rd Highlanders,[13] the new O. C. of the 3rd Batt[on], seems a consequential sort of man and one whom I fancy would prefer to see his subordinates do most of the work. To day we went up from Phylae in a small steamer some ten miles up river, which is much finer above than below the Cateract. Col Coetligen the late Com[dnt] of Cartoum[14] passed through here on his way down the other day. I believe things are pretty quiet in the Soudan now and many people passing down. All the work and glory seems centred round Souakim. Two of our officers are on their way up from Cairo with orders I believe for Berber. There is a large sum of money here for Gordon at Khartoum which someone will have to take through but they have wired to stop it for the present. Col Duncan said he would let me go through with it, but those lively hopes were soon dispelled! I fancy the officers coming from Cairo will take it. I hope to get a trip up to Koroseo[15] or Wadi Halfa[16] if an opportunity offers itself soon. Our tents here at day time are almost unbearably hot: yesterday inside was 105°. They are building stone huts for us which will be an immense boon, and unless they do the same for the men when the hot weather comes I should think most of them would die. They are also talking of sending the 35th on here from Sioot[17] where they now are."

Donne's next letter, again from Assouan, was to his parents and was dated 9th April 1884:

"... A regular family budget arrived here today – letters from Campden Grove, Crewkerne and one from Beadon, who is on his way home and asks for cigarrettes (sic) which I am afraid I shall be unable to supply. I suppose he will be home almost as soon as you get this. Thanks for all the family news – our bi-weekly mail are the events of the week here of course. It seems they are sending some British officers through to Berber also. I suppose we fellows here are no longer thought of in Cairo – I am afraid you must expect dull letters from this out of the way place, for now that we have settled down there is very little to do. I doubt very much if your two Egyptian friends would think Assouan such a nice place if they had the summer to spend there. It is very pleasant here now, and a few days back was the coolest we have had. I think I told you of our sand storm which raged all day. The heat and sand were awful while it lasted. The Souakim Campaign seems at an end. The business is now to extricate Gordon. I wish I could see my way to getting down there but Col Duncan, our CO seems to think there is no chance for anyone here. So things must be as they are ..."

At this point the letter is devoted to a page of family gossip concerning his sisters Anna and Rose, and he then returns to the local situation at Assouan:

"... We often go over to Phylae which is an hour's ride from here. I have been trying a painting of the painted Hall, but the thing seems hopeless as paints and paper dry up like chips in this dry climate. ... Gordon's Soudan policy seems belicose and he has apparently shot two Pashas for treachery – another miserable sort of massacre. I may also state that out of sheer disgust after more than a years hardwork the original English officers have lost most of their energy for the business. The Volunteers whom we sent to Suakim with the Camel Transport apparently ran away at the last battle and 40 were in consequence flogged but there is one consolation in that they were headed in their flight by two Englishmen – the artist to the Graphic and the Special of the Daily News or some paper. Sir W Hewitt did well by dismissing them on the spot and sending them home to their papers branded – let us hope – for ever.
This is the yarn that we heard up here, but I have seen it in no paper yet. A large number of soldiers and others have come through from Khartoum – most miserable looking devils imaginable without arms. One native officer, apparently an exception to his race, had six wounds in his body. You seem to take a rosy coloured view of our position here, but I think it is a case of thus far shalt thou come and no further and as we are building forts and hutting the troops there seems little chance of onward movement down there ..."

He continues:

"... We too are beginning to loose faith in our material considering they are all of the same stock. Did I ever tell you that Sir E Wood had a meeting of C. O's just before we left Cairo, and we unanimously assessed the fighting value of the native officers at several points below that of the men, and even below zero! We were likewise of (the) opinion that the men would be more influenced by the native officers than by their English officers but as these are supposed to be State secrets you must not promulgate them too far. I see an Egyptian Batt[on] is going to Souakim. I think it would be a good thing to get a sporting rifle

Castle, near Sarras, 'Batu el Hazar', Belly of the Rocks, Lower Nile, May 1884.

out here – a small express, or something handy of that sort. This is a poor place for horses. My two 'Bob' and 'Coco' are at present very fit, but I am afraid the sand and heat will do them no good. Bob is a very good bay charger, and Coco a white pony ..."

The next letter from Donne was dated 25th May, but in the meantime he completed a black and white sketch dated 22nd April of the 'Interior of Officers' mat hut, at Kajbar', and a painting of the Castle near Serra, Lower Nile during the month of May.

The letter of the 25th May was in fact the last letter that has survived and the next entry is from the second journal. The letter addressed to his parents reads:

"... The position of affairs does not seem altered much. No one seems to know what is going to happen or how. A Campaigne (sic) in the south for (the) British would as seems to be recognised be madness at this time of year, but they seem to talk of an autumn campaigne (sic) when the expect (sic) of affairs may of course be very much altered. I think we shall remain much as we are now for the summer: more Cavalry Artillery and Infantry are on the way up to strengthen us here, and with outposts at Korosko[18] and Halfa[19] things ought to be pretty safe as far as Egypt is concerned. If British troops are going up we I think ought to go on to Dongola and hold that place against all comers, and secure the river. The heat here is very trying: yesterday it was over a 100 in the shade and more than 90 all night, and the continual mopping and perspiring is to say the least of it 'wearing', and I expect to be able to announce in my next letter the arrival of my old friend Mr Prickly Heat. I am all ready to move to Korosko when the steamers come back: I should have been off before now only I fancy they are stuck in the mud somewhere up stream. I have rec^d the invoice for the rifle and have sent directions for it to be forwarded on to me. I have been collecting empty glass bottles to improve our defences at Korosko when we get there. If you have not sent off 'Palms & Temples' never mind now, as I am pretty weary of temples, the heat disipates all romance ..."

There then followed several passages dealing with domestic matters before Donne returned to the events at the camp at Assouan:

> "... The midday gun has gone off, and the mail boat ought to be coming in, but I see nothing of it. The river is glassy and the whole aspect is that of ferocious heat – and we are not even in June yet. Col Duncan, our Chief, who knows Col Mosse, is nearly driven wild by the flies, and gets about 20 telegrams every day, each one usually cancelling or contradicting the last.
>
> There is to be no leave for Egyptian officers employed up here, so I for one shall not ask for any but sit tight with the grim satisfaction of feeling that at least no one up here can go before me. I was at Corfu this time last year. Wish I was there now. We shall have no Doctors at Korosko and I hope we shall not want them ..."

Donne's second journal commences in September 1884 and therefore there is a gap between his letter of 25th May and the commencement of the journal. During this time he and his battalion moved to Korosko. A number of watercolours were painted by Donne during the first six months of 1884. These were:
Camp of the Egyptian Troops at Assouan, under Colonel Duncan, March 1884.
In May he completed a painting of the "... Castle, near Sarras, 'Batn el Haqar', Lower Nile, May 1884 ...", and in June he painted a picture of his own tent at Korosko which he called "... 120° in the shade, 18th June 1884 ...".

The journal commenced on 7th September and reads:

September 1884

Wady Halfa.
The remainder of the 35th left on 7th September by train to Serra, where the Regt was put into boats to sail up the river to Dongola. They were thus quite the advanced party of the expedition. A few days after the 38th[20] came up and camped near the 3rd Batt[n] E. A. and several steam launches, which from their draught of water and delicate machinery seemed utterly unsuited for the work.
Sir E Wood has been trying his best to get the 3rd Batt[n] sent on, even part way to Dongolo, but our fate is quite in the hands of Lord W.[21] Our chances are improved as Sir E Wood has charge of the Lines of Communication and today the 13th Sep[t] we have actually sent ½ Coy on to Sarras[22] with Capt Eagar,[23] and the Batt[on] seems likely to follow.

10. I rode out to the Naval Camp & had a long day at the Cateract watching the 'Nasif el Kair' (sic) being hauled up the rapids. Everyone works hard, and there are thousands of Esneh & Dongola men to do the hauling, which is sometimes exciting work. 3 sailors were drowned in the rapids on the 12th.

26. Sarras. The Batt[on] was ordered on here on the 18th, and all the English and Native officers were glad to make a move southwards at last. By train 30 odd miles from Halfa[24] we camped on the river bank as usual and the surroundings are much more like that of the Rhine than the Nile. Eagar[25] preceeded us by a few days. There is an old Arab mud brick fort in an island mid-stream about 200 ft high, which looks very picturesque. When I was here in the beginning of May last it was all dry land. The Steamer Nasif el Khair (sic) came in today, victor after her hard struggles over the rapids, but with several holes in her bottom. She is now getting ready to face the Senneh Cataract, which is bad enough, about 10 miles on. The Mounted Inf(antr)y arr(ive)d at Halfa before we left, T. Thornton of 35th, Morse 56th and Livingstone 42nd[26] among them. They all left here today in Nuggas for Dongola – making a very pretty start of it. These Nuggas are fine boats with great cargo capacity, half decked over, and look very like walnut shells in the water, with one big mast and sail amidships. They hold 40 or 50 English soldiers and would take at least 60 Egyptians. We have orders (for) a Company (to be sent) on their way to Dal, about 70

miles or so south meanwhile the 3rd Batt^{on} is converted into a working party to construct a line of rail in the Ambakol direction.[27] They work well at it, and we shall have to camp further out on the desert before long, as part of the embankment is already constructed.

November 1884

10. Tangor[28] – Before we left Sarras the heads of the enemy that the Mudir of Dongola had vanquished in battle arrived. They were not a savory sight being impaled on spears and stuck up for view at the camp, needless to state the Sirdar would not send them on to Cairo. The Nasif el Khair got over the Senneh Cataract on the 24th September.

The 3rd Batt^{on} remained camped at Sarras all October, and meanwhile Sarras increased daily in importance and became the real starting point for the expedition and the railway was pushed on as fast as possible into the desert. Our men began to get rather tired of the monotonous work, when all of a sudden Lord Wolseley ordered a suspension for three weeks, and started himself for Dongola on the 28th October.

We were ordered about the same time to march southwards in detachments with 3 months supply (sic) to work at different stations on the Dongola route – principally for portage work. We got our rations completed by the 30th and I started for Absirat[29] on the 31st. It was a difficult job getting the boats ready. ------left with one Company for Ambako and Eagar was already at Akasheh."

Donne's journal finishes in 1884 at this point and does not resume until March 1885. There is however one letter dated 9th November 1884 which was written by Donne to his parents which amplified his brief notes in his journal for early November 1884:

"... As I am gradually moving southwards. Herewith a rough map of the section of the river from Senneh to Absarat[30] where I am going although at the present rate of progress I don't lay much faith on ever getting there. We are now at Tangor,[31] having been over a week getting here. The work is tedious and the Cataracts very difficult to get up – in fact this one looks now impossible and none of our ships got up yesterday. We took 3 days to get them over Ambigole. You will see I have still a long way to go to Absarat which is supposed to be flowing with milk and honey in comparison to this barren rock part. ...

... (part of the letter is missing) ... is lying near here, the crew being camped on a small cove which looks quite romantic. I was asked by the Graphic special[32] to send a drawing to the Graphic but have had no time as yet.

Two of our boats have been wrecked and there are plenty of other boats lost also. I am curious to see the 38th[33] come along in their boats: having pronounced them a practical failure. I wonder how they will get up these rapids! We live now on stores and a few sheep we have with us I have besides 8 cases of private stores and liquor, which will be a boon if they do not go to the bottom.

Our men are rationed for 3 months. I wonder what Parliament says to all this expense – I am almost out of books and coats which is a serious thing. If we get over Tangor I hope to get myself to Absarat sometime after the 20th. Address me 'Wady Halfa to be forwarded'.

        Donisthorpe A. Donne.

Tangor Cataract. Nov 9th 1884 ..."

Notes to Chapter Thirteen

1. He is referring to his elder sister Anna Jane Merifield Donne who was born in 1855.
2. Major General Charles George Gordon, CB., late Royal Engineers.
3. Lieutenant Colonel J. O. Vandeleur, Royal Sussex Regiment.
    Monthly Army List, April 1884.

4.   Lieutenant E. B. Eagar, The Northumberland Fusiliers.
      Monthly Army List, April 1884.
5.   Sioot, also spelt as Siout now known as Asyut.
6. . Edfou, now known as Idfu.
7.   Esneh, now known as Isna.
8.   Lieutenant Colonel F. Duncan, Royal Artillery.
      Monthly Army List, April 1884.
9.   Major General Sir Ralph Biddulph, KCMG, CB, late Royal Artillery.
      High Commissioner and Commander in Chief Cyprus.
      Monthly Army List, April 1884, page 31.
10.   Major P. D. Trotter, Princess Louise's (Argyll and Sutherland Highlanders).
      Monthly Army List, April 1884.
11.   Phyla also spelt Philae.
      The Public Schools Atlas
      by the Reverend G. Butler DD.
      Published by Longmans, Green & Co, 1894, Map 22a.
12.   Donne's younger brother Lieutenant Henry Richard Beadon Donne.
13.   See note 10.
14.   Donne refers to Khartoum.
15.   Korosko.
      Butler, op cit, map 22a.
16.   Donne refers to Wadi Halfa (Wady Halfa)
      Butler, op cit, map 22a.
17.   See note 5.
18.   See note 15.
19.   See note 16.
20.   Donne continued to refer to regiments by their old title, i.e. '38th' – The South
      Staffordshire Regiment.
21.   General Lord Wolseley, GCB., GCMG.
      Monthly Army List, April 1884.
22.   Sarras also spelt Serra.
      Butler, op cit, Map 22a.
23.   See Note 4.
24.   Donne refers to Wady Halfa.
      Butler, op cit, Map 22a.
25.   See Note 4.
26.   Lieutenant F. G. Todd-Thornton, Royal Sussex Regiment, Lieutenant A. T. Morse. Donne
      gives his regiment as being the '56th' whereas Morse was of the '50th' – the Queen's Own
      (Royal West Kent Regiment), Lieutenant P. J. C. Livingstone, The Black Watch (Royal
      Highlanders).
      Monthly Army List, April 1884.
27.   Ambakol – also spelt Ambukol.
      Butler, op cit, Map 22a.
28.   Tangor – also spelt Tanjur.
      History of the Sudan Campaign, Part II.
      by Colonel H. E. Colville CB, HMSO, 1889, Sketch Map.
29.   Absirat – also spelt Absarat.
      Colville, op cit, Sketch map.
30.   Donne's sketch map was unsuitable for reproduction.
      See map at page 144
31.   See Note 28.
32.   Donne had been invited to become a 'Special Correspondent' for the newspaper The
      Graphic.
33.   The South Staffordshire Regiment.

14   Egypt November 1884 to August 1885

DONNE'S FIRST entry in his journal is dated 3rd March 1885 but two letters pre-date this entry. The first was written on 14th January 1885 at Absarat and was addressed to his 'Aunts':

> "... Many thanks for your Xmas books and letters the former were a great god-send here, & I have been eagerly devouring the contents, as I had absolutely nothing to read. My Xmas mail arr(ive)d here from England only on the 12th January – a sort of Greek Xmas! (sic), and I was quite overwhelmed with letters books papers etc of a whole months collection which were welcome as water to a man in the wilderness. The expedition has now rolled on south or rather "rowed" I should say and I am left here with the sick in hospital like a waif with next to nothing to do.
>
> Bitterness of spirit has now passed away and I am only looking forward to a happy release from this monotony, which I fondly hope will come off about next April ..."

The next portion of the letter deals with family matters. The letter concludes with further comments on his life in Egypt:

> "... Lord Wolseley is expected to get to Shendy[1] tomorrow – suppose they will soon be fighting. I am not a lucky individual in that respect, but shall have more chance of a whole skin to enjoy myself in when I do get away into the world again. I shall go home like a steam engine to see what sport there is to be got out of the old Country whilst I am still young. I am getting quite antiquated and fat through this sort of life ..."

Donne concluded his letter with a postscript which reads:

> "... Another poor chap in the Egyptian Army has blown his brains out – a Col Inglefield. There seems quite a fatality! ..."[2]

Two days later Donne wrote to his parents, again from Absarat:

> "... I have so gorged myself in the last 3 days with all the books and papers you sent out, that I feel something like an over read pig. I am of course deeply indebted to everyone for such a feed, and I got such a heap all at once – a whole months collection in one mail that was quite like an embarras of riches (sic). I think I have received everything you sent out – they came on the 12th January so were rather late for Xmas, but that signifies little. 3 parcels of tabac, socks, almanacs, Figaro, novels, magazines, papers all made up a mail bag to myself. The Figaro is a splendid paper and its illustrations adorn the crimson lining of my marquee, and also the hospital tent. I have next to nothing to do now, so it is well to have something to occupy one's mind, and detach it from the somewhat uncharitable thoughts that sometimes crowd in. The whole expedition has now passed on and there is a dearth of life on the river. I am still detained here, as you perceive but expect to go to Kajbar before long. The advanced troops are supposed to be at Shendy[3] now, and I am only longing with a long long wish for the time when they will be returning. We have had to bury four poor fellows from this little station alone and I am afraid there is another who will not live. Is it not sad – a Col Inglefield of the E. A. has shot himself at Halfa ..."

The next portion of the letter deals with family matters and then Donne continues:

> "... I do not think the natives have any fell intentions against us – not even the bedaween (sic) tribes on this side of the river. At all events with a rifle one ought to be good enough for 6 of them any day. I have grown a beard and am very lazy, and have no troops here to look after. They have been building a water wheel for the last 6 weeks just outside my tent, and now the horrible machine is in working order and threatens one with its distracting noise. So have told the poor proprietor that unless he can make it work without noise that work it shall not. ... The weather is still delightful here – never any rain little or no cloud,

yet still it is a howling wilderness to live in and ones thoughts can only be directed to getting out of it ..."

Whilst Donne was in his camp at Absarat and the expedition was assembling at Shendi the Dervish army had surrounded Khartoum and early in the morning of January 26th, 1885, only ten days after Donne had written his letter home, the leader of the Dervish army, the Mahdi, gave orders for the final assault. At 3.30 a.m. the assault commenced and the Egyptian forces were quickly overrun and when the news of the attack was brought to General Gordon he rose dressed in his uniform, with tarbush and sword and went out on to the balcony of his quarters to confront the Dervishes with a revolver in his hand. A dervish at the foot of the staircase hurled a heavy spear at Gordon and this struck him in the chest. This broke the spell and the remainder of the attackers surged forward and quickly killed Gordon. Gordon was dead and Khartoum was then in the hands of the Mahdi.

Donne recommenced his journal on 3rd March, by which time, of course, Gordon was dead and the whole expedition for the relief of Khartoum had been a failure:

March 1885

3. "Above Handak.[4]

    After such a long pause it is always difficult to resume the thread of a Diary or Journal – but thats my failing, and I shall probably have lots of time now to make up lee way – all today has been an ugly blank, for to do anything but wrap one's head up in a blanket and smoke Virginian was impossible, except to a saint I have seldom experienced a more damnable plague than the sandflies have been: there is no stamping them out like one can flies but they attack one's face in a merciless way — natives and Englishmen alike, and Taha my Egyptian soldier servant was half wild with their bites. They seem to be very local – come and go suddenly: here they swarm but at Korti and Dongola there were none. The Egyptian Army has been doing fine work since I last wrote: I don't believe the English Army would be where they are now had it not been for the never failing help rendered at the Cataracts by our poor little Army who will of course get more kicks than praise when all is over. Most unexpected events have happened: the English army have passed on leaving us in the lurch to grumble over our hard luck and keep up their Communications for them".

(Donne then returns to 1884) –

1884

"I was several days at Tangor, and had great difficulty in getting the Nuggars and boats up the rapids. Our Nuggar was wrecked: the rest were hauled up by sheer force, and were the last sailing boats to pass up. It is a very nasty place with 3 gates – There is a grand view of the whole concern from the high Gebil behind which birds eyed, also plenty of crocodiles about and I had one or two good shots with my new rifle.

The road from Tangor to Akesheh is very rocky, and only by unloading the camels and mules and portaging, could we get the baggage over some of the places. The wind was good and (the) Nuggars sailed right up (the) Akesheh rapid without help so next day we passed on to Dal and Sarkamatto about 6 hours march across an 'Akaba' for the men – here I found Daubeney, S. Worsley, and other officers – & Col Henderson of the 60th[5] dangerously ill. Trotter sailed right up to Sakamatto (sic) in the aftnoon; but a few days afterwards the rapids became very formidable, impassable for large vessels, and the worst obstacle for Whaler boats in the whole Batnal Haggar. There is a 3 mile portage. Here I had another delay before I could get on to my destination having to wait the return of fresh Nuggars to put the men and stores in.

Donne, photographed in February 1885.   It is inscribed 'Stationed at Absarat on the Nile'.

Dal is finely situated with high hills to S. of it and a Pyramid hill off to the S. W., which acts as a guide for those crossing the long Akaba to Absarat.

I had no time to climb them but no doubt the view of the river would have been very extensive, and a good point to 'map' the district from. From Dal south the banks become much more fertile and populous, and that blasted dreary aspect of the Batn el Hagar disappears. Some of the larger houses are quite 'Baronial' in style and have a castleated appearance with high mud flanking towers.

They don't forget, either, to display their travelled wisdom, a love of China, by displaying a plate over the door, a sign that some of the family have travelled W(est) as far as Cairo, or may be to Europe.

Whilst I was here Lord Wolseley passed through to Halfa and Le Marchant came up from Dongola with a convoy. ...

The Capt(ain) had again wrecked himself in the rapids, and lost a good deal of his Company stores; the Nuggar had heeled over & sunk. I had to put him under arrest for disobeyance of orders, and took him on with me seeing that he marched all the way with the men.

At Amara there are the remains of a temple but I did not find it, I crossed over in the Nuggar to see a proposed station at Sikket El Abd,[6] the head of the road to the Oasis of Selimah, and continued the journey by boat to Say Island,[7] where after a long march the men arr(ive)d and camped.

Next day we cleared Say Island and got on as far as Souardeh[8] – a large village near which several hippopotami can often be seen and even fired at, one put his head out of the water once close to one of the whalers and there seem(s) no doubt whatever of their actual existence there.

On the W(est) bank above this village are some fine ruins of 2 temples – one with only one column apparently standing now, the other the ruins of Solib, which are the finest I have seen S(outh) of Phylae. It is but little known and apparently Pharaonic (sic) in date, the ruins look very fine standing on elevated ground hear the river. I had time on hand and made a sketch of them.

The next day took us down to the great bend in the river at Colehmatto,[9] from whence an Akaba on (the) W(est) bank leads in 3 days to Dongola. It was here that the Soudan Railway was to have been carried over the River but it has (never) been completed so far.

The river now ran due East so we had to tack along the bank for want of a fair wind, and we stopped near Agge for the night – the following day we towed up past the old fort of Tinareh[10] – an ancient Berberi stronghold with an apparent history, and there are many similar ones in the Sukoot[11] and Mahass[12] Districts. They all have great high flanking towers which look imposing in the distance. By flukes of wind we managed to get into our destination Absarat that night 23rd November – a place that I shall have reason to recollect as having afforded me a two months residence of sometimes amusing and exciting and sometimes highly monotonous existence.

The next day 24th (November 1884), the Company pitched camp and I rested once more in my magnificent red pavilion, the admiration, not to say the envy, of the whole line of communication and all passers by.

I was appointed Station Commandant of Absarat and whilst holding that appointment, the whole expeditionary force passed up – either in whalers on the river or by camel route on shore – and not till the end of January (1885) was I relieved of my duties there.

I entertained heaps of those passing up to the front, some old friends and many new ones. In December it was found necessary to form a hospital & Dr Boyd made his appearance. Poor Eagar made away with himself at Kajbar on 27th Nov[br].[13] Col Grant[14] happened to be there at the time of the disaster, but what actually prompted him to shoot himself will I imagine remain one of those strange mysteries that often perplex men, but certain it is that his loss to the Batt[on] was much felt, for he was a hardworking officer and was apparently suffering from some melancholia at the time. But he had a strange dislike of the

Egyptians which often caused us to disagree – when I arrived at Kajbar, he was already buried. Gen[l] Earle[15] since killed in action arrived with St Aubyn next day from Dongola and put the station straight under Barrow of the 9th Br" (sic).[16]

Major-General W. Earle commanded the River Column and had been given, by Lieutenant General Sir Garnet Wolseley, Colonel Henry Brackenbury as his second-in-command and under this leadership the River Column continued to advance under Wolseley's orders. On 10th February a squadron of the 19th Hussars which had been scouting along the left bank encountered an Arab force which was holding a line of hillocks. As the main column rounded the eastern end of the ridge the enemy opened fire and two or three men were hit. After a short advance the General halted the column under cover and despatched a company of the South Staffordshire Regiment to occupy the spur and another company to line the rocks on the left of the advance and so keep down the fire from Jebel Kirbekan. The column was then advanced about 300 yards over a spur into a narrow valley bounded by rocky ridges leaving a company of the South Staffordshire Regiment in occupation of the spur to keep down the fire from the summit of Jebel Kirbekan. However the fire increased and Earle ordered Lieutenant Colonel P. H. Eyre, Commanding the South Staffordshire Regiment to take two companies and endeavour to storm the ridge by its western shoulder. These companies were exposed to such heavy fire from the summit and from hillocks to the south that, after climbing about one-third of the way up the shoulder, they were forced to take cover under a cluster of rocks. It was whilst in this position that Lieutenant Colonel Eyre was critically wounded.

During this time two companies of the Black Watch were moved to some high ground to the right front and from there could see some of the enemy making their way to the river about 400 yards away and escaping by swimming across. General Earle ordered them to move to the bank and prevent the enemy from crossing. At the same time three remaining companies of the South Staffordshire Regiment, and four companies of the Black Watch, under command of Lieutenant Colonel W Green were ordered to advance and swing round to their left so as to face four koppies which were held by a strong force of riflemen. General Earle then advanced the two companies of the Black Watch which had been on the extreme right. The move enabled the river bank to be cleared and at the same time the main force were ordered to advance and clear the hillocks until they attained a position on the rocks about 400 yards distant from them, the intervening ground, being open, was swept by enemy rifle fire. The two right companies of the Black Watch, supported by a company of the South Staffordshire Regiment, successfully stormed the hillock nearest the river and having taken it were able to bring flanking fire on the main enemy position who showed no sign of abandoning the hill. As General Earle was about to give the order to assault the main position a body of spearmen charged down the hill towards the nearest company of the Black Watch, which under command of Lieutenant Colonel Green was advanced to the left front. The Arab spearmen were forced to retreat but not before the Black Watch had received a number of casualties including the death of Lieutenant Colonel R. C. Coveny. The order was then given to charge, the troops on the western hillock also being ordered to advance simultaneously with a frontal assault.

With bagpipes playing the Highlanders advanced at a steady double over the open ground and took the bases of the two rocky pyramids and then continued advancing by scrambling up the rock strewn slopes. A desperate stand was made by some of the enemy on the summits of koppies and, at the moment of victory for the British, General Earle was killed. His death was described by his second-in-command, Colonel Henry

Brackenbury, as follows "... The assault was over, and the two main koppies were in our hands; the troops were searching the sconces and holes among the rocks; and there was, as there must always be after such an effort, some need to collect them and form them up for fresh work. Between the crest of the two main koppies there was a depression forming a small flat plateau, on which was built a stone hut some 10 feet square with a thatched roof. General Earle was engaged in forming up the men in ranks on this plateau, not more than 10 yards from this hut, when a sergeant of the Black Watch said 'There are a lot of men in that, and they have just shot one of our men'.

General Earle ordered the roof to be set on fire ... our men had set the roof on fire, and my attention was attracted for a moment by seeing a native, who rushed out from the side door of the hut, bayoneted by one of our men. As I turned my head back towards the General, I saw him fall, shot through the head from a small square window in the hut, close to which he had approached. He lived only a few minutes, tended to the last by his Aide-de-Camp, Lieutenant (J. T.) St Aubyn (Grenadier Guards), and by the Senior Medical Officer, Surgeon-Major (C. H.) Harvey ..."

The command of the River Column then devolved upon General Brackenbury and the final assault of Jebel Kirbekan took place at 12.30 p.m.

At sunset the bodies of Major-General Earle and Lieutenant Colonels Eyre and Coveny were buried "... side by side at the foot of a solitary palm tree on the river bank ..."

Donne makes no further comment on the action at Kirbekan, nor does he made any further comment on the death of General Earle. His journal continues:

"I rode back to Absarat on the 28th Nov(emb)er stopping a night at the large village of Dulgo on the way. Opposite which are the remains of an ancient town and Temple, now known as Sayseh. I crossed the river to see them and found only 3 columns standing and these very knocked about, and apparently used as a quarry. I expect Sayseh is about the same antiquity as Solab. My old friend Bent of the 38th[17] passed in his whaler on the 30th and sent him on his way rejoicing with a bottle of ale. Troops now began passing pretty thick, and there were often 5 or 600 Camels in camp, and it was with the greatest difficulty we could sometimes ration them all. I was seldom a day without guests who came to feed or sleep. Bridge of (the) 38th came in suffering from dysentry,[18] and Verner of (the) Rifles[19] apparently on a sporting trip. Baker and Woodhouse were also frequent visitors. Byng & Rodney of (the) Heavy Camel C.[20] dined on (the) 9th. Col Forster of (the) 46th arr(ive)d (on the) 12th also Col Blundell District Com[dant] who took up his quarters at Absarat.[21] Gordon of Cyprus [22] passed and dined & slept on the 18th for the last time, poor chap, as he was lost in the Bayuda desert, and never again heard of. On the 15th Carmichael of the 5th Lancers[23] dined: he was killed at Abu Clea: Sharpe, 35th,[24] passed through (on the) same day with whalers. On the 21st Dec(ember) the Egyptian Corps passed, and we had quite a Bim-bashi's dinner with Woodhouse, Marriott, Carter and self. Poor Guthrie RA[25] also passed the same day, he always reminds me of Malta. He was also numbered amongst those who 'remained' at Abu Clea, and as I heard, died in great agony from blood poisoning. Heaps of others also passed up amongst them Col Primrose, The Vienna Attache[26] who was Com[dant] at Korti, and died at Abu Fabmah afterwards in April. Then everyone passed on. Work became less, and things began to assume a decided air of monotony. I had tried hyena and wolf shooting but failed. I had discovered all their haunts and hiding places in the hills now. Crockodile (sic) shooting was also a failure. The hospital of 20 beds very soon filled up from the whalers and convoys, and I buried four men, also one man of Sussex was picked up drowned a few miles north.

Abby RN and Boyd[27] made up the Xmas dinner which was not at all bad under the circumstances. The Christmas batch of papers and books did not arrive until ages afterwards, and the time soon slipped away to the (new) year, which was born without apparent difference coming over our lives ..."

Donne thus concluded his notes in his journal covering the last seven weeks of 1884. He then moved on to 1885 but only recorded a few entries for that year:

1885

"Col Blundell, District Com^{dant} [28] left for Dongola. There was certainly no manner of work for him to do at Absarat, and the Sirdar, Sir E Wood also arr(ive)d here on the 1st Janaury with a large staff and following travelling in the usual luxurious fashion of Generals. I gave him my tent for dinner whence for me I had a most sumptuous repast. This party left at daybreak the 2nd for Korti. The 50th & 18th[29] passed soon after in whalers, completing the whaler convoy ..."

On the 29 March 1885 Donne wrote home to his Mother giving details of his experiences at camp:

"Debbeh.
Here I am at Debbeh, you will perceive – the real place to spend a happy summer in, but for how long a period my somewhat sepulchral quips will date from here is as uncertain as anything else. March is waining fast and we have already a smart crack of heat, which makes all realise what the coming agony is to be with only water to wash it down with – but better that than nothing! Yesterday in the tents the glass went to 116° and (the) day before was 110°, so one is beginning to pour a little. The dried bricks baked in the sun for a few hours, and were ready to build with! I came up the river in whaler boat from Dongola in 5 days with my Egyptians without mishap: they tracked and rowed very well, but it was hot work baking all day in the sun when there was no wind. My men are now employed building huts for Sir E Wood & staff by day and on picquet duty at night. Sir E. W. is expected here tomorrow and is to command the whole of the Nile Column from here. The English troops now here will, I understand, be withdrawn, so I shall be left alone in my glory with no other Egyptians nearer than Dongola. Sir E. W. you know has quitted the E. A. and Grenfell[30] reigns in his stead. Sir O Lanyon and Kitchener[31] are now here on

The interior of an Officer's mat hut, Kajbar, 22 April 1884.

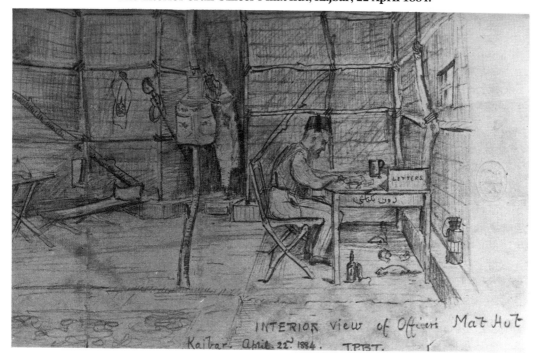

Wood's staff; if I remain I suppose I shall be Commandant.

We have 2 forts, 1 with 250 Bachi Bazouks of the Mudirs; the other for the English (man), but no one expects any of the Mahdi's people to come thus far, but precautions are necessary as the Darfur & Kordofan roads come in here. In a fit of unusual generosity I sent you off a roll of sundry sketches – in various stages of completion; none of them finished: I want you to keep the temple ones, as they were more or less of a series. The beautiful ruins of Solib are there portrayed, and the Absarat sketch of my tent is for you, long since promised. If Anna[32] likes to make use of the other drawings for publication, such as Tangur,[33] Tinareh, Sarras or even the Absarat one, or Solib, you can do so, but they would be rather late in the market, and if not published please keep them. None of those in particular have been in the papers. Now then for War news. Reuters telegrams make us all jump, as England seems to have the old Jingo spirit again revived, and is ready we are all glad to see, to shew a bold front to Russian designs. It seems a touch and go now, and the Naval people are going back to their ships. I hope this will be a Turkish alliance, and if so perhaps a Turkish Contingent would become a reality, and I should try for that. In any case war with Russia will draw all troops north out of this which sounds comforting ...”

The remainder of the letter dealt with family matters. Donne produced a black and white sketch of an officer's mat hut at Kajbar which was dated 22nd April 1885. He also painted two water colours during this period of the campaign, these being:

The Nile expedition, 1885, and

The Nile expedition – conveying stores to the front along the Abu Fakmak - Dongola Reach, 1885.

The last entry in his second journal reads:

“... Kajbar. 16.4.85.   Have just returned from Debbeh ...”

10th Sudanese Battalion going down river.

Unfinished sketches by Donne – Dongola, April 1885.

Unfinished sketch by Donne – Nile craft, 1885.

Unfinished sketch by Donne entitled 'Two more of the guns'.

With the conclusion of the second, and very short journal the remainder of the Donne story can only be told from his letters that have survived. The next letter was written from Absarat and dated 3rd July 1885 and was addressed to his Mother:

"... As there is an English mail leaving tonight, just a few lines to acknowledge yours and Fathers letters from Cheltenham where you have been no doubt relaxing. There has been a lull in the evacuation programme – why I know not, and a lot of counter ordering, but the wheel has begun to go the right way again today, and Boyd and the Hospital have disappeared North after having been here about 7 months. But this is the 3rd July, and no sign of my being uprooted – in fact it appears the last lot have not yet left Dongola. So it is as doubtful as ever when I shall be off, and even more so off to England.

It is impossible to put a date on anything, so dont let my movements influence any of yours. I have not yet received either of the 2 parcels, perhaps they are delaying them at Halfa,[34] the post is naturally erratic now ...

Like most of the other stations, we have had our little fire here – the Egyptians were burnt out, and most of their kit with them, and the safety of the rest of the camp was simply owing to there being not a breath of air at the time. The illumination was fine, and the palm trees blazed up like rockets. The ammunition had a wonderful escape. There were 6 boxes with 3,600 rounds in the fire, but although the wood casing was entirely burnt off 4 of them, the contents did not explode! Had I known they were in the fire at the time I should not have been so keen on going near it! The heat that these huts develop when on fire is so intense that it is impossible to save anything.

My CO Trotter[35] is still at Kajbar. You need not fear the result of my having little fights with him, he is too well known along the line to be able to do much harm now. The business I alluded to is settled – I wrote him a letter from here charging him straight with what amounted to a dishonest report, and as he has not answered I presume he has "swallowed the pill" which was all I wanted. Gen Grenfell[36] has asked me to re-engage in the E. A. so I said I would provided leave was forthcoming, and that I could pass my English exams, which is impossible down here. So I suppose Egypt will be my H^{d}Q^{trs} for a year or so more. I am getting very anxious about my promotion – as steps are going, and I have as yet passed neither exam for promotion, and they are both very stiff. I can only pray that the 2 officers above me have passed, and stave off the evil day a bit.

We have had some terrible hot days – which quite wear one out, and as I have very little to do here, it is a melancholy existence. All though otherwise well, I feel exceedingly weak and incapable of much action. I hope it will not last more than 10 days longer, as I hear Dongola may be evacuated today, and streams of convoy boats are going down with sick and stores. A fine young Cr Sergt of the 50th[37] died here yesterday on his way down of enteric. The number of officers who have died (during) this campaign is extraordinary, and I regret none more than poor Lt Col Gordon of the 93rd[38] who died at Suez. He was Commissioner in Cyprus and did me many good turns and such a 1st class soldier.

I have taken to living in (a) tent again in preference to a hut which is hot and stuffy, and where animals of all sorts abound. Scorpions become more frequent as the Nile rises. We have had 3 sand storms lately, from the South. The Nile rises slowly: it has risen in all 220 centimeters.

... There is now absolutely no such thing as fruit or vegetable to be got here. Living on rations is not condusive to health. Plunge me suddenly into London, and I should buy up all your fruit shops – and have soles for breakfast ..."

Donne concludes this letter with a postscript:

"... Mrs Eagar was kind enough to send me a small supply of paints the other day – kind was it not but if I had half-a-dozen boxes I don't think I should ever paint this river again ..."

The final letter surviving from 1885 is the one written to his Mother in August of that year giving news of his impending leave:

"... Another scrap from your wandering Jew – just to tell you that in about a week I hope to be off to Cairo. I have got my relief here, and am only waiting the result of a Court to get away. I might have remained here as O.C. Egypt[n] Troops – which I am now, but nothing was good enough but leave – which I forced on the General. He wrote and told me "I did not know you were keen on leave", so I wired him "I feel played out and leave a necessity" and also have written to say that I was so keen on getting away that I intended to get leave "at any sacrifice". I was very much annoyed at the way he had rounded on me – I am commanding a small army here – Camel Corps Artillery and my own regt – 1000 men – but hope to hand over to Major Surtees, Coldstream Guards,[39] a very nice fellow, as soon as possible. So when once I get started you will find this strange harum scarum creature routing you out in London Town. They are *not* going to give us a medal after all, so I only get a bar on the old one inscribed "Nile 1884-5" and, as I believe the 4th (Class) Osmanich from the Sultan. Better than nothing! ..."

The letter concluded with comments on various family events.

Notes to Chapter Fourteen

1.   Shendy – also spelt Shendi.
     History of the Sudan Campaign, Part II.
     by Colonel H. E. Colville, CB.
     HMSO, 1889, Sketch Map.
2.   Major L. E. C. Inglefield, Leinster Regiment. Died at Wady Halfa, Upper Egypt 5 January 1885.
     Monthly Army List, February 1885, page 793.
3.   See note 1.

4.   Handak – also spelt Khandak.
     Colville, op cit, Sketch map.
5.   Donne continued to refer to regiments by their old pre-1881 title, i.e. '60th' refers to The
     King's Royal Rifle Corps.
6.   Sikket El Abd – also spelt Sakyet el abd.
     Colville, op cit, Sketch map.
7.   Say Island – also spelt Sai Island.
     Ibid.
8.   Souardeh – also spelt Sauarda.
     Ibid.
9.   Colehmatto – also spelt Koyeh Matto.
     Ibid.
10. Tinareh – also spelt Tinari.
     Ibid.
11. Sukkkot is shown on the Sketch map of The Nile between 2nd and 3rd Cataracts.
     Colville, op cit, Insert on Sketch map.
12. Mahass is shown on the Sketch map of The Nile between 2nd and 3rd Cataracts.
     Colville, op cit, Insert on Sketch map.
13. Lieutenant E. B. Eagar, The Northumberland Fusiliers,
     Monthly Army List, 1884.
14. Colonel R. Grant, Royal Engineers,
     Commanding Royal Engineers, on the Staff.
     Monthly Army List, 1885.
15. Major General W. Earle CB, CSI.
     Monthly Army List, April 1884, 34a.
16. Major S. D. Barrow, Bengal Staff Corps.
     The Campaign of 1882 in Egypt,
     by Colonel J. F. Maurice,
     Reprinted by J. B. Hayward, 1973, page 127.
17. Captain W. H. M. Bent, The South Staffordshire Regiment.
     Monthly Army List, April 1884, 417.
18. Lieutenant W. C. Bridge, The South Staffordshire Regiment,
     Monthly Army List, April 1884, 418.
19   Captain W. W. C. Verner, The Rifle Brigade (Prince Consort's Own),
     Monthly Army List, April 1884, 568.
20. Major the Hon C. C. G. Byng,
     1st Life Guards serving with the Heavy Camel Regiment.
     Quarterly Army List, 31 March 1887, page 1233.
     Lieutenant Lord Rodney, serving with the Heavy Camel Regt. With the Camel Corps up the
     Nile, by Count Gleichen.
     Reprinted by E. P. Publishing Ltd, 1975.
21. Colonel H. B. H. Blundell.
     History of the Sudan Campaign, Part I.
     by Colonel H. E. Colville, HMSO, 1889, page 238.
22. Captain W. H. Gordon, The Royal Welsh Fusiliers.
     Monthly Army List, April 1884, 359.
23. Major L. M. Carmichael, 5th (Royal Irish) Lancers,
     Monthly Army List, April 1884, 90,
24. Lieutenant R. G. A. Sharp, Royal Sussex Regiment,
     Monthly Army List, April 1884, 410.
25. Lieutenant J. D. Guthrie, Royal Artillery.
     Monthly Army List, April 1884, 152.
26. Colonel The Hon E. H. Primrose, Grenadier Guards.
     Monthly Army List, April 1884, 257 and 34.

27.   Surgeon T. Boyd. In charge of the Field Hospital at Absarat.
       Quarterly Army List, 31 March 1887, page 1224.
28.   See note 21.
29.   Donne is referring to the following regiments:
       18th – The Royal Irish Regiment.
       50th – The Queen's Own (Royal West Kent Regiment).
30.   Brigadier General F. W. Grenfell.
       Monthly Army List, April 1885, 75b.
31.   Colonel Sir W. O. Lanyon, KCMG, CB,
       and Brevet Major H. H. Kitchener, Royal Engineers.
       Monthly Army List, April 1884, page 34a.
32.   Anna Jane Merifield Donne, Donne's elder sister born 1855.
33.   Tangur – also spelt Tanjur.
       Colville, op cit, Sketch map.
34.   Halfa – Donne is referring to Wady Halfa.
       Colville, op cit, Sketch map.
35.   Major P. D. Trotter, Princess Louise's (Argyll and Sutherland Highlanders).
       Monthly Army List, April 1885, 545.
36.   See note 30.
37.   50th Regiment – The Queen's Own (Royal West Kent Regiment).
38.   Brevet Lieutenant Colonel R. W. T. Gordon,
       Prince Louise's (Argyll and Sutherland Highlands).
       Monthly Army List, April 1885, 545.
39.   Surtees is shown in the Monthly Army List, April 1885 as 'Lieutenant H. C. Surtees',
       Coldstream Guards.

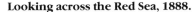

Looking across the Red Sea, 1888.

Above: Donne in his Egyptian Army uniform. The photographs, dated November 1885, were taken at the 'Alexander Bassano Studio, 25 Old Bond Street, London W'.

Left: A further study from the Alexander Bassano studio, dated 'Xmas 1885'.

Below: Donne's 1866 examination – special certficate of proficiency, 'distinguished in military law'.

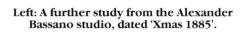

EXAMINATION FOR PROMOTION.

SPECIAL CERTIFICATE.

15   Suakin and Toski

DONNE EVENTUALLY managed to obtain leave and arrived in England during the latter part of 1885. There is no record of his movements during this time but it was during this period of leave that he became engaged to Cecil Frances Grace Hughes who was the younger daughter of the Reverend Robert Edgar Hughes and the Granddaughter of Sir Thomas Collingwood Hughes, 8th Baronet of East Burgholt Lodge, Manningtree, Suffolk.

It was during this leave that Donne took his promotion examination in London in January 1886 and on the 15th February he received a letter from the Military Education Division, War Office, addressed to him at the Egyptian Army, War Office, Cairo advising him that he had passed and "... will be recorded as qualified for promotion to the rank of Major ...". He was also sent a 'Special Certificate' for attaining a "... higher standard of proficiency entitling him to a Special Certificate & was 'distinguished' in Military Law ...".

Donne returned to Egypt after taking his promotion examination and had rejoined the Egyptian Army. In August 1886 he was stationed at Suakin[1] and wrote to his mother and this is the only letter that has survived covering the period between his return from England in January 1886 and his return to England for his marriage later that year. The letter reads:

"Sauakin.   12th August 1886.

I must write you a few (lines) either on business or pleasure to acknowledge your last letters, which arrived yesterday. So you did get my letters after all which I had thought lost. Thank Eva for her letter and the Father for his business one – which I must answer in this. So you must retail out what is necessary.

You seem (to be) having a very charming time in the Alps. Yes I do wish I could have a little change from this monotony, but I have got into the way of getting leave at the wrong season I fear, however it is for Cecil's sake that I am coming home in the autumn if I can, otherwise I should wait till next summer. Any change will do one good after a summer here, which just now is fairly trying and every one howling with prickly heat. I have got it worse than I ever had it in my life and the only remedy is to grin and bear it. It also deprives one of the pleasure of drinking – our only delight for every drop one swallows aggravates the nuisance. However in other respects we are most fortunate, for the place is wonderfully free of insects, not even flies or mosquitos to disturb one. I think it is too hot for them! We have just had a heavy storm of wind and rain – the first since I came to Sauakin – blowing down tents, huts and all and flooding the men out, but it cooled the air a little and reduced the climate a bit. I am still in command here, and shall be till the 19th, when probably some one will come down. So I shall have had a good spin of it, and if I can get the extra pay, better still. When do you intend going home? I dare say you will be able to give me a shake down again. I hope to go up to Cairo in October if I can. I have written to Gen[l] Grenfell to that effect ..."

The next section of the letter concerns family financial matters and is concluded by Donne giving his mother advice on the mail situation:

"... I have so little time to write, and as we get such little notice before the mails go out ...".

Donne obviously obtained leave in October as he had planned as on 8th November he married Cecil Frances Grace Hughes at St Mary Abbotts Church, Kensington. Donne was soon separated from his wife and was back on duty with the Egyptian Army in December 1886.

He was now under contract to the Government of H.H. the Khedive of Egypt for service with the Egyptian Army. The contracts were renewed annually and the three contracts that are with the Donne papers cover the periods 1st December 1886 to 9th August 1887; 9th August 1887 to 31st December 1887 and from 1st January 1888 to 9th August 1889. All three were between "... Major General Sir F. Grenfell, K.C.B., Sirdar ..." and "Captain B. D. A. Donne, Sussex Regt".

It was during 1887 that Donne was appointed Commandant of a newly formed 10th Sudanese Battalion which he had raised at Luxor. Little is recorded in the Donne papers of the work entailed in the formation and the training of the new battalion but in November the Battalion embarked for Suakin. There is a report dated 6 November 1887 complimenting Donne on the excellence of his unit and the report reads:

"... I wish to bring to the notice of the Sirdar[2] the excellent manner in which the 10th Batt[n] embarked for service.

For three days before their departure the Batt[n] had not a single prisoner.

The steamer to remove the Batt[n] arrived at about 8.30 am. the camels of the camel corps the water tanks (full) and baggage were at once embarked and at 1 pm. the men of the 10th Batt[n] paraded in marching order and were marched to Quarantine Island where they were embarked by Companies in the most orderly manner the steamer sailed at 3 p.m.

I said a few words to the men on parade telling them how satisfied I was with their good service and behaviour here, that I would look after their families during their absence and also that I hoped they would soon return.

On board the ship before leaving I asked the men if any of them wished to tell me anything but beyond two men giving me money for their families the remainder said they were quite happy and only wished me to accept their compliments.

The women of the battalion although they suffered at the departure of their husbands behaved in the most orderly way throughout.

Everyone present remarked that it was the most orderly embarkation of troops they had seen. I think the officers and men of the Batt[n] deserve great praise and I should be much obliged if the Sirdar would express to the Battalion his approval.

(Signed) H. H. Kitchener.[3]

6.11.87. ..."

The following notes were added to the document:

"... A.G.

Please send this letter to Donne Bey and tell him to inform his Batt of the Sirdars complete satisfaction, both at this creditable embarkation & subsequent march from Kosseir to Keneh.

The short period taken – and the excellent condition of the men on arrival reflects great credit on him and his officers – & shows the good state of discipline prevailing in the corps.

(Signed) F. Grenfell MG.
Sirdar.[4]

22 Nov 87.

OC 10th Batt E. A.

Memo of Sirdar and letter of O.C. Eg Troops Suakin passed for your information and action.
            By Order.

Henry Hallam Parr.   A.G.

22.11.87
W.O. Cairo ...[5]"

Donne led his battalion on another march crossing from the Nile to the Red Sea when the 10th Battalion was required to reinforce the garrison at Suakin during the period that it was under attack by the dervish forces led by Osman Digna. The relief of Suakin

Captain B. D. A. Donne's contract to serve in the Egyptian Army as Kaima Kaw (1st Commandant) from 1st January 1888 to 9th January 1889.

finally came with the Battle of Gemaizah which took place on 20 December 1888 and resulted in the defeat of the forces lead by Osman Digna. The force opposing the Dervish Army was a combined British and Egyptian army made up of the 20th Hussars, 24 Company Royal Engineers (only seventeen members took part in this action), 2nd Battalion, The King's Own Borderers and 1st Battalion The Welsh Regiment of the British Army,[6] and from the Egyptian Army the 9th, 10th, 11th and 12th Sudanese Battalions, and the 3rd and 4th Battalions Egyptian Army. The 1st Brigade, Egyptian Army was commanded by Colonel H. H. Kitchener, and although the Battle commenced at 6 a.m. with a vigorous artillery fire the actual advance did not begin until 7.30 a.m. and the enemy were in complete retreat by 8 a.m.

It was estimated that some 500 of the enemy were killed and the loss of the combined British and Egyptian force only amounted to six killed and two officers and forty-four wounded.[7] The complete account of the battle is given in the work "Mahdiism and the Egyptian Sudan" by Major F. R. Wingate.[8] Donne received a further bar to his Egyptian Medal for 'Gemaizah 1888', was 'Mentioned In Despatches' on 24 December 1888 and was given a Brevet rank of Major.[9]

Donne continued to serve with the 10th Sudanese Battalion after the action of 1888 and the first surviving letter leading up to the Nile battles of 1889 is dated 16th June 1889 and was written to his Father from Wady Halfa. The letter reads:

"... In a few days time we are actually going to assume the offensive and at any rate long before you get this the results will be noised abroad, if results there are. Col Wodehouse[10] has got permission at last to try and destroy the Dervish position at Sarras, where they raid from, before they are reinforced by the new Emir Wad (en) Negoumi.[11] So we are going to cross the river to the west bank, and march on Sarras – 2½ days march from here across the sandy desert skirting the Cataracts. The force we are taking is to consist of all we can spare, (leaving 1000 men in garrison).

3rd Batt[n]		500
9th "	Soudanese	550
10th "	"	550
13th "	"	550
Cavalry		200
Artillery		4 guns.

Allowing for leaving or dropping men to keep our lines clear 1500 men will probably be the assaulting force. The enemy are said to be entrenched in a 'bourg' so if they stand as they are pretty sure to do, it will be a bigger business than Suakin, and there may be obstinate fighting. Of this force I shall be the 3rd senior officer present.

17th June.   If this business comes off you will hear of it before you get this. I think our chief enemy will be the sun as there is no shade, and we shall be quite 5 days about the march. Today however there is a diversion in the direction as the telegraph is cut between this and Korosko, so perhaps there is a raid down there. At any rate if accidents should happen to me, I am sure you will know how to impart it to Cecil. My telegraph address is to you.

Leave does not seem any clearer, but if this expedition comes off I shall be able to get away directly afterwards. I am glad Cecil is having a quiet time in Ireland and she seems very happy there.

It is fairly hot here, but not so bad as Assouan, and we hope the river is really on the rise now but it is awfully low still ..."

Donne then discussed a number of family matters before continuing with his final comments to his Father which were dealing with his contact addresses:

"... If you should have reason to write or wire to Egypt concerning me "Grenfell Cairo" will be your best address. "Donne Wady Halfa" will reach me, or "Hudood Wady Halfa" is the official wire of the Commanding Officer up here ..."

The next letter was from Donne to his wife in England which was written after the battle of Argin which was on 2nd July 1889. The letter was undated but was written before the Battle of Toski on 3rd August 1889. The letter gives details of the preparation for the battle:

"... Since mine of the 20th to you at Seaton nothing has changed. There seems to be a sort of inaction on both sides – both waiting for reinforcements. Today we have captured and killed fewer than any day. I dont understand our inaction for I should like to worry them much more. I wrote to my father on the 22nd, but as it was hurriedly posted I had no time to send you one too. My indisposition soon passed off. I went up that p.m. to view the enemy's camp or Dehm, as they call it, and had a lovely shot with my small rifle at their patrol which came down. Negoumi's clerk deserted and (has) given us an accurate account of their numbers. We know now that they left Dongola or Sarras with six thousand fighting men and now have 2,800 left. So 3000 are either killed or deserted. The women and children are numberless ... perhaps three or four thousand more, and their camp still looks enormous. Negoumi does not pretend to notice his losses! He left Sarras with 520 horses ... now 132 are left, and they have from three to four hundred riflemen.
The Sirdar, Kitchener, Settle and (the) H^{d}Q^{tr} staff are living in our house at Assouan. I am glad the Sirdar is there. I spend part of my time on board (the) steamer here, and always eat and sleep on shore ..."

After a few passages of personal comment to his wife, Donne continues with his narrative of local events:

"... 25th (July). Perhaps today you will be starting for England ... Such a nice looking black deserter has come in to us – his brother is in the Battalion. He is genuinely glad to be rid of the Dervishes, and for trying to desert after Arghin, they gave him 500 courbeg stripes. His back was still quite raw. Ngoumi (sic) exercises much terrorism over his people and keeps them from deserting.
The other Emir, Makeen el Nur, has already passed north of Halfa, and I expect will join Ngoumi today or tomorrow. He is said to have a purely fighting force with him, some say 700, others even 1500 men, with 100 camels and 200 horses. I expect Ngoumi will advance when he receives this reinforcement, and he will have an imposing force if he keeps them together, but there is an IF!
    Last night a party of men and women came down for dates, and two women were killed. These poor wretches suffer more than the men. We reckon that their force is now reduced by 3000 people; yet it seems to make little difference to them. There is no doubt that Ngoumi started with:

Fighting men	5780
Women, children and slaves	6000
	11780

It is not quite clear what they intend to do with the latter when they advance. We are getting up 20,000 sandbags from Cairo.

(The letter then deals with personal comments for his wife).

26th. This morning I hear the mail will not be in today – perhaps tomorrow. Kitchener is coming up to look round, which will make Wodehouse quite jealous. News says the enemy intends pushing north at once, now that they have been reinforced. If so it will I hope bring matters to some climax, as he will be further than ever from supplies, and nothing to eat in front, unless he can attack and defeat us, or get command of the river.
    Just got a telegram from Sir Edwin Arnold of (the) Daily Telegraph, asking if I will wire news to that paper, so I sent off a telegram today, but stupidly made a mistake! so do not much fancy doing amateur 'special'! They want news of (the) impending battle – how

blood-thirsty they are at home. I hope it wont be a very big battle, if there is one, for Arghin was quite enough for my nerves for one day, or for a whole year.

27th July. I have just written an article on 'The Invasion of Egypt' to Sir Edwin Arnold to see if he likes to publish it in his Daily Telegraph, but probably by the time it reaches England it will be valueless. If published I asked him to send you a copy at Seaton. ...[12] Wodehouse has given the gun we captured at Arghin to the Regiment; it is a brass cannon in good condition, one wheel a little broken. It has Ismail's name on it and was made in 1873. We are much longing for a post. Kitchener[13] will probably bring letters this evening.

28th. Your – letters have come – with Kitchener. ...

The Dervishes are moving north this a.m. Beech[14] killed six with his cavalry and Gordon[15] got seven more, so we keep up our average with little or no loss to ourselves. I expect we shall soon be moving after them ..."

Donne concluded his letter on the 28th July and closed with personal comments to his wife who was, at that time, still living in Ireland and had not moved to Seaton as he had expected.

Donne's next letter was written on the day before the Battle of Toski on 3rd August. The letter gives a graphic description of the area before the battle. (After opening the letter with personal comments to his wife he recounts the activities since his last letter of 28th July):

"... Sent from Toshki (sic) Aug 2nd, 1889.

Yesterday I rode out to see the deserted camp or Dehm of the enemy, it was a long ride, and the sight when we arrived an extraordinary one. There were over sixty dead lying about, and several still living, having been left behind to die of hunger and thirst; they were a piteous sight as you can imagine. Some had crawled a short distance towards the river and then died, and around the Djem (sic) were from two to 300 graves. This will give you some idea of the frightful mortality amongst this invading horde. They have been there 18 days. The whole plain was strewn thick with abandoned debris, hundreds of spears, many rifles, large drums, saddles, and every description of article; it was something like a battlefield. Many of the miserable creatures who came in here are starving; in two days we got several hundreds, beside more than 160 fighting men killed or captured. They had been eating the leather thongs that are used to bind things together! One woman had a lot of baked camel, with the hair scraped off.

Beech,[16] with his cavalry has lots of small skirmishes, and has killed a large number of enemy, and brought in lots of loot, such as arms, quilt armour for horses, tent shades, etc. I have a large copper drum, and brass head ornament for horses, besides a lot of spears etc.

Here we are already at the end of July, and with the heat of August to face; but one does not feel the heat so much when knocking about in this way as when perhaps stationary like Assouan. But still it is very excessive in the middle of the day and one drinks oceans!

The general opinion is that this whole business will now be settled at one blow. In fact what is left of Ngoumi's army ought to be annihilated; none of them ought ever to return. They must be smitten and blotted out! Their numbers decrease daily; for instance yesterday they lost 57 men. Mr Ngoumi is reported to be angry with his advisers because he has not found the expected country full of dates to eat and cultivated villages to settle in, but he is still moving north in his dogged determination to carry on till the death I suppose. We are behind him and Kitchener[17] in front of him at Toski, with a similar force to ours.

When the two are joined under Grenfell[18] the force would number say 3,700 men, perhaps more. I estimate the enemy's fighting force that he could put against us as 2000; you see we shall well out-number him on the final day ... if there is one.

Yesterday I rode out behind the big temple to view his camp from afar. It was several miles off but one could see white tents and black masses. David has just come back from patrolling all night in the steamer. He captured 67 people, including 20 men, 1 camel, 5 donkeys, and killed 8 men, 5 camels, 6 donkeys. They killed a splendid camel of Ngoumi's brother. When he came back to the same place in the morning, he found not only the camels and donkeys cut up for food, but the men too! It is becoming a campaign of daily horrors!

1st August. We have now been a whole month on this campaign and there is no doubt that a single action will now soon settle it. Indeed deserters when they see our forces, think we might have done so long ago. We are now on the steamer going north to rendezvous at Toski where Grenfell is, and it is a change to be moving again. I think the General will take some decisive action now, which you will probably hear of before this reaches England. At any rate we shall have all the confidence on our side!

(The letter is punctuated at this point with some personal comments for his wife, but he then continues):

It is blowing hard today, and the river is quite rough. We have just put in to the bank and caught three men with spears, and further on we were fired on by a few riflemen behind rocks, but no harm was done. We replied with the Gardner gun.

Toshki (sic) 2nd August. Here we are in a fresh village, and all the troops are here with the Sirdar. He rode round the lines to see us this morning. The English cavalry are here as well as our own, so we have a fine mounted force of over three hundred cavalry and eighty camelry (sic). As an opportunity of posting may come at any moment I will close this now ..."

The Battle of Toski took place in the morning of 3rd August 1889 and only two British regiments took part in the engagement these being the 20th Hussars and the Royal Irish Rifles.[19] The Egyptian Army under command of General Grenfell formed the main attacking force. The artillery opened fire at 9 a.m. and the battle was virtually concluded by 2 p.m. The Egyptian Army consisted of the 1st Brigade made up of the 9th, 10th and 13th Sudanese Battalions, a total of 1450 men, and 2nd Brigade consisting of the 1st Egyptian Battalion, 2nd Egyptian Battalion and the 11th Sudanese Battalion. The detailed account of the action is contained in Major Wingate's authoritative work.[20] For this battle Donne received another bar for his Egyptian Medal, this was the bar 'Toski 1889', and was again Mentioned in Despatches on 4th August 1889.

Donne is mentioned in Wingate's account of the Battle of Toski and in his book he describes the disposition of the troops at the start of the battle as follows:

"... whilst Nejumi was making his dispositions the 1st Infantry Brigade, under the command of Major Hunter, had, under cover of the rising ground, and unseen by the enemy, followed in the rear of the mounted troops, and at 10 a.m. siezed a rocky position some 1500 yards in length and directly opposite, and 800 yards distant from the hills now bristling with Arab banners and riflemen. These troops were disposed as follows: 9th under Major Lloyd on the right, 10th under Major Donne in centre, and 13th under Captain Kempster on the left, while the artillery massed under Major Rundle, occupied the ridge between the 9th and 10th. The mounted troops supported on the right of the infantry. The 2nd Infantry Brigade, coming up shortly afterwards, remained in support to the left rear of the position ..."

Steady volley-firing was maintained for about half-an-hour but at this time a harassing enfilade fire was experienced by the Egyptian force from some Arab riflemen concealed in between boulders on a high hill on the right but these were soon driven out and killed by a detachment of the cavalry.

It was uncertain as to the extent of the enemy force in the rocks and Colonel Wodehouse, who commanded the infantry division, was directed to move his line to the right with a view to enfilading the enemy's left flank. After moving only some 500 yards towards the right front the line overlapped the left of the enemy's position and Major Lloyd seeing that there were a large force of enemy about to charge from behind the hill, halted his battalion and reinforced by his reserve company opened fire on the Arabs who then rushed from their cover and charged the 9th. The line held and the men fired with great steadiness causing the enemy's charge to halt and the Arabs were then forced to retire leaving 150 men dead on the hill-side. The 9th Battalion now advanced and, being reinforced with a company of the 2nd Egyptian Ballalion under command of Captain Martyr, seized the first hill inflicting more losses on the enemy.

General Grenfell, having seen the Arab charge repelled by the 9th Sudanese Battalion, ordered the whole line to advance towards the enemy's position, which was then under continual shell fire from the artillery. A large force of the enemy arrived opposite the centre and attempted to charge the 10th Sudanese Battalion, commanded by Donne, but were repulsed by heavy rifle-fire and the 10th, together with the 9th Sudanese Battalion, advanced and secured the sandy ridge connecting the hills from where they were able to fire on the enemy who were still massed behind the centre position.

General Grenfell, who was by then at the top of the hill first seized, seeing the 13th Sudanese Battalion had been checked in front of the detached hill on the extreme left of the line, sent orders that the hill should be stormed at once. The battalion, supported by the 1st Battalion on the left, had suffered severely from enfilading fire from a number of enemy riflemen concealed behind some rising ground.

In a few minutes some seventy men had been killed or wounded but the 13th Sudanese and 1st Egyptian Battalions, lead by Major Hunter and Captains Kempster and Coles, stormed the hill and captured it after a very closely contested hand-to-hand battle during which Major Hunter received a spear wound in the arm. After winning the hill the enemy repeatedly attempted to regain it but after three unsuccessful attempts abandoned it. Over thirty standards were captured during this part of the action. Only one hill remained in possession of the enemy and the 9th and 10th Sudanese Battalions had already almost surrounded it whilst the 1st Egyptian and 13th Sudanese were taking the other hill and now the 13th moved to the right and completed the outflanking movement. The battalions rushed the hill at the point of the bayonet and drawing the Arabs out inflicted heavy losses and on this hill captured some seventy-five standards.

During this, and the previous operations, the 2nd and 11th Battalions on the far left had materially assisted in the battle by providing heavy flanking fire on the enemy concealed by the rocks from the fire from the troops making the frontal attack. The artillery at the same time operated on the left flank at a 600 yard range. By 11.30 am the first position had been captured and the enemy retreated towards the hill where their temporary camp was situated. At this stage of the battle the Nejumi attempted to rally his retreating force and despite two Egyptian Squadrons and the 20th Hussars attempting to complete the route the Nejumi escaped to the hills.

At noon the general advance was again ordered, this time on the enemy's second position, and the 11th Sudanese, together with the 1st and 2nd Battalions, led the attack supported by the 1st Brigade. The artillery shelled the enemy position and the mounted troops on the right of the line also advanced. During the artillery attack on this second position a well directed shell brought down the largest banner, which was later found to be that of the Nejumi, and it was thought that at that time he received his second wound.

On gaining the heights little opposition was encountered as the enemy were again in full retreat and the camp site that they had just abandoned was captured by the Egyptian troops. Masses of tents, equipment, drums, swords, spears and chain-armour were captured as well as a large number of men, women and children.

With the fighting apparently over a camel was observed on the line of retreat, surrounded by about forty of the enemy. The laden camel and the party were fired on by a troop of cavalry and the camel and a number of the men were hit. The cavalry called upon the remainder to surrender but as they approached the Arabs, including those that were thought to have been killed rushed the troopers and a fierce hand-to-hand encounter followed. Having broken off the engagement the Arabs returned to the camel and then reformed and charged again which resulted in the whole party being killed except one man who succeeded in escaping on a passing horse. The cavalrymen examined the camel and its burden, found it had been carrying the dead body of an important chief, and under the direction of Captain MacDonald it was taken to Toski where it was at once identified as the body of the Nejumi.

After this event the pursuit of the enemy continued for about two miles but owing to the exhausted state of the horses the pursuit was abandoned. The 'cease fire' was sounded at 2 p.m. and the last of the enemy were seen escaping through a gorge in the range of hills bounding the south-west of the Toski plain. The troops eventually reached camp at 5 p.m. having fought for the whole day without food and with very little water. The defeat of the Arab force had been complete and on the 3rd, the day of the battle, and the following days some 4,000 prisoners and deserters were taken, 147 standards captured and 4,000 spears and a large number of rifles, swords and other arms were all impounded. It was estimated that the Arab force lost 1,200 men killed while the Egyptian force losses were comparatively light with 25 killed and 140 men wounded.

A week after the Battle of Toski Donne posted a letter to his Mother from Halfa giving details of the action:

"... It is my turn to write to you now, and your last was from Hake's in London. Although still in the field this campaign is practically over. The irresistible Dervishes who crossed our frontier on 30th June 12000 persons are now a flying mass of fugitives begging for food & life. We estimate having killed 2,500 fighting men since the first shot was fired and I believe all the Emir Wad Saad[21] has with him in his retreat are 200 men only. How are the mighty fallen!

He is trying to get over our frontier and next time they come they will know where it is. I suppose you saw the text of Negoumi's letter to the Sirdar. In the great fight at Toshki (sic) all their important leaders fell, and for the Egyptian army it is a splendid success, as we not only fought them in the open, but for the first time in these Soudan fights fought them in line and not in (a) square. They were utterly routed leaving over 1000 dead on the field – or rather sandy plain, and it cost us 120 killed and wounded, quite enough for such savages! or semi-civilized savages, as they know the art of war, and are no mean foe to face. In their chief position when we captured most of the flags they lay in heaps and our Soudanese soldiers hacked and hewed until the sand was soaked in blood. Our own soldiers are but civilized savages for a dead body is as much attraction to them as to a vulture – and they always set fire to slain bodies of their enemies. The Dervishes were simply mown down in hundreds as they attempted to charge and those who remained were shot or bayoneted as they threw their spears at our men, or were charged by the cavalry. It was not a very pretty fight, but there was no resisting the fearful fire of our line.

All the Chief Emirs fell – their Commander

        Wad el Negoumi

and   Abd Haleem

        Makeen el Nar

        Wad Jabarrah[22]

the chosen of the khalifa have all gone to the paradise they expect for fighting the 'Turk' as they call us, and the hippocrites – brutes in reality who have brought untold suffering on miserable women and children and who well merit the bayonets of our men. They are slave hunters out of work really! Under the ban of an extraordinary fanaticism, which renders them bold in fear of their Khalifa. 'Sons of dogs' as our soldiers call them "we have no fear of them when they invade us here"! and indeed they fight them with a real hatred the Baggara and the Faaleen races are the curses of the Soudan and even we Englishmen can take a savage joy in destroying them – say nothing of the black whose country they devastate with fire and sword, men, women & children. Before we had the order not to shoot them when they came in it was quite a pleasure to give them to our men to execute. Now they are all spared and cared for alike.

Aug 8th. Here we are on our way back to Halfa and shall probably have to march to Sarras, although my men are nearly bootless and in rags. All along the banks today on our way up the Berberis have been giving us a real ovation – dancing shouting, firing guns to express their joy at their deliverance and our triumphal return. We displayed all our captured flags from the steamer. I have told you that I have such nice trophies for Cecil. Several very fine standards, drums and spears.[23]

But it is at Assuan where we count to make our entry with all the spoils of war. How nice war is when it is over! But very horrible when being waged! I have seen my fill of blood and suffering. Address me still at Assuan. Love to you all at Seaton.

from your loving son,
Donisthorpe Donne ..."

This is the last letter that has survived from Donne's service in Egypt following the battle of Toski. The work of Donne during that action was however officially recognised and the following extract was forwarded to Donne:

"... El Kaim Donne Bey,
... ... extract from Horse-Guards letter is forwarded for your information.
By Order,
H. H. Kitchener.

25.11.89   A.G. ..."

"... 7700   Horse Guards,
War Office,
13 Nov 89.

Sir,

With reference to the recent distinctions and Promotions conferred upon certain officers in recognition of their Services during the action at Toski on the Nile, I am directed by the Commander in Chief to acquaint you that His Royal Highness has caused the following officers to be noted for future consideration, as specially deserving of Extra-regimental promotion on account of their Services during the action and of the strong recommendation of Major Gen[l] Sir F. N. Grenfell KCB Sirdar of the Egyptian Army on their behalf.

I am further to inform you that although the undermentioned officers who were favourably brought to notice in your Despatch have not been granted on this occasion any honour or reward, a record has been made of their good services in the field of action of Toski.

Brevet Major B. D. A. Donne,
   Royal Sussex Regiment (Employed with the Egyptian Army).
I have the honor to be
   Sir
Your obedient Servant,
(Signed) G. B. Harman ..."

During the period 1888 and 1889 Donne completed a number of paintings depicting events of the campaign and in particular events concerning his own 10th Sudanese

Battalion. These were:

A soldier of the 10th Sudanese Battalion;

10th Sudanese Battalion going down river, near Arment, 21 November 1888, en route to Kosseir;

Relief of Suakin, 10th Sudanese Battalion marching across the desert from the Nile to Kosseir on the Red Sea, 1888;

10th Sudanese Battalion at halt in the desert near Bir el Morela at a rain pool after a 2 day hard march, November 1888;

Suakin during the investment by the Dervishes;

A sortie from Suakin before the battle of Gemaizah, 1888;

Three soldiers of the 10th Sudanese Battalion.

In addition to the Donne paintings there are in the Donne collection five photographs of the 10th Sudanese Battalion including one of the Battalion's band.

**Soldiers of the
10th Sudanese Battalion.**

Relief of Suakin – the 10th Sudanese Battalion marching across the desert from the Nile to Kosseir on the Red Sea, 1888.

10th Sudanese Battalion at halt in the desert near Bir el Morela at a rain pool after a two day hard march, November 1888.

Saukin during the investment of the Dervishes.

A sortie from Suakin before the battle of Gemaizah, 1888.

The 10th Sudanese Battalion on parade at Luxor. The lower picture opposite shows their band.

Notes to Chapter Fifteen

1. Sauakin – also spelt Suakin
    History of the Sudan Campaign, Part II.
    by Colonel H. E. Colville
    HMSO, 1889. Sketch Map.
2. The Sirdar was Major General Sir F. W. Grenfell, KCB, ADC.
3. Brevet Colonel H. H. Kitchener, Royal Engineers attached to the Egyptian Army.
4. See note 2.
5. Manuscript Memorandum AG 0135 dated 22 November 1887.
    (Documents of Egyptian War Office, Cairo).
6. Mahdiism and the Egyptian Sudan
    by Major F. R. Wingate, DSO, RA,
    Published by MacMillan & Co, 1891.
    Pages 365 – 369.
7. Wingate, op cit, page 368.
8. The book was published in London during 1891 with an introduction by
    "... Major-General Sir Francis Grenfell, KCB, Sirdar of the Egyptian Army ...".
9. Army Form B 199.
    Record of Service of Benjamin Donisthorpe Alsop Donne.
10. Brevet Lieutenant Colonel J. H. Wodehouse, Royal Artillery.
    Attached to the Egyptian Army.
    Monthly Army List, 1888, page 34b.
11. Donne is referring to 'Abderrahman Wad en Nejumi'.
    Wingate, op cit, page 239.
12. There is no record of Donne's article having been published.
13. See note 3.
14. Donne is referring to Veterinary Surgeon (Ranking as Lieutenant) J. R. Beech, CMG, who
    was serving with the Egyptian Army cavalry.
    Monthly Army List, September 1888, page 34b.
15. Lieutenant W. G. Gordon, Royal Engineers serving with the Egyptian Army.
    Ibid.
16. See note 14.
17. See note 3.
18. See note 2.
19. Wingate, op cit, pages 420 and 421.
20. Wingate records in his book that "the infantry brigade taking part in the action at Toski
    had, when the orders were received for their advance to take up positions, just been
    dismissed from morning parade and were preparing to have breakfast.
    Ten minutes after the order had been given the troops started forward without food and
    with only their water bottles filled. Each man was carrying 100 rounds of ammunition ..."
21. Donne refers to Emir Ali Wad Saad.
    Wingate, op cit, page 432.
22. See note 11.
23. The Drum and standard brought home to England by Donisthorpe Donne were presented
    to the National Army Museum by Donne's Grandson Lieutenant Colonel William
    Donisthorpe Shaw.

16   Egypt, Cyprus and Service in the U.K.

AFTER THE Nile Campaign of 1889 Donne continued to serve with the Egyptian Army and in 1890 he relinquished command of the 10th Sudanese Battalion. For his services during the Nile Campaign he was awarded the 3rd class of the Medjidie by the Khedive. He had, then, both the 4th class of the award, which had been promulgated in the London Gazette of 23rd October 1885 and also the 3rd class.[1] After his relinquishment of command he was then employed on staff duties and as the Commandant of the Egyptian Army Military School. He remained in Egypt until May 1893 when he returned to England and was ordered to rejoin the 1st Battalion of his own regiment, the Royal Sussex Regiment, on 9th October 1893.[2]

During his time in Egypt in 1891 and 1892 Donne completed a number of paintings which were entitled:

The Mosque, Cairo, 1891;

Cairo, the Citadel, early morning;

Cairo, the Citadel, midday;

Alexandria;

Aboukir Bay, 1892;

Aboukir Fort, 1892;

Cairo, a street scene;

The Pyramids, 1892;

and two studies of local ships. Donne completed his attachment with the Egyptian Army and made arrangements to travel back to the United Kingdom taking in many of the countries that he had previously visited or served in including Cyprus. Before he left Egypt he completed a number of paintings during the months of January to April and these included the following studies:

The Valley of the Kings, 1893;

Karnac, Luxor, 1893;

An Egyptian village scene, 1893.

**Donne
photographed in 1891.**

He departed Egypt in May and apart from his notes on his visit to Cyprus his journal, or diary, of his travels does not appear to have survived. However his movements can be followed by the paintings that he completed during this extended journey back to England. He does not appear to have been accompanied on this trip by his wife who was, no doubt, at home in England caring for their two children. By this time Donne had two daughters, one Alice Grace Merifield Donne had been born on 2 September 1887 and the second daughter, Evelyn Cecil Donisthorpe Donne, had been born on 4 December 1889.

Cairo – the citadel at mid-day. (Courtesy of Mrs Michelle Cooper.)

Cairo in early morning, 1893. (Courtesy of Mrs Michelle Cooper.)

Alexandria.
(Courtesy of
Mrs Michelle Cooper.)

The Mosque,
Cairo,
1891.

Aboukir Fort, 1892.

Aboukir Bay, 1892.

Opposite: The Pyramids, 1892.

Studies of local ships.

Valley of the Kings, 1893.

**Karnac,
Luxor, 1893.**

**An Egyptian
village scene, 1893.**

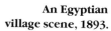

**Unfinished sketch
by Donne;
the Pyramids, 1892.**

Donne travelled from Syria to Cyprus on the Ship 'Niger' and his notes on this part of his travels have been entitled 'Cyprus Revisited' and read:

"... Before dawn the next morning, the "Niger' was already off Cape St Andreas the extreme point of the Carpas promontory and by the time dawn broke was pointing her bows across the Bay of Salamis. Bit by bit, as the rising sun began to illumine them, I could make out familiar points on the landscape, and as we glided onwards across a glassy sea towards Cape Greco, I could make out, in the distance, the walls of famous Famagusta. Then the proud outline of Buffavento and the Pentaktylos Mountain appeared in the far distance, and as the bay of Larnaka opened, the long white outline of the low lying town came in view, mirroring itself in the glorious expanse of tranquil waters. Larnaka is by no means an attractive place, or at all calculated to favourably impress new arrivals with the Island, but the lovely morning light showed her at all events in her best array. The first boat was soon alongside as we dropped anchor as near inshore as possible, bearing the blue ensign, the only visible token of English occupants.

There was little or no change in the place since my former visit some 12 years previously. Not a house seemed to have been altered. There was the same Commissioner's house on the Scala occupied indeed by the same official who has reigned there ever since. But a new iron pier jutted out from the shallow shore to make a landing easier than it was in 1881. Landing on that occasion in one of the ship's boats of H.M.S. 'Monarch', the Midshipman in charge got her broadside on to the surf and we all got a severe ducking – including General Sir A. Cunningham, who was a passenger on board. But now we disembarked on this fine new jetty, and were assisted up by a Zaptieh in the old familiar garb I had seen introduced in 1881. Not a stitch of their uniform had evidently been altered since my time.

After the easy formalities of the trim little Custom house had been submitted to, – it seemed a veritable pleasure after the horrors of the Syrian Ports – I had leisure to stroll through the town. Although still early there were few signs of life about. The old cobble-paved bazaar street was just the same as formerly but all the English established Mercantile houses had gone. Larnaka that boasted a race-meeting and a club in 1881 had dwindled again into the insignificant seaport of Turkish times – with but its three English officials to add to its importance and population. Before proceeding to Nicosia I went to seek a breakfast with my old friend Major Chetwynd, the Police Commandant and acting Commissioner of the District,[3] and I found him in much the same place, and indeed occupation, as I had left him many years before and living with Mr Morton, now promoted to the Head of the Island Customs. Besides the pleasure at being once more in this 'Enchanted Island', a hearty welcome, and a chat over the many chances and changes that years carry with them, soon passed the time, as I had to be on the Nicosia road by 9 o'clock. With 3 Cyprus ponies harnessed to an old chaise, the 28 miles is now covered in 4 hours. Fortunately for me a very heavy thunderstorm the previous day had deluged the country and rendered the usually dusty road pleasant to travel over. Passing through the uninteresting plains of Larnaka and the bare white chalk hills, hardly a living creature or peasant's hut is seen until a small inn is reached some 13 miles inland. Here the ponies rested from their hard trot or hard canter which they had maintained nearly the whole of this dreary way. On the telegraph wires that follow the road I counted some 15 or 20 small Cypriot owls perched at various intervals. These were the only creatures I saw and seemed emblematic of the dormant condition that Cyprus exists in. Resuming our way, the Messaria plain began to open before us and the craggy peak of Buffavento and the Carpas range made the landscape more deserving of Cyprus.

Then we passed the Village of Piroi, but not until the last of the undulating hills was topped and we had passed the Leper Farm on the opposite side of a small ravine, did the tall minarets of Nicosia come in sight. All seemed so familiar, yet so novel, to me for the trees and eucalypti planted 12 years before had grown up and almost hidden the old Turkish ramparts and now formed pleasant avenues of approach. Villas too had sprung up on the

West of the town mostly occupied by the English officials, and formed a pleasing addition to the scene with their gardens and trees. Away in the distance the long low building of Government House was almost hidden amid the trees that had grown up around it – what 15 years ago when Sir Garnet Wolseley pitched his camp there was only a barren eminence. Beyond again Mount Troodos, in the dim mid-day distance, still showed a few lingering streaks of the winter's snow, and already seemed to invite to its cool plateaux those who were fortunate enough to escape from the scorching plains beneath. I was lucky enough to arrive at Nicosia before the annual Troodos migration takes place, and found a kindly welcome under the roof of an old friend and Wellingtonian – Law, who, once Commissioner of Kyrenia, was now Queen's Advocate of the Island. It was in the very same villa where I had years ago lodged soon after my Chief, Colonel Gordon, had built it. Now it was enlarged, improved, and hedged round with shrubbery and garden and other new villas had cropped up around it.

Let me take the reader for a stroll through the interesting old town. At first all the streets and houses, even the ramparts, seemed smaller to me than years ago, but it was only the mirage that time and busier and more important scenes doubtless reflected on my imagination. I found my way exactly through the confusing narrow little streets that seemed to lead to nowhere; but all the houses, pleasant courtyards, overhanging windows, Greek ladies, even the stones and bazaar shops were identically as I had last seen them. Even the Zaptiehs of my whilom Police hung about the same places as before. If the town had been in a state of Rip Van Winkleism for the last 12 years, the reproduction could not have been more complete.

I looked into a Greek 'Caffeniss' (coffee house) in the Bazaar and saw sitting there in the same uniform, the very energetic police official who had formerly served under my orders. I addressed him by name and said I wished him to come at once with me to the Buyuk Khan – he rose and joined me with a sort of wondering look and I could easily see that he was puzzled. My conversation evidently still more perplexed him. Reluctant as a police officer to confess ignorance of someone who was evidently well acquainted with the place, he was driven at last to ask me who I was. "Surely" I said "you know the Commandant of Eleven years back?", "But I can well excuse you if you do not, for I may have changed and you have not".

How interesting it was to see again the old gate of the Lusignan Cathedral - Santa Sophia, with its white washed portals and old Turks sauntering in and out to prayer, all looking so solemn and deserted, yet so calm and peaceful. Those weather-worn walls and buttresses that have seen the Christian ousted and again reassert himself, seemed to endure for all time amid the even tenor of the tranquil, mouldering old town.

Of old friends and fellow-officials there were many left serving on in the Island, some in the same, a few in higher office. But many had left and still more who had laboured hard in the regeneration of the Island and done grand service to the flag, had passed away, leaving their tracks in the sands of time to be filled by others. Foremost amongst them I may mention:

Mr. Samuel Brown, Chief Island Engineer,[4] to whom Cyprus is indebted for its roads, bridges and piers – who died in Hong Kong.

Colonel (Major General) A. H. A. Gordon, the reorganizer of the Cyprus Military Police who died on his way home from China in 1893.

Lieutenant Colonel Gordon, the first energetic Commissioner of Nicosia who died at Suez after the Suakin Campaign of 1885.

Captain Gordon, Assistant Commissioner of Famagusta, lost in the Bayuda Desert 1885, and never heard of again.[5]

Captain Croker, Adjutant of Police and Cyprus Pioneers, accidentally killed at Chicago 1893.

Sir Elliot Bovill,[6] Chief Justice and universally esteemed who was carried away by cholera in the Straits Settlements 1893.

Mr Langdon Rees, of Smyrna, who started the first Island Journal called the Cyprus

Herald in 1881, and liberally supported the Turf. He died in Cairo in 1891, as respected there as he was mourned in Cyprus and the English Levant.

Captain Inglis, Commissioner of Famagusta, who died in Nicosia in 1883.

To these I may add, although not officially connected with this Island, Sir Samuel Baker, whose work on Cyprus – "Cyprus as I saw it in 1879" – is a well known and standard book, and Mr Grenville Chester a frequent visitor and well known in Egyptian and archaeological circles.

Colonel Bowlby, 20th Foot (1893).[7]

No one knows the work of an English official in Cyprus unless he has been there to see. The Public Works, the Law, the Police, the Customs, Education – all are admirably worked, and with wonderful economy, and it is uphill work too, with two antagonistic races and two foreign languages to combat; and yet there seems to be a brand of ineffectiveness laying its heavy hand upon the whole, which damps all ardour and exposes a restiveness not to be surprised at – any way?

It is because its light has gone out, and illuminated another more fortunate locality. Its trade may yet increase and bear better fruits, its wine trade and customs may show better results, and law and crime improve in future years as education and communications improve, but stagnation and debt will for ever cloud it as long as Egypt overshadows it in importance and the burden of the Tribute (payable to Turkey) is unremoved.

Some talk of Cyprus becoming the trade Emporium of the Levant, some of the facilities of making a port at Famagusta, others the Euphrates Valley Railway to India and the East

affecting its importance and making it a 'place d' armes' of the Mediterranean. It is inconceivable that anything of the sort will be effected in our time – if even in the time of our great grandsons. It has no attractions to make it a trading centre – as witness the failure in 1878.

There is no harbour in the Island, and to convert the long-deserted, unhealthy Famagusta – that a Greek cannot even live in – into a harbour of the necessary size would cost millions that no mad-man even would think of flinging away, in the face of the many fine ready-made ports along the Asia Minor Coast and Skenderoon Bay (Iskanderun). Let us even suppose the Euphrates Valley railway to be an accomplished fact, and Famagusta capable of accommodating and docking steamers, the real trade outlet and mail route is much more likely to be the Bosphorous or Smyrna – and indeed is already rapidly tending that way, by the rail to Angora now opened.

Whatever the views held by the Island officials on the future prospects of their – or rather our – island, it would be treading too much in the sphere of Politics and Strategy to pursue the subject further with any advantage to myself or the reader. But certainly it is that our possession of Cyprus, as of our other interests in the Inland Sea – whether they tend toward the Euphrates Valley, the Suez Canal, or a grand port at Famagusta capable of floating a 15000 ton ironclad – must depend entirely on sea power. As long as our Naval power is adequate in the sea, Cyprus has no superior value to us than many other Islands would be in the Levant ..."[8]

Donne had commenced his travels from Egypt and before arriving in Cyprus visited a number of countries and then embarked for Cyprus from Syria. His journies can be followed, not from notes, but from the sequence of his paintings and these are listed in order to show his progress on his homeward journey:

Jerusalem, a street scene, 1893;
Jerusalem, the Dome of the Rock, 1893;
Lebanon, Beirut, 1893;
Damascus, Courtyard of the Great Mosque, 1893;
Mar Saba, 1893;
Baalbek, 1893;
Baalbek, the Temple of Jupiter, 1893;
A Crusader Castle, 1893.

Right:
Lebanon –
Beirut,
1893.

Opposite: Jerusalem,
The Dome of the Rock,
1893.

Far opposite:
Jerusalem,
a street scene, 1893.

Above: Mar Saba, 1893.

**Top left: Damascus, courtyard of the
Great Mosque, 1893.**

Left: Baalbek, 1893.

A Crusader Castle, 1893.

Baalbek – the Temple of Jupiter, 1893.

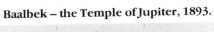

Donne embarked from Syria and journeyed to Cyprus where, as has already been recorded, he spent some time and during his stay on the island completed a further three studies of the island, these being:

Limassol from the Acropolis of Amathus, 1893;

Limassol from the sea;

Cape Gata and Mount Troodos, 1893.

Limassol from the sea, 1893.

Limassol from the Acropolis of Amathus, 1893.
(Courtesy of H. M. Williamson.)   **The Sea of Marmora, 1893.**

Cape Gata and Mount Troodos, 1893. (Courtesy of H. M. Williamson.)

He departed from Limassol and may well have completed the latter two sketches from the vessel whilst slowly leaving the Port of Limassol and proceeding along the coast. He next visited the island of Rhodes where he completed three paintings, these being:

Rhodes, as seen from the anchorage, 1893;

Rhodes, 1893;

The Gateway, Rhodes, 1893.

Rhodes seen from the anchorage, 1893.   **Rhodes, 1893.**

Below: Greek island craft at Smyrna.
(Courtesy of H. M. Williamson.)

The Gateway, Rhodes, 1893.

Island craft at Smyrna, 1893. (Courtesy of H. M. Williamson.)

He then appears to have travelled north stopping off at Smyrna and then the island of Imbro (Imbros), and then continued his voyage to Turkey. It was during this part of his homeward journey that he painted a further six paintings which he entitled:

Greek island craft at Smyrna, 1893;

Island craft at Smyrna, 1893;

The Island of Imbros, 1893;

The Sea of Marmora, 1893;

Coastline of the sea of Marmora, 1893;

The Golden Horn of Scutari, 1893.

The Island of Imbros, 1893.

Coastline of the sea of Marmora, 1893.

Unfortunately without his diary or journal to refer to it is difficult to know exactly which route he then took to reach England, but he did complete one further painting at this time which indicates that he did not take a most direct route as his final painting from his travels depicts Bagnoli, near Naples.

Donne rejoined the 1st Battalion as a Substantive Major (he had been promoted to that rank whilst still serving with the Egyptian Army, on 28 December 1888) which was at the time stationed at Dublin. During the following year the Battalion moved to Fermoy, Ireland and Donne remained with the 1st Battalion until warned for embarkation to join the 2nd Battalion which was then serving in India.

The Golden Horn of Scutari, 1893.

Bagnoli, near Naples, 1893.

Donne after his return from Egypt, circa 1895.

Notes to Chapter Sixteen

1. Army Form B 199.
    Record of Service of B. D. A. Donne.
2. War Office, Horse Guards, letter 112/35/438 dated 12 August 1893.
3. Major the Hon E. J. Chetwynd, formerly of the 61st Regiment of Foot.
4. Samuel Brown, Government Engineer
    Appointed 13 August 1880 (Cyprus Gazette No 58 dated 11 September 1880).
5. Captain W. H. Gordon, The Royal Welsh Fusiliers.
    See also Chapter 14, Note 22.
6. Sir Elliott Charles Bovill held various legal appointments in the Government of Cyprus
    including Judicial Commissioner of the Queen's High Court of Justice for Cyprus from 26
    November 1881 and President of the Court of Temyiz from 12 June 1882.
    The Private Journals of Lieutenant Donisthorpe Donne.
    by George Georghallides,
    published in the Journal of Greek-Cypriot Studies, 1969, page 50.
7. Major H. R. Bowlby, 20th Regiment of Foot.
    He was appointed Chief Commandant of Military Police and Inspector of Prisons on 1
    April 1879 (Cyprus Gazette No 17, dated 2 April 1879). His services were terminated on
    1 December 1880 when the two Cyprus Police Forces were amalgamated. (Cyprus
    Gazette No 62 dated 26 November 1880).
8. It is quite probable that the comments included at the end of his notes on his return visit
    to Cyprus were intended to be used in a book that he was writing at the time of his death
    in 1907 dealing with the Study of Mediterranean Sea Power.

Malta – HMS Ramillies in the Grand Harbour, 1896.

P and O liner 'Himalaya' leaving Valetta, 1896.

17   India, South Africa and Retirement

A LETTER sent from the War Office to The General Officer Commanding, Cork District dated 13th April 1896 warned Donne that he was to be ready to embark as from 13th May 1896 to join the 2nd Battalion, Royal Sussex Regiment in India as the Second in Command.[1] Donne handed over his duties in Ireland and proceeded to England and had leave in London. It was whilst at 75 Upper Richmond Road that he received a letter from the War Office, dated 10th June, 1896, advising him that he was to embark on the Peninsular and Oriental S. N. Coy's steam ship 'Himalaya' at London on 3rd July. He was permitted to take on board with him "... 80 cubic feet of baggage ...".

Once again Donne's diary, or journal, for this voyage from London to Bombay has not survived but we are able to trace his passage by a number of paintings that have survived and show that he visited Gibraltar, Malta, Egypt and then through the Red Sea. The paintings that illustrate his journey are:

Gibraltar, The Rock, 1896;

Malta, HMS Ramillies in the Grand Harbour, 1896;

P & O liner 'Himalaya' leaving Valetta, 1896;

Egypt, Cairo, 1896;

Red Sea – Jedda, 1896;

Donne disembarked at Bombay and then travelled across India to the Oudh to join his Battalion at Fyzabad. The battalion remained at Fyzabad until ordered to join the Tirah Expeditionary Force in 1897. The Battalion moved to Fort Jamrud and it was whilst at that location Donne found time to complete one painting which he called "Fort Jamrud, North West Frontier". The Battalion marched as part of Expeditionary Force from Fort Jamrud to Lola China where they encountered heavy sniper fire. From there they marched over the Alachi Pass to Karamna and Burg. The 2nd spent Christmas in the

Gibraltar – The Rock, 1896.

Egypt – Cairo, 1896.

Red Sea – Jedda, 1896.

Bazar Valley and then marched south to cover the flank and rear of the 2nd Brigade which was retiring to the Khyber Pass having destroyed a number of 'hostile' villages. 'D' Company surprised a party of Afridis who were attempting to follow and despite the advantages of the Afridi's having knowledge of the area and being skilled hill fighters the 2nd Battalion extracted themselves with few casualties. The retreat of the 2nd Brigade was brought to a successful conclusion due to the work of the 2nd Royal Sussex Regiment in drawing off the tribesmen. The terrain in which this action was fought consisted of ridges and spurs and was extremely rough and difficult and covered with scrub. Two NCO's were killed and because of the terrain their bodies were never recovered. The Afridis in an attempt to demoralise the 2nd Battalion sniped the camp all the following night. The unit then withdrew towards Ali Masjid and as they did so the attacks from the tribesmen became less frequent. New Year 1898 brought new tasks to the battalion in that the men were occupied with stone clearing, sangar building and in mounting picquets. In one small skirmish a picquet of seven men were attacked from the rear at close range with rifle fire and with large stones but were able to hold off the enemy for more than an hour before the tribesmen withdrew.

With the organised resistance by the tribesmen at an end, the Brigades of the Tirah Expeditionary Force were broken up and reformed. The 2nd Battalion remained on the North West Frontier performing picquet duties, building blockhouses until the hot weather was over and on being relieved the battalion moved back to Sialkot and Amritsar.[2] For his service on the North West Frontier and in the Tirah Campaign Major Donne received the India General Service Medal, with clasps 'Tirah 1897-98' and 'Punjab Frontier 1897-98'. Major L. L. Gordon in his book 'British Battles and Medals' shows that the 2nd Royal Sussex Regiment received their India Medal (1895-1902) and clasp 'Tirah 1897-98' for their service in the Swat Valley.[3]

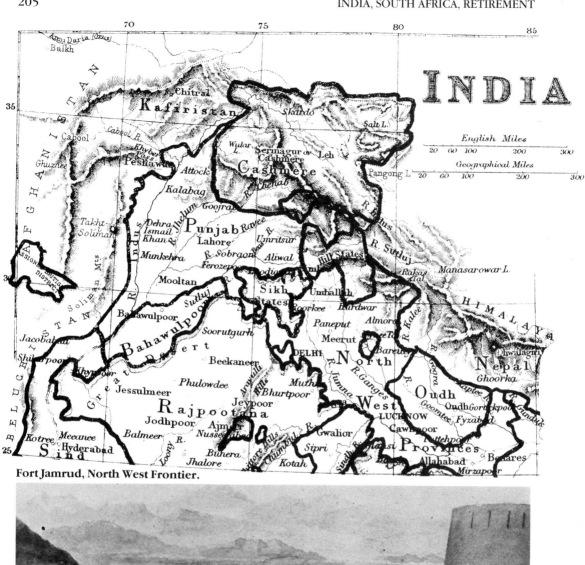

Fort Jamrud, North West Frontier.

2nd Battalion, 35th Regiment, at Fort Jamrud, North West Frontier.

With the return to peace-time soldiering in India Donne was able to move around the country and it was during the latter part of 1898 that he painted The Red Fort at Agra and also Mussoorie (which was one of the best known hill stations in Northern India).[4] During his tour of duty in India Donne painted two water colours of the Taj Mahal. One he called 'The Taj Mahal, 1897' and the second 'The Taj Mahal, with cranes in flight', this second painting was also dated 1897 and both would have been painted before he moved with his unit to the North West Frontier and the Tirah Campaign. His younger brother Beadon, who later became Colonel H. R. B. Donne, CB, CMG, was also an excellent artist and painted the Taj Mahal during his tour of duty in India. His illustration of this magnificent building shows it in an early morning mist.

Donne's tour of duty in India was shortened as he was selected for promotion to Lieutenant Colonel and appointed to command the 1st Battalion. His promotion to Lieutenant Colonel dated from 15th October 1898 and Donne returned to England to join the 1st Battalion which was then stationed at Aldershot. With the outbreak of the war in South Africa the regiment fully expected to be one of the first regiments to be placed on active service but to their bitter disappointment they were warned for service in Malta. The history of the regiment by G. D. Martineau[5] records that at Malta the men went about their duties "... with long faces and villainous tempers ...". The regiment was eventually mobilised for active service in South Africa and departed from Malta on 20 February 1900 on the steamer 'Pavonia'. The regiment had a five or six weeks voyage to the Cape and arrived there at the end of March. Donne, who was at this time the Commanding Officer, found time to complete one painting whilst on board which he called "Off Cape Town, the tablecloth mist".

The regimental history records that "... The Battalion under Colonel Donne, being sent up to join Lord Roberts' Army at Bloemfontein, now formed part of General Bruce Hamilton's 21st Brigade for the advance to Pretoria, begun on May 3rd ...". The Battalion came under fire for the first time at Welkom Fire and then moved on to Winburg. They had marched one hundred miles but Lord Roberts soon urged his troops forward in pursuit of his policy of not letting the enemy rest.

The next action was at Zand River where the Royal Sussex drove the Boers from a heavily defended position at the point of the bayonet and in doing so captured a great deal of Boer equipment. On the following day the regiment were permitted to rest until noon and then started a long march to Kroonstad. The regiment was next in action at Diamond Hill, where the conflict lasted two days having commenced on 11 June. Three battalions were mentioned for their excellent conduct during the long fight and these were the Royal Sussex, Derbyshires and City Imperial Volunteers.

The regiment then moved on to Heidelberg where a pleasant greeting awaited the regiment. Some of the ladies from the town met the regiment marching in and presented it with a banner, handworked in silk, with a portrait of the Queen (Victoria) on one side and the Union Jack on the other. An inscription read "... Presented to The Royal Sussex Regiment by the Ladies of Heidelberg, 23rd June, 1900 ..." Colonel Donne thanked the ladies on behalf of the regiment and the regimental band struck up, and the regiment marched off to camp, led by the Sergeant Major, carrying the flag.

The Red Fort at Agra, 1898.   **Mussoorie, 1898.**

The Taj Mahal, with cranes in flight.

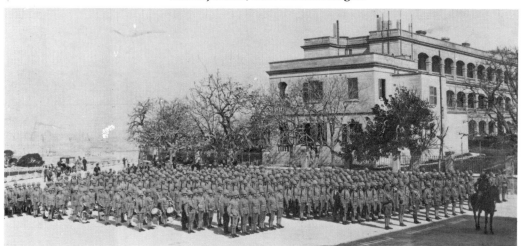

Parade at Malta.   **Lieutenant Colonel B. D. A. Donne at Malta.**

Lieutenant Colonel and Mrs Donne.

The regiment remained at Heidelberg for four days and was accommodated in the railway goods-sheds and a few tents found in the town. It also gave the regiment the chance to re-equip with boots and some items of uniform. Donne took the opportunity to paint another picture, the second that has survived from his tour of duty in South Africa. This is listed as 'Looking across the town of Heidelberg, South Africa'.

Colonel Donne led his regiment further south and as they were accompanied by an enormous wagon convoy of 180 vehicles the advance was very slow. They moved through Villiersdorp, Frankfort, Reitz, Bethlehem and Stabbert's Nek and then came into action again at Retief's Nek. The attack against Marble Kop cost the regiment four killed and thirty-six wounded but it was considered that the action helped to bring about a disorganisation of the Boers in that area and led to the surrender of five commandos to the Royal Sussex Regiment.

During 1901 five companies of the regiment were detached under command of the Second in Command[6] to act as escort to the convoys working to supply General Hamilton's mobile column and Major du Moulin organised a part of his Royal Sussex force to act as mounted infantry and commenced to play the Boers at their own game.

Of all the letters that Donne would have undoubtedly written whilst he was on duty in South Africa only two have survived. The first was written from Johannesburg, South Africa, dated 27 November 1901, and was written to his sister Rose. In it he reveals that he has been away from duty due to illness:

> "... Many thanks for yours of Nov 1 & card enclosed. ...
> I've had a pleasant stay here of 14 days in a sort of convalescent home altho' I'm as fit as can be again. It is very much more interesting here than down in the Orange Colony and this house was built by B. Bamati the Millionaire. I'm off tomorrow back to Bloem-Springfontein and the monotonous work of the Claims board.
> I suppose it takes you a long time to get letters to George. Cecil & the children are going

Off Cape Town – the tablecloth mist.

to holiday at Brighton, but I still have to write them through Exmouth.

Buller does not get much sympathy out here: the army have not forgiven him the horrible mess he made of things in Natal - in fact his entire lack of any sort of general ship. The wonder was that he was not superseded long ago. ...

I should like to try & get home on leave in the spring if all goes well. The Boers are being mopped up at a fairly good rate and when we have reduced them by a few more thousand it ought to tell considerably ..."

The letter was concluded with various messages to other members of the family and signed 'Donisthorpe Donne' but carried a postscript:

"... P.S.   If I do not get an extension of command this time next year I shall be a free man! So life is worth living for now! ..."

The last letter from the Donne collection is the letter he wrote from South Africa on 28 June 1902 to his eldest daughter Alice Grace Merifield[7] which showed that the Royal Sussex Regiment were on the move again. His letter reads:

"... This will be my last letter from Bethulie: we are all off almost at once to concentrate at Bloemfontein, so all busy collecting and packing up. I enclose you (sic) some of the new 1d O.R.C. stamps. They will probably be scarce some day. There is one error in the whole sheet of 240: no stop after "colony"! I have two of them. The painting you sent me was indeed a surprise, and you have made immense strides! Its a pity it was torn up, but you will be able to do plenty more, for it is only practice and scribbling that makes a good painter. I never began to draw with colours until I was 20, so you have had great advantages. The best way to learn is to watch other people.

I enclose a post card for Evelyn I am sorry I can get none out here, but there may be some in Bloemfontein.

Yours was a very nice long letter of June 1. I have got several more interesting envelopes for you: some the Boers used when they occupied the Colony in 1899. I am glad you like the stamp picture, but perhaps you can do a better one ...".

Looking across the town of Heidelberg, South Africa.

The middle section of the letter was devoted to family matters but then Donne returns to current events in South Africa:

"... All the Coronation show here was broken off because of the King's illness. The people were disappointed after all the trouble & expense, but it must have been terrible in London. We all hope he will soon recover. I dont know yet when I shall be able to get away, but I hope sometime in July. I am very sorry to have to go out in camp again, but am getting rid of all the claims work which is a very good thing.

Lt Colonel Beadon Donne[8] in India wants us to adopt a motto with our crest that some of the old Donne's used to have "Vivit post funera Vertus" (Virtue survives death). So you

Officers of the Royal Sussex Regiment in South Africa. Donne is at the centre, in lighter tunic.

must write to Grand Papa Donne and ask him about it. Bye the bye. I hope you and Evelyn both write to him sometimes, as he is very fond of you both, and is always pleased to get little letters. So be sure and write to him: you know he is one of the best amateur painters living; you can tell him all about my medals and clasps if you like. It is nice for Mummy getting the furniture of the London flat, & the pictures too: I hope she has also got the silver tea caddy with the Hughes family coat of arms on it, as it is a family heirloom. You must learn how to clean and polish plate someday ..."

Donne concluded this letter with messages to his two daughters and signed himself as "Donisthorpe Donne".

Donne was awarded the Queen's South Africa Medal with four clasps, these being 'Wittebergen', 'Diamond Hill', 'Johannesburg' and 'Cape Colony'[9] and also the King's South Africa Medal (1901-1902) with the two clasps 'South Africa 1901' and 'South Africa 1902'. He was also created a Companion of the Bath (CB) for his services in South Africa.[10]

Donne returned to the United Kingdom and was promoted to Colonel in October 1902 and for a short while the C. O. of the 35th Regimental District. He was appointed Colonel in Charge of the Home Counties Regimental District Record Office in 1905 a post he still held at the time of his death.

With his return to England the Donnes purchased a property Spring Grove, Isleworth, and his interest in painting then changed and he became absorbed with painting old naval vessels. In 1903 he painted 'Sailing Ships, the Sailing Squadron of the Royal Navy, 1903', and in the following year painted "HMS Implacable' and 'To be sold – The Camperdown' and 'The Hannibal' (neither are illustrated in this book). In 1906 he completed another naval study which he entitled 'Towing the Caledonia to the Breakers Yard' and this work was dated September 1906 (not illustrated).

Sailing ships – the Sail Squadron, Royal Navy, 1903.

Flagship off Malta in the 'Fifties.   Man of War leaving the Grand Harbour,
                                                                                Valetta.

The old Arethusa being towed away in Portsmouth Harbour.

Cleaning ships.

Ships on a beach.

These were to be his last paintings, however in May 1907 he exhibited his sea studies at a Naval and Military Exhibition which was held at Bruton Street, London. Apart from the previously mentioned naval works he also exhibited a fine study of a naval ship in full sail which he called "Flagship off Malta in the 'Fifties'". He received acclaim as an artist for his sea studies but unfortunately four months later he died suddenly at his home 'Collingwood' at Spring Grove, Isleworth, on 23rd September 1907, of a heart attack.

Obituaries were published in The Times, Daily Telegraph, Morning Post, the Daily Graphic, The Globe and the Pall Mall Gazette.[11]

The funeral took place on Friday 27 September 1907. The funeral cortege departed from 'Collingwood', at 2 p.m. and the details of the Procession were given in a Garrison Order dated, at Hounslow, 24 September 1907. The order gave the following detail:

"...   Procession.
(a)   Firing Party, Depot Royal Fusiliers, under Major Legge.
(b)   Band, King's Dragoon Guards.
(c)   Band, 5th & 7th Battalions, Royal Fusiliers.
(d)   Gun carriage.
(e)   Chief Mourners.
(f)   Funeral party (all available Non-Commissioned Officers and men of) King's Guards.
        Permanent Staff of Militia, Royal Fusiliers
        Representatives of the Royal Sussex Rgt (sic).
        Departments.
(g)   Officers, in reverse order of seniority.
(h)   Other Mourners.
(i)   Private Carriages.
                                                Detail.
(2)   The Gun Carriage will be drawn up at the entrance to the House.
(3)   The firing party will be drawn up 2 deep, one pace interval between files, facing the House. The Bands, Funeral party and Officers will be formed up in two ranks at one pace interval and eight paces from each other facing inward in front of the Gun Carriage.
        The above to be in position by 1.45 p.m.
(4)   The Officer Commanding King's Dragoon Guards will arrange for the Gun Carriage and Union Jack.
(5)   All Officers not on duty will attend.
(6)   Attention is called to Section 210 Infantry Training. The detail given therein will be followed.
(7)   Dress for all ranks – Review Order. Officers will wear mourning bands on the left arm of the tunic ..."[12]

    A report of the funeral recorded that:

"... On the arrival of the procession at Heston the coffin was taken into the Church, and the first part of the burial Office was recited, and after this it was taken to the grave prepared in the new portion of the Churchyard, where the body was duly committed to the earth in the presence of a large assembly, the ceremony ended by the accustomed three volleys fired over the grave by the hundred men of the Royal Fusiliers.

... the impressive ceremony closed by the buglers sounding 'The Last Post'."

Thus ended the life of 'Donisthorpe Donne' (as he always preferred to be called), a soldier and an artist who was, perhaps, typical of his time and was a true Victorian 'Officer and Gentleman'. He was a good officer, who was trusted and liked by his men, and was, without doubt, an accomplished amateur artist.

At the time of his death Donisthorpe Donne was working on a manuscript of a book dealing with the Mediterranean and intended to include in his work details of his journeys in the Mediterranean area, his studies of the sieges by the Turks of the Great Venetian fortresses in Cyprus, Crete and Rhodes as well as his observations on the development of Cyprus.

He was already the author of the first English book to be printed and published in Cyprus. His book, which was published in 1885, was entitled Records of the Ottoman Conquest of Cyprus – and Guide and Directory to Cyprus.

In addition to this little known work he was a keen Egyptologist and for his work in that field he was made an Officer d'Academic Francaise for the services he rendered to Egyptology.

Memorial stone
of Colonel
B. D. A. Donne, CB,
in the cemetery
at Heston church.

**Medals and decorations of Colonel B. D. A. Donne, CB. The Companion of the Bath
is shown separately, above.**

Notes to Chapter Seventeen

1.   War Office letter reference 112/35/506 dated 13 April 1896.
2.   A History of the Royal Sussex Regiment,
     by G. D. Martineau,
     Published by Moore & Tillyer, 1955 page 126.
3.   British Battles and Medals,
     by Major L. L. Gordon,
     Published by Gale and Polden Ltd., 1962, pages 273 and 274.
4.   Handbook for Travellers in India, Burma and Ceylon,
     Published by John Murray, 13th Edition, 1929, page 423.
5.   See note 2.
6.   Martineau, op cit, page 137.
7.   Alice Grace Merifield Donne was born on 22 September 1887 and was baptised at the
     Parish Church, Kensington.
     She married in 1909 to Neville Frederick Shaw MA.
8.   Donne's younger brother was serving in India on the staff of the Headquarters, Bengal
     Command as an Assistant Adjutant General.
     "Lieutenant Colonel Henry Richard Beadon Donne". He had assumed that appointment on
     5th April 1900.
     Monthly Army List, December 1901, page 27.
9.   See details of Record of Service at Appendix A.
10. Two Years on Trek,
     by Lt Col L. E. du Moulin,
     Published by Murray & Co, 1907. Appendix D.
11. The Times, Wednesday 2 October 1907.
     The Daily Telegraph, Wednesday 25 September 1907.
     The Morning Post, Tuesday 24 September 1907.
     The Daily Graphic, 25 September 1907.
     The Globe, 25 September 1907.
     Pall Mall Gazette, 25 September 1907.
12. Order issued by Garrison Adjutant, Hounslow, dated 24 September 1907.

Colours of
the 35th
Regiment
of Foot,
later the
Royal
Sussex
Regiment.

Record of Service of
Benjamin Donisthorpe Alsop Donne

Details have been obtained from the officer's own copy of the Army Form B199, and other official documents.

Date of birth   — 4 October 1856
Place of birth   — London

Promotions and Appointments

Appointed Sub Lieutenant, Unattached list.	10 September 1875
Appointed Sub Lieutenant, 35th Foot	10 September 1875
Promoted Lieutenant, 35th Foot with antidate	10 September 1875
Promoted Captain, Royal Sussex Regiment	20 October 1883
Granted Brevet Major	28 December 1888
Promoted Major, Royal Sussex Regiment	10 February 1892
Promoted Lieutenant Colonel, Royal Sussex Regiment	15 October 1898
Promoted Colonel	15 October 1902
OC No 35 Regimental District as Colonel	27 January 1904
Appointed Colonel in Charge of Home Counties Infantry Record Office	15 September 1905

Medals and Decorations

Companion of the Bath
Egyptian Medal, with clasps 'The Nile 1884-85'
                             'Gemaizah 1888'
                             'Toski 1889'
India Medal, with clasps 'Punjab Frontier 1897-98'
                         'Tirah 1897-98'
Queen's South Africa Medal, with clasps 'Cape Colony'
                                         'Johannesburg'
                                         'Diamond Hill'
                                         'Wittebergen'
King's South Africa Medal, with clasps 'South Africa 1901'
                                        'South Africa 1902'.
Khedive's Egyptian Star, for 1882.
4th Class Medjidie (Egyptian Award).
3rd Class Medjidie (Egyptian Award).
3rd Class Osmanich (Egyptian Award).
Officier d'Academie Francaise.

Sketches and Paintings by Donisthorpe Donne not included

The following list of Donisthorpe Donne sketches and paintings has been compiled from a manuscript list found with the Donne papers, written by Donne, and lists of paintings sold to private collectors. The following is in the order given in Donne's manuscript with the additional paintings added in chronological order based on the known travels of the artist.

Malta, Pembroke Camp, 1879	Whereabouts unknown
Malta, Valetta, 1879	Whereabouts unknown
Malta, St Elmo, 1879	Whereabouts unknown
Malta, St Elmo, 1879 (second painting)	Whereabouts unknown
Malta, Salvatore Gate, 1880	Whereabouts unknown
Malta, Valetta Ditch, 1880	Private ownership
Malta, Grand Harbour, 1880	Whereabouts unknown
Malta, View of Citta Vecchia, 1880	Whereabouts unknown
Malta, 'Inconstant' saluting, 1880	Whereabouts unknown
Sicily, Palermo (July 1880)	Whereabouts unknown
Cyprus, Turkish Quarter, Limassol, 1880	Whereabouts unknown
Cyprus, River Garilis (Garyllis), 1880	Whereabouts unknown
Cyprus, Machera (Makheras) Monastery, 1880	Whereabouts unknown
Cyprus, View from the top of Troodos, 1881	Private ownership
Cyprus, Nicosia from Buffavento Castle, 1881	Whereabouts unknown
Cyclades, Polino (Polykandro) Island, 1881	Whereabouts unknown
(Donne visited this area in April 1881)	
Greece, The Acropolis, April 1881	Whereabouts unknown
Cyclades, Syra harbour, 1881	Whereabouts unknown
Chios (Scio), the Encampment, 1881	Whereabouts unknown
Turkey, Chanak and Dardanelles, 1881	Whereabouts unknown
Cyprus, Kyrenia Hills and St Hillarion (Hilarion), 1882	Whereabouts unknown
Cyprus, View from Hillarion (St Hilarion Castle), 1882	Whereabouts unknown
Cyprus, Ghikko (Kykko) Monastery, 1882	Whereabouts unknown
Cyprus, Sea Gate, Famagusta, 1882	Whereabouts unknown
Cyprus, Famagusta Harbour, 1882	Private ownership
Cyprus, Mount Troodos from Nicosia, 1882	Whereabouts unknown
Cyprus, View from Ramparts, Nicosia, 1882	Private ownership
Egypt, Madinet Habou (Habu), Thebes, 1883	Whereabouts unknown
Egypt, Plains of Thebes, 1883	Whereabouts unknown
Egypt, Goorneh, 1883 (Gourna)	Whereabouts unknown
Egypt, Temple of Goorneh (Gourna), 1883	Whereabouts unknown
Egypt, Interior of Edfou, 1883	Whereabouts unknown
Egypt, Karnac (Karnak) from the Sacred Lake, 1883	Whereabouts unknown
Egypt, Cairo from the Mameluke Tombs, 1883	Whereabouts unknown
Egypt, The Pylons of Edfou, 1883	Whereabouts unknown
Egypt, The Great Temple, Abu Simbel, May 1884	Private ownership
Egypt, The Painted Hall, Phylae	Private ownership
Egypt, Phylae (Philae), 1889	Private ownership
Egypt, The Rock of Abuseer (Abousir) (date unknown)	Whereabouts unknown

Egypt, Nubia, Temple at Wady Sabooa (sic)
    (date unknown)   Whereabouts unknown
Egypt, Nubia, Ruins of Gorjan Tava (sic) (date unknown) Whereabouts unknown
Egypt, Cairo, Bab Essoushlik (sic) (date unknown)   Whereabouts unknown
Sudan, Saukin, April 1886   Private ownership
Rhodes, 1893   Private ownership
Arabia, Mount Sinai, 1896   Private ownership
Red Sea, HM Steamer 'Tor', 1896   Private ownership
Red Sea, Yarbo, 1896   Private ownership
England – To be sold – 'The Camperdown', 1904   Whereabouts unknown
England – The 'Hannibal' at Portsmouth 1904   Whereabouts unknown
England – Towing the 'Caledonia' to the
    breaker's yard, 1906   Whereabouts unknown
Malta, Flagship off Malta in the Fifties
    (date unknown – exhibited in 1907)   Whereabouts unknown

Bibliography

'An Officer who was there' *Suakin, 1885.*
   Kegan, Paul, Tench & Co, 1885.

Barthorp, M. *The North West Frontier, A Pictorial History 1839-1947.*
   Blandford Press.

Butler, The Rev G. *The Public School Atlas.*
   Longmans Green & Co, 1894.

Cavendish, Miss A. *Tel-el-Kebir, 13th September 1882.*
   The Royal Engineer Journal, Vol 92, No 3, September 1982.

Colvill, Colonel H. E. *History of the Sudan Campaign.*
   H. M. S. O., 1889.

Creswicke, Louis. *South Africa and the Transvaal War, Vol VI.*
   Caxton Publishing Co.

de Cosson, Major E. A. *Days and Nights of Service with Sir Gerald Graham's*
   Field Force at Suakin.
   John Murray, 1886.

du Moulin, Lt Col L. E. *Two years on Trek*
   Murray & Co., 1907.

Elliott, Maj-Gen J. G. *The Frontier 1839-1947.*
   Cassell, 1968.

Georghallides, G. S. *The Journal Notes of Donisthorpe Donne.*
   The Journal of the Society of Greek-Cypriot Studies, 1969.

Georghallides, G. S. *A Political and Administrative History of Cyprus 1918-1926*
   (with a survey of the foundations of British rule).
   Cyprus Research Centre, Nicosia, 1979.

Gordon, Major L. L. *British Battles and Medals.*
  Gale and Polden, 1962.

Haggard, Lt Col A., DSO. *Under Crescent and Star.*
  Wm Blackwood & Sons, 1896.

Keshishian, Kevork K. *Romantic Cyprus.*
  Printco Ltd, Cyprus, 1972.

Magnus, Phillip. *Kitchener, Portrait of an Imperialist.*
  J. Murray, 1958.

Martineau, G. D. *History of the Royal Sussex Regiment.*
  Moor and Tillyer, 1953.

Maurice, Col J. F. *The Campaigns of 1882 in Egypt.*
  Reprint by J. B. Hayward, 1973.

Nevill, Capt H. L. *Campaigns of the North West Frontier.*
  J. Murray, 1912.

Nutting, Anthony, *Gordon, martyr and misfit.*
  Reprint Society, 1966.

Rogers, Col H. C. B. *Troopships and their history.*
  Seeley Service & Co, 1963.

Simkin, Richard. *The War in Egypt.*
  George Routledge & Sons, 1883.

Steevens, G. W. *With Kitchener to Khartum.*
  Wm Blackwood & Sons, 1898.

Symons, Julian. *England's Pride.*
  Hamish Hamilton, 1965.

Thurston, H. *The Travellers Guide to Cyprus.*
  Jonathan Cape, 1967.

Wilson, Col Sir Charles W. *From Korti to Khartum.*
  Wm Blackwood & Sons, 1886.

Wilson, H. W. *With the Flag to Pretoria, Volumes 1 & 2.*
  Harmsworth, 1900-1901.

Wilson, H. W. *After Pretoria, The Guerilla War.*
  Amalgamated Press, 1902.

Wingate, Major F. R. *Mahdiism and the Egyptian Sudan.*
  MacMillan, 1901.

Army Lists, 1874-1908.
Hart's Army List.
Illustrated London News, 1878-1880.
London Gazettes.
The Graphic, 1878.

Overseas References.
Cyprus Gazette, 1878-1883.
Cyprus Herald, 1881-1885.

Second study of the colours of the 35th Regiment.
(The first is reproduced as a colour plate, on page 126.)

Index

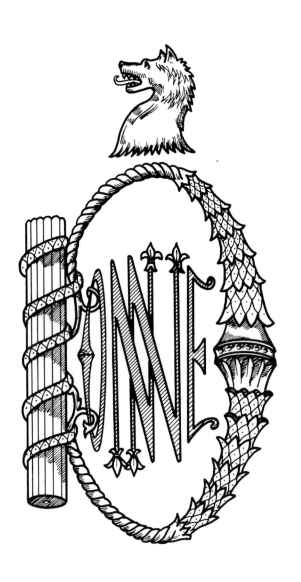